CO⋏
IN STUDENT AFFAIRS

Complex Cases in Student Affairs provides students and professionals with a deeper understanding of how problems in student affairs might be addressed through the application of relevant theory/research and practical considerations of professional practice. Featuring 22 original cases situated at a range of different types of institutions, this important text covers many functional areas, represents the experiences of a diverse set of student populations, and addresses a variety of complex and intersecting issues that student affairs professionals regularly face. A clear process for applying theory to practice along with case-specific questions prompts readers to engage with the issues presented in the cases, identify and analyze problems, and construct robust solutions. Whether you are a student affairs or higher education graduate student, faculty member, early student affairs professional, or staff supervisor, reading, analyzing, and crafting resolutions to the cases in this book will better prepare you to effectively consider and address the challenges of the field.

Michael G. Ignelzi is Professor of Student Affairs in Higher Education in the Department of Counseling and Development at Slippery Rock University, USA.

Melissa A. Rychener is Coordinator of the Intercultural Preparation and Competency Curriculum at Duquesne University, USA.

Molly A. Mistretta is Assistant Professor of Student Affairs in Higher Education and Clinical Mental Health Counseling in the Department of Counseling and Development at Slippery Rock University, USA.

Stacy A. Jacob is Assistant Professor of Student Affairs in Higher Education and Graduate Coordinator for the Department of Counseling and Development at Slippery Rock University, USA.

COMPLEX CASES IN STUDENT AFFAIRS

PREPARING EARLY CAREER PROFESSIONALS FOR PRACTICE

Michael G. Ignelzi,
Melissa A. Rychener, Molly A. Mistretta,
and Stacy A. Jacob

Routledge
Taylor & Francis Group

NEW YORK AND LONDON

First published 2018
by Routledge
711 Third Avenue, New York, NY 10017

and by Routledge
2 Park Square, Milton Park, Abingdon, Oxon, OX14 4RN

Routledge is an imprint of the Taylor & Francis Group, an informa business

© 2018 Taylor & Francis

The right of Michael G. Ignelzi, Melissa A. Rychener, Molly A. Mistretta, and Stacy A. Jacob to be identified as the authors of this material has been asserted by them in accordance with sections 77 and 78 of the Copyright, Designs and Patents Act 1988.

Library of Congress Cataloging-in-Publication Data
A catalog record for this book has been requested

ISBN: 978-1-138-69961-8 (hbk)
ISBN: 978-1-138-69962-5 (pbk)
ISBN: 978-1-315-51645-5 (ebk)

Typeset in Sabon
by Apex CoVantage, LLC

Contents

Preface

ORIGINS OF THIS BOOK

This book is the result of a process that started about 10 years ago, when my then student affairs graduate program faculty colleague, Melissa Rychener, and I decided that we wanted to change how comprehensive exams were conducted with our master's students. We had inherited a comprehensive exam format that we were of 'two minds' about. We both liked that the existing exam was an oral presentation because it gave students an opportunity to speak about what they had learned during their graduate studies. We were committed to sending students into the field who could both effectively write and talk about what they knew. However, what we didn't like about the exam format was that it was an hour-long, somewhat unstructured conversation, where a panel of three faculty members from our department asked students questions about concepts across all of the coursework they had completed and how they might apply those to professional practice. As you can imagine, this comprehensive exam generated much anxiety for students because they had little idea what they might be asked, and correspondingly felt their preparation for the exam had insufficient focus. I'll never forget participating on my first comprehensive faculty panel where before we could begin the exam the student became physically ill (i.e., vomited), and we had to reschedule. I remember thinking that a process that created this level of anxiety was not necessarily conducive to learning. Students also questioned the utility of this format to the professional work they would soon be performing. Over time, Melissa and I found ourselves in agreement with their complaints.

The Student Affairs M.A. program at Slippery Rock University is housed in the Department of Counseling and Development. Around this time, our counseling faculty colleagues started to explore changing the comprehensive exam for their counseling program students to a case presentation. For these majors, this process meant preparing an oral case presentation on a client whom they were working with in their counseling internship. The proposed presentation was focused on having students analyze their clients and their issues—utilizing theories and concepts from their coursework. Students would then be asked to apply that analysis in designing appropriate counseling goals and treatment plans. Melissa and I were intrigued with this format because we both appreciated and valued case-based learning approaches. We used case studies from a variety of sources in our teaching, but we were not initially clear on how we might develop a corresponding comprehensive case-based exam for our student affairs majors.

After much consideration and discussion, our department faculty decided that we would all change our required comprehensive exam to case-based formats. The way we initially managed this change for student affairs exams was to adapt an existing case from the literature for each new exam cycle. All students in a particular cohort were asked to analyze and propose resolutions for that case in individual 45-minute oral presentations followed by 30 minutes of faculty questioning. We immediately noticed an improvement in the process. Students were more engaged, recognized the relevance of applying their program learning to a 'real-life' situation, and their anxiety was significantly lessened. Melissa and I were largely happy with this shift because it encouraged students to study and prepare together, enhancing their collaboration and shared learning. We also felt that this case analysis process better mirrored the way complex situations are actually reflected upon and resolved in professional practice.

However, there were still problems. With everyone preparing their exam on the same case, some students had an advantage based on the functional student affairs areas and related issues focused on in the case. Certain students could relate to the presented case more easily due to their particular interests and fieldwork experiences. Another issue arose out of a change we instituted regarding who listened to the case analysis presentations. We began including both faculty and students in the audience because the faculty valued these collective learning experiences. We wanted our students to hear each other's analyses and proposed resolutions to the case, as well as to have the opportunity to engage in the rich conversations that occurred during the question-and-answer portion of the exam. To accomplish this goal, we had case analyses presented in our internship course sections with all student members of a particular section participating. While this process generated a valuable shared learning experience, student case analyses (which were necessarily scheduled over a number of class sessions) had many similarities in terms of the theories and concepts utilized and the case resolutions proposed.

A couple of years into this shared case format, we decided another alteration to address the aforementioned problems was needed. We moved to the model that we have used ever since, in which students write their own cases for analysis. Our student affairs majors take two fieldwork courses, a practicum in the fall semester of their second year and an internship in the spring. We built a case-writing assignment into the practicum curriculum, where students generate ideas for an interesting, complex case and write several drafts of their case with guidance and feedback from their practicum instructor. The case a particular student writes may have a relationship to something they have experienced or observed in their fieldwork (Graduate Assistantship or external internship), but it is largely a fictional case. The goal for case writing is to produce a realistic story that is complex and detailed enough to allow for analysis through a number of theoretical/research content areas the student has studied in their program courses (e.g., environments and cultures, student learning and development, diversity, organizational behavior and leadership, law and ethics). The final draft of a student's case is then analyzed by that same student for their comprehensive exam (what we now refer to as their culminating experience) during the spring semester internship course.

This final alteration to the culminating experience project addressed all of the problems associated with the single assigned case format, and in many ways likened the experience for students to the process of writing a thesis. I draw this comparison because as with the production of a thesis, the student chooses the central focus of the experience, is largely in charge of the content of the project (i.e., writing the case), and is in control of crafting the project's outcome (i.e., the case analysis presentation). While students find writing their case and the case analysis challenging, they are fully invested because it is *theirs*. They also realize that they understand the challenges of their case and its potential resolutions better than anyone else because of the significant time they spend researching and reflecting on the problems in their case.

The creativity and quality of case analyses because of this process significantly improved. The faculty members who have been involved in this experience—the four authors of this book—agree that our students' ability to apply theory to practice in a comprehensive and integrated manner is greatly enhanced through this culminating project. More important, students recognize the utility of this culminating experience to their future work in the field, and successful completion of their case analyses generates noticeable confidence in their competency.

CASE STUDIES

We felt it was important to trace the process of the creation of our current culminating experience model because that process resulted in a 'happy accident' that is the centerpiece of this book—the case studies written by our master's students. After several years of having students write their original case studies, we realized that they had generated wonderful situations and narratives that had promise for use as teaching tools with other student affairs graduate students and early professionals. Their cases are different from most student affairs cases available in the literature on several accounts. First, they are longer, more detailed, and raise more complex and nuanced issues than most existing cases. Second, they often put a younger, less experienced professional at the heart of the case as the key student affairs administrator and/or decision-maker. Third, most cases contain extensive student and staff dialogue giving the reader a sense of the lived experience of those involved in the case. The dialogue is particularly useful in doing developmental analysis. Fourth, these cases do not lend themselves to formulaic or easy solutions; they are 'messy', as are real-life situations, with competing character and/or institutional interests. And fifth, because these cases were written for the purpose of engaging in a comprehensive theoretical and conceptual analysis, they are broad and rich for potential use in a variety of student affairs courses or professional staff trainings.

At the heart of this book are 22 original cases. Twenty-one of these cases were selected by the four faculty members who supervised their writing: Stacy Jacob, Molly Mistretta, Melissa Rychener, and me. It is a collection of some of the best cases produced by our master's students over the past eight years. These cases have been rewritten and revised under a co-authorship agreement with our former students who originally wrote them for their culminating experience. One of the 21 cases has two former student co-authors, as portions of their original cases were combined to produce the version in this book. There is one additional case in the book that was co-authored by a current student affairs professional in an important functional area (student conduct) that we felt should be included in this collection. It should be noted that most of these cases have been shortened from their original, student-written versions to provide more usable cases for teaching and learning. In our rewriting and editing, we carefully attempted to retain the rich issues and narratives reflected in these cases by their original authors that make them valuable tools for analysis and instruction. If you feel after reading these cases that we were successful in this effort, most credit should go to the student authors who gave us such wonderful material with which to work. If we were less than successful with some of the cases included here, we gladly accept the blame.

INTENDED AUDIENCES

One intended audience for this book is teaching faculty in student affairs and higher education graduate preparation programs and their students. This case book is designed for use in both particular student affairs courses and across the courses in an entire program. We also think this book can be of value to student affairs supervisors in their staff training efforts, particularly when aimed at new or early professionals in the field.

ORGANIZATION OF THE BOOK

The first three chapters of this book, which are directly written to student affairs graduate students and early student affairs career professionals, describe the ways cases, such as the ones presented in this book, can be utilized to enhance learning. Chapter 1 argues the importance of using relevant theory to inform our understandings and approaches to student affairs work. The value of applying formal theory and research to the situations we are presented with as professionals is emphasized. Chapter 1 also describes the benefits of and methods available for using case studies in learning how to apply theory to real-life professional situations and dilemmas. Chapter 2 shares two valuable approaches for analyzing complex cases using relevant formal theories from the student affairs field. These approaches, which grew out of our work with students on their culminating experience case analyses, are flexible and adaptive to the identified issues that particular cases present. Our goal is to suggest a process that is well matched to the varied and complex nature of situations student affairs professionals are charged to address. Chapter 3, building on the results of doing a robust case analysis, turns to crafting theoretically sound and realistically effective resolutions, both short and long term, to the issues and problems particular cases present. Emphasis is placed on the importance of designing actions and interventions informed by and consistent with the preceding theoretical analysis. Designing realistic potential resolutions to the case, which take into account context and available resources, is also stressed. These three chapters, which include examples connected to a case in the book, are meant to be read before engaging with the other cases.

Chapters 4–25 each contain one co-authored case for reading and analysis. Each case is preceded by a short reflective abstract, whose purpose is to direct the reader toward consideration of important themes and issues raised by the case. Each case is followed by a few case-specific questions for consideration and discussion. These questions are provided for additional reflection and to complement the more comprehensive process of analyzing the case and crafting potential resolutions as described in Chapters 1–3.

At the end of the book is an index for all 22 cases presented. Cases are indexed by student affairs functional areas, institution type, student populations, salient issues addressed, and theoretical content areas covered. This index allows the reader to find cases, by chapter, which match their interests for a particular case among the aforementioned categories.

The authors of this book believe that the best way to learn to effectively apply theory to professional practice is to *practice doing so*. The cases contained herein, along with the analysis, resolution, and question processes suggested, provide a useful vehicle for gaining the necessary practice required to enhance this critical proficiency. Whether you are a student affairs or higher education graduate student, faculty member, early student affairs professional, or staff supervisor, we sincerely hope that you will find reading and working through the rich issues in the book's cases engaging and facilitative of your continued learning.

—Michael G. Ignelzi

Acknowledgments

The authors of this book would like to acknowledge the good work of their Slippery Rock University students, many of whom have their work represented in this volume. However, it should be noted that for every case in this book, there were several more just as intriguing cases from which we could have chosen. Over the years, we have all read many wonderful cases from our students and this is but a sampling of their hard work over the past several years.

We would also like to thank our families that have supported us before, through, and beyond the writing of this book.

We are deeply thankful to our student Alexander W. Rizzutto for his copyediting talents, good humor regarding our many needs, and attention to detail. We are also indebted to Jillian Pavlick for her work on the case chapter index. Her contribution will helpfully guide faculty and supervisors involved in professional development training in using the book.

Finally, we must thank the Panera Bread in Cranberry Township, PA for providing an excellent space in which we could meet to solve the problems of the world, laugh, and eventually find a path to completing this book.

PART I

INTRODUCTION

Chapter 1

Why a Case Study Approach?

Michael G. Ignelzi and Melissa A. Rychener

INTRODUCTION

As a professional staff member, whether it's your first year or your 25th, you will face situations that catch you off guard. You will be asked questions that you aren't sure how to answer. You will find yourself in the midst of events unfolding in ways that you never expected. The professional work of the student affairs division can be confusing and overwhelming, but it will also provide you with many opportunities to make a positive difference in the lives of students . . . if you thoughtfully prepare for your profession.

Most student affairs preparation programs seek to teach the theories and perspectives that help new professionals make sense of the world of student affairs on college campuses. As essential as this theoretical base is for effective professional practice, becoming a skilled navigator of the unpredictable waters of campus life requires practice as well. Together with our students, we have developed a book of case studies straight out of our experiences on college campuses. Reading, analyzing, and crafting resolutions to these cases will better prepare you for the challenges that await you in the field— whether you are in the captain's seat or part of the crew.

One of the lessons of experience is that there are almost always more options for responding to questions or crises than might be obvious at first glance. When faced with a crisis, however, we may find ourselves responding instinctively, seemingly automatically, to the complex situations that present themselves. These 'automatic responses' may create more unanticipated problems than they resolve.

What we advocate for in the following pages is an approach that begins with reflection, an attempt to understand the problem itself, the perspectives of the people involved, your own analysis, and the relevant thinking (theories) of scholars in our field. Out of this reflection and analysis, you will form nuanced responses that take into account all of these perspectives. These responses take into consideration short- and long-term solutions and intended as well as unintentional consequences. By creatively analyzing and thoughtfully resolving real cases, you will gain the kinds of experience that will allow you to be a more effective student affairs professional.

PERSONAL AND FORMAL THEORIES

For the purposes of the opening Chapters (1–3), we ask that you read the case "Student Veteran Support and Discrimination" (Chapter 4) before continuing. We are utilizing this case as an example of the type of real-life situations student affairs professionals face in their work, and we are relating specifics about the case analysis approach and process in these opening chapters to that case.

Now that you have read the requested case, consider the following question: "If you were in the position of Tabitha Cole, Financial Aid Officer in the case, what might you do to address the concerns raised by the veteran student, John, and the related issues experienced by other veteran students at Southeast Community College?" Once you have thought about this question and noted a few of your ideas, return to reading this text.

Based on our experience as instructors in presenting complex situations/problems to our students, we expect that most of you experienced and/or approached this task in one of two ways. Some of you probably experienced difficulty in constructing an answer to this question. That is understandable because you have likely never thought about this scenario before, and you may not feel you have the knowledge or experience to address the multiple, complex issues the case presents. For others, however, you may have thought of one or several ways Tabitha Cole might begin addressing the issues raised by these veteran students. If you generated one or more potential resolutions to the issues raised in the case, identify the source or basis of your resolution ideas. In other words, what information, experiences, sensibilities, and/or values did you utilize to come up with your answer? When individuals are first presented with such real-life cases and questions, we have found that most rely heavily on life experiences that may have some overlap with the case, on their related beliefs and values about such situations, and on their personal feelings and sensibilities about the particulars of the case.

These bases for understanding and decision-making that we all use represent our personal theories. These theories consist of the complex accumulation of our own experiences, thoughts, beliefs, values, and feelings that we apply to understanding situations and making decisions that we face in both our personal and professional lives. While our personal theories are the accumulation of the sources noted above, we may experience them as intuitive or instinctive views; they are not always the product of conscious reasoning. When you experience a strong sense of what should be done in a situation but can't easily explain or articulate the rationale for that judgment, it is likely that an internalized personal theory is being utilized. In such instances, we just feel or believe that we know the best or right thing to do.

Personal theories are valuable sources of information and decision-making because, regardless of our ability to clearly articulate their origins, they are usually based on a complex, internalized set of factors that represent our best current thinking and response to an issue. As such, individuals should pay meaningful attention to these personal theories in considering how to respond to and resolve situations in their personal and professional lives.

Personal theories, however, have limitations, particularly when used as the sole source of making decisions in complex situations, such as the veteran's case. First, by definition, personal theories are highly personalized; they are largely the product of our own experience, thinking, feelings, beliefs, and values. As such, they are largely limited to our perspective, which may substantially differ from other equally valuable or superior perspectives on the situation. Making decisions, particularly in a professional context, solely from our own personal perspective does not effectively utilize the available knowledge (e.g., theory, research) relevant to the professional field in which we work.

Formal theories, derived from the literature relevant to our professional field, can both support and/or challenge our more intuitive perspectives or personal theories. Formal theories have the advantage of being researched and/or reviewed by content experts, which invests these theories with evidence to support their validity or trustworthiness, and their utility. Such information is tremendously valuable in providing studied understandings and perspectives that can inform our own views. Formal theory is not meant to supplant our personal theories, but rather to provide useful material to enhance our current understandings and to consider in modifying and further developing our own perspectives.

A second limitation of personal theories is that they may not be supported by a rationale that can be clearly articulated to students or professional colleagues, so that they can understand the basis for decisions being considered or made. Regardless of what actions are taken by Tabitha Cole to attempt to resolve issues in the case, individuals affected will want to know and have a right to know the rationale for those actions. Utilizing professional knowledge (i.e., formal theory and research) to inform our personal theories provides a more common, professionally accepted information base and language from which to support those actions with others. It also allows for clearer communication about the considered outcomes among interested parties and as a basis for evaluating those outcomes.

Last, our personal theories may contain biases and/or limitations based on the particulars of our life experience and related beliefs/values. Our personal theories are directly related to our larger 'worldview', which is necessarily influenced by the contexts, cultures, and individuals we have experienced and those we have not. Whether or not Tabitha Cole has any experience in her life with the military, veterans, or veteran's issues, the nature of that experience, and the feelings and beliefs she has constructed from them, will inevitably influence her personal theories about how to best address the concerns raised by John. To the extent that Tabitha's views may be ignorant due to a lack of experience or unintentional bias, formal theories and research, combined with carefully listening to the views of veteran students at SCC, may inform her about best practices for understanding and assisting veteran students.

THE RELATIONSHIP BETWEEN USING FORMAL THEORIES AND PROFESSIONALISM

Student Affairs is a multidisciplinary professional field. Formal theories and research that are taught in graduate preparation programs are drawn from both student affairs and other disciplinary fields including, but not limited to, human development, organizational behavior, person/environment studies, law, higher education, multicultural studies, women's studies, and LGBT studies. These areas of study collectively have much to offer to our understanding of both students, the primary service recipients of student affairs practice, and higher education institutions, the contexts in which student affairs work is performed. Moreover, the theories and research from these disciplines provide useful guidance on how student affairs practitioners can effectively create conditions within collegiate contexts to enhance student learning, success, and wellness.

As in any profession, relevant formal theories and research findings are taught in student affairs preparation programs to ensure that practitioners have some common body of knowledge and standards to employ in their professional work. As discussed earlier, the personal theories of individuals are primary and valuable, but are insufficient when not informed by the more formal theories, research, and standards of a profession. An important goal of student affairs education is to assist in developing practitioners to identify and examine their personal theories in light of the formal theories of the discipline. This process may lead to confirmation, modification, or occasionally, rejection of a particular personal theory. This reflective educational process results in practitioners developing more informed, complex, and adaptive personal theories for use in professional practice.

Some individuals working in the student affairs field, mostly those who have little or no graduate education in student affairs, argue that having a caring attitude for students, good communication skills, and good judgment are most critical to success as a student affairs practitioner. While we acknowledge such professional characteristics are important, we agree with Carpenter (2001) who asserts, "Being a good person or good with students is not enough to be a student affairs professional any more than doctors or lawyers or mechanics are valued for their affability" (p. 311). To illustrate this view, imagine that your medical doctor, who has a good "bedside manner", is treating you for a serious medical condition. She suggests a particular form of treatment to address your illness. When you ask her reasoning for prescribing this treatment, she tells you that this form of treatment makes sense to her, it has seemed to help a couple of her other patients, and she trusts it would help you as well. When you question her for further medical details about why she thinks this treatment would be the best course of action for you, relevant research on this treatment for someone with your particular condition, and for comparative information on alternate forms of treatment, she is unable to adequately answer. We suggest, regardless of her other qualities, you look for another doctor!

While student affairs professionals do not make decisions about the treatment of medical conditions, they make decisions and advise students on issues critical to students' learning, development, and wellness. Students and the higher education institutions that employ student affairs professionals have the right to expect that those professionals' judgments and actions are informed by current knowledge and best practices from relevant theory and research. Student affairs professionals should be cognizant of the personal theories they utilize, those theories should be supported by formal theory and research, and professionals should be able to effectively apply and explain those theories to others. Whatever courses of action Tabitha Cole chooses to pursue in the Veteran's case, the aforementioned criteria should be met.

There is an additional benefit to those student affairs professionals who learn to utilize the knowledge of their discipline in the ways described here. Academic environments, the central home for the generation of theory and research, and the individuals who inhabit them (e.g., faculty, academic and student affairs administrators) recognize and value the ability to utilize theory and research in addressing complex problems. The degree to which you master the reflective and applicative use of theory and research in your work as a professional will significantly influence how you are viewed and evaluated within your institution and the larger student affairs profession.

MASTERING THE USE OF THEORY IN YOUR WORK

So how do you learn to master the use of theory in your work? First, you must become familiar with and study the relevant historical and current theory of the profession. If you are in a student affairs preparation program, this will largely occur through your active engagement with the literature and experiences you are exposed to through your academic courses. If you are a practicing student affairs professional, this process continues by staying current with new theory and research in the field through regularly reading relevant literature (e.g., books, journal articles) and participating in professional development opportunities (e.g., conferences, workshops, trainings). Being an engaged student affairs professional involves seeing oneself and behaving as a life-long learner, and pursuing valuable learning opportunities, whether as a student or as a full-time professional and whether or not those opportunities are required.

Immersing yourself in the relevant knowledge of our field is the easiest part of the process. More difficult is internalizing and integrating that knowledge into your own thinking, and learning how to apply theory to practice. The process of internalizing and integrating professional knowledge into our thinking involves uncovering and comparing our personal theories to the formal theories and research of our field. When reading and studying course material, we encourage students to engage in the reflective activity of considering how a newly learned theory or concept compares with their current understanding (i.e., their personal theory). Questions for consideration include: What are the similarities and differences between the formal theory or concept and your own personal theory? How do you make sense of that? What are the strengths and limitations of the formal theory to your understanding of the phenomena it purports to explain? Does the formal theory have value for informing your current personal theory? If determined useful, how might you modify your personal theory in light of the newly learned formal theory or concept? Through this on-going reflective process, supported by course discussion, activities and assignments, students internalize and integrate knowledge from the student affairs field into their developing personal theories of professional understanding and practice.

Learning to apply theory to practice is often difficult because it involves applying generalized, often abstract concepts to real-life situations within a particular context. Situations and persons are more complex than any theory; no one theory is able to account for the variety of differences in persons and situations we must address as student affairs professionals. As such, a theory typically cannot be applied in whole, but rather concepts from multiple theories (personal and/or formal) need to be combined to effectively understand and address the complexity of real-life situations and problems. This complicated task requires both careful reflection and practice.

CASE STUDIES AS A TOOL FOR APPLYING THEORY

How can early professionals ensure they have sufficient opportunities for this needed reflection and practice? You can, of course, directly apply your fledgling, evolving theories to your real-life work as student affairs graduate assistants, interns, or new professionals, but this is often impractical or ethically questionable. It can be impractical because early professionals may not yet hold positions or responsibilities that place them in situations where they have the professional autonomy or authority to effectively implement their ideas. More critically, applying your 'under construction' theories to real-life professional situations, where actual consequences are at stake for students and other constituent groups, raises ethical concerns related to what extent it is acceptable to affect the outcomes and welfare of others in the service of your own learning.

We contend that utilizing the case study approach to learning is a superior method of learning to apply theory to professional practice. This learning approach avoids the difficulties discussed previously, while still providing rich, real-life situations to consider and explore. The cases provided in this book, such as the Veteran's case, allow readers to imagine themselves in key professional roles with the complex responsibilities of analyzing the issues raised in the case and crafting effective resolutions to those issues. Considering and integrating formal theories/research with your current personal theories is at the core of this endeavor. Reflectively analyzing and designing resolutions for these cases effectively mirrors the process that competent professionals utilize when addressing real-life situations in their work. Improving your competency with this process will improve your competency of applying theory in your real-life professional work.

Perhaps more important, using the formal theories and research of the discipline in a reflective, comparative process with our own personal theories allows us to come to a more intimate and complex understanding of how our ideologies and beliefs guide our professional practice. The process of comparing our own theory making with theories of the field allows us to find shortcomings in our own analysis as well as to develop a greater understanding of our values, biases, and sources of motivation. For example, we might find ourselves relating to Tabitha Cole's empathetic response to John's experience. This might spur us to learn more about veterans or to recognize that we would feel isolated working in an organization that didn't dedicate adequate resources to supporting the student populations that it promised to serve. This might help us to define our job search criteria or help us to articulate questions to potential employers. If we were struggling to construct an organizational response to the problems in the case, we might go back to our organizational behavior course to assist us in brainstorming alternate responses when our own experience was insufficient. This process would add breadth to the organizational responses at our disposal going forward.

As we have discussed, case studies help us to develop the processes of analysis and reflection needed to create responses that draw upon our personal theories and the theories of the scholars in our field and related fields. The process of comparing our personal theories with those of others helps us to better understand what motivates us and what limits our understanding. Additionally, examining our own responses to situations, how we make sense of them, and how we frame resolutions provides us with important clues about our own values. This insight can help us to know ourselves as professionals, influence our career choices, and shape our practice.

Now that we have explored case studies as an important tool in developing reflective student affairs practitioners who are able to create and apply theory, let's look at how the case study approach can be used in graduate education in student affairs and in professional education and training.

USING CASES IN A MASTER'S PROGRAM

Case studies have become the cornerstone of professional education in disparate fields such as business, medicine, and law (Garvin, 2003). Professionals in these fields must be prepared to wrestle with complex, "ill-structured problems" (Kitchener & King, 1994) in a rapidly evolving work environment—like those encountered by student affairs professionals. Cases, like those published by the *Harvard Business Review,* are central to the approach used in some professional education programs. Similarly, the cases in this book are complex, multifaceted cases designed to elicit critical thinking and in-depth analysis. You are encouraged to creatively engage with the issues raised in each case, applying appropriate theoretical lenses to gain deeper understanding, and then drafting resolutions out of this analysis.

CASES WITHIN ACADEMIC COURSES

Within student affairs preparation programs, cases can be used within content courses—such as student development or organizational behavior. For example, in a course on organizational theory, you could be assigned to work in groups to identify and analyze the organizational issues present in a particular case and craft a resolution of these issues out of your analysis. Class discussion and even exam questions can be contextualized within the issues of the case, thereby encouraging you to more deeply understand abstract theoretical concepts and connect them to concrete examples within a relevant professional context.

Example

Two of the organizational issues that emerge in the Veteran's case are the director's role overload and competition for scarce resources within the division (Bolman & Deal, 2013). The Director for Student Success, Luke, oversees several functional areas. Perhaps Luke is too stretched to provide adequate attention to any of these areas. Luke responds defensively to the veteran student, John, when he tries to address the gaps in services for veterans. Luke's defensiveness may demonstrate the dysfunction of an overly competitive environment within the division. Understanding this dynamic may inform a case resolution in which the department reorganizes these functions in a way that gives them more resources and attention.

CASES AS CAPSTONE ASSIGNMENTS OR IN PROFESSIONAL EDUCATION AND TRAINING

Rather than focusing on case issues relevant to just one course content area (such as organizational behavior, in the example above) a more complete way to look at the cases in this book is to consider the issues from the theoretical perspectives in courses across the curriculum. One way to do this is to use these cases as the culminating or capstone assignment for a master's program. This kind of cross-disciplinary case analysis can also be utilized in the training and continuing development of student affairs professionals. Case analysis and resolution can take place at staff meetings or one-on-one professional development meetings.

For this purpose, students and professional educators may be asked to apply concepts from student development, leadership, diversity, organizational behavior, legal and ethical issues, etc. In your role as a student or professional, you could be asked to generate issues relevant to each of these areas of study and then develop a resolution out of this analysis across disciplinary boundaries. In addition to helping you to better understand and contextualize theory, through such processes, you learn to integrate concepts across disciplines, which is a better approximation of how theory is used, and useful, in practice.

Example

In the Veteran's case, John Brown's development can be viewed from the perspective of Baxter-Magolda's theory of self-authorship (2011). In the analysis, Tabitha's mentoring style could be compared to Luke's approach in relation to fostering John's self-authorship. This developmental analysis would complement the organizational analysis in which role overload and an unhealthy competition for scarce resources leads to a reorganization of the division. Tabitha listened to John's perspective and encouraged him to find his voice, which helped John to create his own solution to the problems he was experiencing. On the other hand, Luke questioned John's approach, perhaps because Luke felt that his authority was being undermined in a competitive environment. Luke seemed to be more focused on preserving his own reputation rather than supporting John's growth, even in an organizational structure that gave him a perhaps unrealistic set of responsibilities. An organization with a focus on supporting the development of students would be wise to consider how these structural, organizational decisions affect student learning and growth.

USING CASES TO UNDERSTAND INSTITUTIONAL TYPE AND FUNCTIONAL AREA

Institutional Type

How an institutional type shapes the student affairs learning environment is best understood in context. Most entry-level student affairs professionals have limited experiences across institutional types, and they sometimes underestimate the importance of this variable to their career trajectories and the decisions that they face within the context of higher education. The cases in this book are situated in different types of institutions, and you are invited to consider how the issues of the case and the case resolutions might be affected by institutional type. Throughout the text, you are asked to consider how the outcome of a case might be different if it was situated in a different institution.

Example

Promised resources for veteran students are not available at an under-resourced community college. At a better resourced community college or other institution, perhaps the situation for veterans might be different. Also, contrasting how the two staff members respond to the veteran student's dilemma makes it clear that the Division of Student Affairs has inconsistent values in relation to empowering and advocating for students. Perhaps this is indicative of an approach to hiring and promotion that fails to recognize and reinforce student affairs competencies—which may point to a lack of resources for recruitment and professional development.

New professionals in particular need to be aware of differences among institutions and institutional type in terms of professional orientation to and support of the values of the field.

Functional Area

Like many students who enroll in student affairs preparation programs, you may have clear ideas about the functional area(s) in which you hope to work. By considering a variety of cases located in diverse functional areas, you have the opportunity to think about how issues cross areas and how student affairs professionals collaborate across areas. You also have the opportunity to consider how the values of the field transcend the functional area.

Example

Tabitha, the Financial Aid Counselor, advises and advocates for the veteran student because of her student affairs perspective and her broad view that takes into account the needs of students beyond her formal role as a financial aid advisor. In contrast, Luke, the Director for Student Success, lacks this student affairs orientation. Students and new professionals reading this case may be challenged to think about how the professional orientation of colleagues and supervisors may influence their professional development more than the functional area.

CASE STUDY APPROACH HIGHLIGHTS THE IMPORTANCE OF REFLECTION

Harkening back to the introduction of the chapter, case studies capture a moment in time and allow you the luxury of reflection to identify issues, to seek to understand these issues from a variety of theoretical perspectives, and to develop case resolutions out of this analysis. This ingrains in new professionals a habit of mind that reminds you to step back from the pressing events of the day and consider a variety of ways of looking at these situations, informed by the best thinkers and theories in our field. It is only after this analytical process that resolution is sought. By using this problem-solving process, issues are more likely to be understood within an institutional, professional, and functional area context and in relation to other issues affecting the institution. The interests and motives of colleagues, supervisors, and students are more fully recognized and explored as well. It is our hope that the case study learning approach will ultimately inspire better and more informed decision-making in our field.

In conclusion, the case study approach advocated in this book invites students and professionals in the field of student affairs to grapple with complex cases in an effort to become better prepared to meet the challenges of serving college students. In the following chapters, you will gain more insights into how to approach the situations described in the cases, identify critical issues, and apply formal and personal theories to analyze these issues and craft resolutions.

REFERENCES

Baxter Magolda, M. (2011). *Authoring your life: Developing an internal voice to meet life's challenges*. Sterling, VA: Stylus.

Bolman, L. G. & Deal, T. E. (2013). *Reframing organizations: Artistry, choice, and leadership* (5th Ed.). San Francisco, CA: Jossey-Bass.

Carpenter, S. (2001). Student affairs scholarship (re?) considered: Toward a scholarship of practice. *Journal of College Student Development*, 42(4), 301–318.

Garvin, D. A. (September–October 2003). Making the case: Professional education for the world of practice. *Harvard Magazine*. Retrieved from http://harvardmagazine.com/2003/09/making-the-case-html

Kitchener, P. S. & King, K. A. (1994). *Developing reflective judgment: Understanding and promoting intellectual growth and critical thinking in adolescents and adults*. San Francisco: Jossey-Bass.

Chapter 2

Analyzing a Case Study

*Stacy A. Jacob, Stefanie M. Centola,
and Kara Werkmeister*

INTRODUCTION

In Chapter 1, you learned why the authors of this book consider using
case studies as highly beneficial for your learning and why we believe that
learning from case studies can inspire you to become a highly developed
decision-maker and practitioner in the field. However, you may have been
left wondering how to approach learning from a case study or how to use
theory to create viable solutions to problems. The theories that you are
learning in classes, or have learned, may seem to be relevant or important
to situations you encounter in cases (and also in real life because cases are
meant to be a reflection of real life) but you may be asking yourself, "How
is knowing theory going to make me a better practitioner? I understand
theory, but what do I do with it?" In this chapter and in Chapter 3, the
authors will present ways in which students can effectively create theory-
driven solutions. This chapter will prepare you for creating those solutions
by discussing two methods for analyzing a case, and Chapter 3 will present how to use that analysis to create solutions for the problems presented
in a case. The discussed methods for case analysis are the result of several
years of working with student affairs students at Slippery Rock University
on their culminating projects in the Student Affairs in Higher Education
program. If you have not already done so, now would be an excellent time
to read the first case in this book about student veterans entitled, "Student
Veteran Support and Discrimination" by Kara Werkmeister and Stacy A.
Jacob. This case will be used as an example throughout this chapter as we
explain how to analyze a case.

ANALYZING A CASE CONTENT AREA
BY CONTENT AREA

The first method for analyzing a case centers on examining a dilemma through the lens of a single content area such as organizational behavior, student development, or diversity and then repeating the process for other content areas. As you may have noticed in the previous chapter, all of the cases in this book are multidimensional and can be analyzed through the lens of several course content areas. In fact, most of the cases in this book contain a broad array of perspectives that cut across several content areas in student affairs/higher education. While this first method may be most suitable for use from a single content or course perspective, it can also be used to analyze a case through several content areas—area by area.

As you may have read in the preface, Slippery Rock student affairs students must write a complex case, analyze it through five different content lenses, and then provide long-term and short-term solutions to their case for their culminating project. These five content lenses represent the major classes that all of our student affairs students are required to take: higher education environments, cultures, and students; developmental issues; organizational and leadership issues; legal and/or ethical issues; and diversity issues. We also include an "other" lens in which students can analyze the case through any relevant theory from other courses, or independent reading and research. You may refer to Appendix A to see the outline the Slippery Rock faculty provides to students completing the assignment.

To use a single content lens, you must first identify a content area through which you will view the case. For the purpose of this chapter, we will look at the case through an environmental/cultural theory content area and we will look at how chapter co-author, Kara Werkmeister, analyzed this case as a student. Before we begin, examine the following outline that briefly demonstrates how Kara applied environmental theory to the case:

Higher Education Environmental, Cultural, and Student Issues

1. Issue: Physical structure of Student Veterans Center and lack of resources in said center
   - Strange and Banning (2001)—Architectural or environmental probabilism, physical features of an environment
2. Issue: Person-environment incongruence between John Smith and the Student Veterans Center
   - Astin (1993)—Typology of students, "Social Activists"
   - Strange and Banning (2015)—Person-environment congruence

3. Issue: Chilly climate for student veterans at the university
   • Peterson and Spencer (1990)—Climate, "Perceived climate," and "Psychological/felt climate".

Once you pick a content area (in this example and case we used environmental/cultural theory), you need to identify the main issue or issues present in the case in that content area. In this case, Kara chose three main environmental issues: the physical structure (Strange & Banning, 2001) of the Student Veterans Center and the lack of resources that are allocated to it, the person-environment incongruence (Strange & Banning, 2015) between John Smith and the Student Veterans Center, and the climate (Peterson & Spencer, 1990) for student veterans at the university.

Once you have identified the issues within the case using a content area, you need to identify useful theories within that content area that are helpful in explaining the issue. You should name, reference, define, and explain the parts of the theories that you choose to apply to the issue(s). You should also demonstrate which parts of the case are examples of the theories you used by employing quotes from the case. Once you have worked through all the issues and theories in a content area that apply to the case, you will find you have a thorough and detailed analysis through a single content area. In order to fully understand what we have explained previously, let us now look at Kara's analysis in the following paragraph:

> From an environmental/cultural perspective, the first issue in this case is the physical structure of the Student Veterans Center and the lack of resources in the center. John, our main character in the case, is directed to utilize the Student Veterans Center as a source of support during his difficult time at college. However, when John locates the center, it is described as, "It has a few couches, an American flag, and no door to separate the room from the rest of the center." John is quoted saying, "It's just a room."

According to Strange and Banning (2001), "architectural or environmental probabilism" (p. 14) explains the relationship between physical environments and the behavior within those environments. Strange and Banning (2001) explain this concept by utilizing an example of a welcoming entrance to campus: the welcoming entrance does not *cause* entry, but the probability of entry is increased with the proper design. Once you understand probabilism, you begin to understand how a physical environment can, according to Strange and Banning (2001), communicate nonverbally. Physical artifacts on a campus such as signs, symbols, and specific structures can reflect the campus's values. These physical features of a campus, according to Strange and Banning (2001), "can hinder or promote learning" (p. 31).

When looking at the institution in the case, Southeast Community College is depicted as an environment that is military friendly, but the physical features of the campus can be analyzed in opposition to this welcoming slogan. The Student Veterans Center, which is housed within the Center for Student Success, does not provide resources, aside from couches, and is essentially a room with a few couches and no door. The room is described by the Center for Student Success's director, Luke Moore, as a "safe space for students"; however, it is not designed for students who may seek quiet and reprieve from crowds because of the lack of privacy. The dearth of resources, both human and physical, in the Student Veterans Center at Southeast Community College communicates a message that is in opposition to the military friendly tagline the school advertises.

The environmental and cultural viewpoint uncovers the second issue in this case: the person-environment incongruence (Strange & Banning, 2015) between the Student Veterans Center and John Smith. John, as evidenced in the case, wants to help the university become a better place for military-connected or military-affiliated students. However, as John pursues his idea of creating resources and support for students similar to him, he is met with resistance and a lack of initiative and encouragement from the Center for Student Success's director, Luke Moore.

According to Strange and Banning (2001), in (1968) Astin wrote *The College Environment* in which he, "analyzed the collective activities of college students as an observable and measurable source for understanding the impact of a particular campus environment" (p. 40). Strange and Banning (2001) also note that in 1993 Astin identified a typology of college students, empirically derived from self-reported student responses to the C.I.R.P national freshman survey, which assesses student behaviors, attitudes, expectations, values, and self-concept" (p. 41). Of the seven student types Astin highlights, the "Social Activist" type provides insight on John Smith's behavior. Astin (1993) defines the "Social Activist" type of student as a student who is interested in "participating in community action programs, helping others who are in difficulty, influencing social values, and influencing the political structure" (p. 39). John fits this typology in that he has taken it upon himself to create a group for students that not only helps others but also advocates for social issues on the campus; all on a volunteer basis. However, John is not met with an equally student-focused and volunteer-oriented environment in the Student Veterans Center. In this case, the description of the students at Southeast Community College aligns with Astin's (1993) Hedonist type. This type is incongruent with John's "Social Activist" type. The problem may also be compounded by the fact that Luke may not be accustomed to working with John's type and could cause part of the frustration felt by John.

Strange and Banning (2001) explain the importance of person-environment congruence, stating that

> the degree of person-environment congruence is predictive of an individual's attraction to and satisfaction or stability within an environment . . . since people are presumed to prefer and be satisfied with a state of congruence rather than incongruence, a person is not likely to be attracted to an environment that bears little resemblance to his or her characteristics.
>
> (pp. 52–53)

While John was originally attracted to the Southeast Community College for its military friendly tagline, which one would assume is tied to support for students in distress, an appreciation for volunteers, and community service/social support, he found the environment of the Student Veterans Resource Center to be incongruent with his "Social Activist" typology. And, as Strange and Banning (2001) explain, a "lack of congruence must lead to dissatisfaction and instability" (p. 53).

In addition to the incongruence and instability of the environment John experiences in relation to the Student Veterans Center, the third environmental/cultural issue worthy of analysis is the climate at the university in relation to student veterans. As described throughout the case, John experiences many issues of discrimination, discomfort, and a lack of support and acceptance at the university; all of which are related to his status as a student veteran. John highlights his discomfort at the university both in the beginning of the case when speaking with his financial aid counselor, where he is quoted saying, "It just seems that some of the people on campus here don't thank me for my service quite as nicely as you did," as well as in his final statement in the case to the Dean of Students when he says,

> I have been discriminated against here [at the university] countless times . . . I am made fun of by classmates and peers. And when I sought support and resources, I found that the Student Veterans Center was just a room . . . I worked to create a support group for military connected students . . . and was told that this will not be supported or funded. . . . I am a veteran, and I have never felt more unsupported, unappreciated, or disrespected than I have on this campus.

Tierney explains that "climate has long been seen as an important concept related to individual performance." Climate, as defined by Peterson and Spencer (1990), "can be defined as the current common patterns of dimensions of organizational life or its members' perceptions of and attitude toward those dimensions" (p. 7). Peterson and Spencer (1990) point out that climate is about current attitudes and perceptions versus culture, which is about deeply held values and beliefs. There are three different categories of climate delineated by Peterson and Spencer (1990) "objective climate," "perceived climate," and "psychological, or felt climate"— "perceived climate," and "psychological, or felt climate" are the most salient to this case (pp. 12–13). "Perceived climate focuses on cognitive images that participants have of how organizational life actually does function and how it should function. These perceptions may be accurate or inaccurate, but they represent reality from the perspective of the participants" (Peterson & Spencer, 1990, p. 12). Conversely, "psychological, or felt climate . . . is the motivational, rather than perceptual, dimension that describes how participants feel about their organization and their work" (p. 13). Examples "include measures of members' loyalty and commitment, their morale and satisfaction, their beliefs about the quality of effort or involvement, and their sense of belonging" (Peterson & Spencer, 1990, p. 13). Combining Peterson and Spencer's categories of climate with John's perceived and felt experiences illustrates what student affairs educators refer to as a chilly climate (see the work of Hall and Sandler) for student veterans at the university.

ANALYZING A CASE ISSUE BY ISSUE

The second way you can analyze a case is by examining the case issue by issue. This past year, co-author Stefanie Centola created a second way to analyze a case. To Stefanie, and for the case she wrote, the content area by content area approach was not working. She saw that several content areas might fit under a single issue and analysis of an issue could be more thorough when looked at through multiple content areas. Stefanie successfully presented her case analysis using an issue-by-issue approach, and our second method for analyzing a case emerged. In this method, you identify several broad-based issues in a case and analyze the issue through any content area that informs that issue.

In order to construct the analysis through issues, there must be multiple issues identified within the case. To help identify the main issues in the case, focus on pinpointing the problems that need to be addressed and/or aspects in the case that seem to need a change. Once the main issues are identified, it is important to determine the "how" and "why" behind each issue to better understand that issue. In other words, determine how the issue may be present within the case and why the issue is a problem for the college or university. To do so, use your coursework and the theories, research, and ideas you have learned to support the hows and whys. By defining issues, this type of analysis combines the different content areas into one issue instead of focusing solely on one content area. Applying multiple content areas to each issue can help students understand how content areas can be deeply intertwined with other content areas. This method is especially useful in assisting students in their understanding of the complex nature of student affairs work and in articulating that complexity in their professional work. To better understand the analysis through issues, let us see how co-author Stefanie Centola used the case to find an issue and how she defined the "how" and "why":

> **Issue 1:** The lack of veteran support on a military friendly campus.
> **How could this happen:** Environmental probablism
> **Why is this a problem:** It violates ethical standards of the profession as defined by ACPA.

Now let us look at how Stefanie fleshes out the analysis of one of the issues present in the case, the lack of veteran support on a military friendly campus, and how she uses the "how" and "why" to create a theory driven analysis.

The first issue in this case is that there is a lack of veteran support on a military friendly campus. To understand how the lack of veteran support is a problem and why it is an issue for the college that proclaims itself as military friendly, we will be analyzing the through an environmental and ethical lens.

First, the environmental perspective will be examined in relation to the lack of veteran support on the Southeast Community College's campus. John Brown decides to seek out the Student Veterans Center after consulting with his financial aid advisor, Tabitha Cole. The Student Veterans Center is located within a space called the Center for Student Success. When John finds the center, he realizes it is just a room within a larger center that supports clubs and organizations such as Greek Life, Multicultural Connections and Volunteer Opportunities. Because the Student Veterans Center lacks both personnel support and resources, John does not feel as if his needs are being met despite the college's advertisement as a military friendly place. According to Strange and Banning (2001), physical features are important factors in creating a first impression at an institution and the ways in which the physical environment influences behavior can be seen through three different perspectives: architectural determinism, environmental or architectural possibilism, and environmental or architectural probablism. Within this case, the perspective that will be closely examined is environmental probablism. "Environmental probablism emerged to capture the probabilistic relationship between physical environments and behavior" (Strange & Banning, 2001, p. 14). In other words, environmental features such as layout, location, and arrangement can create behaviors that are likely to occur (Strange & Banning, 2001). Since the arrangement and layout of the Student Veterans Center is poor, this may result in the lack of visitors to the center, whereas a warm, inviting room filled with resources and a support staff may encourage more frequent usage. Another possibility for the lack of use of the Student Veterans Center may be its location. If student veterans are seeking support and hands-on resources in a private place, an office that encompasses so many other tasks and offices may not best serve their needs. Viewing this issue from the environmental perspective, and understanding the impact of environmental probabilism can help us comprehend the lack of veteran support on the Southeast Community College's campus.

Now that the lack of veteran support on Southeast Community College's campus can be understood through an environmental content area, we can move on to examining why the lack of support is a problem on the military friendly campus through an ethical content area. Southeast Community College prides itself on being a military friendly campus. When John Brown decides to invest in the support opportunities for veterans, he finds that the Student Veterans Center consists of an empty room with an American flag and some couches. John is confused because he did not feel supported and he was not given any resources as a student veteran. When Tabitha Cole, the financial aid professional, reaches out to the Director for the Center for Student Success, Luke infers that there is not enough professional staff to serve all the needs of each veteran student. The director also suggests that Tabitha refer the Counseling Center to John for further assistance. There is a Student Veterans Center; however, there is no personnel support or actual resources for student veterans.

How can Southeast Community College pride itself on being military friendly if there are not any specific resources or professional support for student veterans? Clearly, the institution is not upholding the promise of being military friendly and thus an ethical issue arises. The ACPA Ethical and Principle Standards (2014) provide ethical standards that outline professional practice and behaviors. Standard 3—Responsibility to the Institution states that "student affairs professionals share responsibility with other members of the academic community for fulfilling the institution mission" (ACPA, 2014, p. 4). Within this standard, section 3.1 states that "professionals will contribute to their institution by supporting its mission, goals, policies, and abiding by its procedures" (ACPA, 2014, p. 4). In this case, professionals should adhere to the military friendly and supportive mission that is espoused by the university. It is apparent that the Student Veterans Center is not supportive and not a resource for students; therefore, the professionals within the office, specifically the director, do not adhere to the ethical standard of responsibility to the institution (ACPA, 2014, p. 4). Section 3.4 states that "professionals will assure that information provided about the institution is factual and accurate" (ACPA, 2014, p. 4). The campus advertises itself as military friendly but after examining the resources for student veterans, it is clear that people on campus are not dedicating resources to support the advertised claim and are not consistent with the military friendly image that the institution advertises.

NEXT STEPS

Now that you know how to analyze a case through two different methods, you are ready to provide theory informed solutions. Chapter 4 discusses how you can begin to connect the theoretical analysis of a case with possible resolutions. Second, it will walk you through a series of concepts that will help you to think about creating theory-driven solutions and instruct you on how to develop such solutions.

REFERENCES

American College Personnel Association (ACPA). (2014). *ACPA Ethical Principles & Standards*. Retrieved from www.myacpa.org/sites/default/files/Ethical_Principles_Standards.pdf

Astin, A. W. (1968). *The college environment*. Washington, DC: American Council on Education.

Astin, A. W. (1993). An empirical typology of college students. *Journal of College Student Development*, 34, 36–46.

Hall, R. M. & Sandler, B. R. (1982). *The classroom climate: A chilly one for women: Report of the project on the status and education of women*. Washington, DC: Association of American Colleges.

Peterson, M. W. & Spencer, M. G. (1990). Understanding academic culture and climate. In Tierney, W. G. (Ed.), *Assessing academic climates and culture, new directions for institutional research*, No. 68 (pp. 3–18). San Francisco, CA: Jossey Bass.

Strange, C. C. & Banning, J. H. (2001). *Educating by design: Creating campus learning environments that work*. San Francisco, CA: Jossey Bass.

Strange, C. C. & Banning, J. H. (2015). *Designing for learning: Creating campus environments for student success*. San Francisco, CA: Jossey Bass.

APPENDIX A: STUDENT AFFAIRS CASE ANALYSIS OUTLINE

Higher Education Environments, Cultures, and Students (3–4 Minutes)

Describe environmental and cultural elements of the case.

Discuss an environmental theory or elements of the campus culture relevant to the case.

Developmental Issues (5–7 Minutes)

Identify the relevant developmental issues embedded in this case.

Discuss 2–3 particular theories/concepts that illuminate your understanding of the developmental issues you identified and specifically explain how they do so.

Organizational and Leadership Issues (5–7 Minutes)

Identify the relevant organizational, leadership and management issues embedded in this case.

Discuss 2–3 particular theories/concepts that illuminate your understanding of the organizational/management issues you identified and specifically explain how they do so.

Legal and Ethical Issues (3–4 Minutes)

What 1–2 legal issues will you discuss with legal counsel, and what case law will inform your questions?

Discuss 1–2 ethical standards and general ethical principles that are relevant to this case.

Diversity Issues (3–4 Minutes)

Discuss the systems of oppression (discrimination, prejudice, "-isms," ethnocentric monoculturalism) that are operating in this case.

Discuss how differences in cultural values contribute to the problems visible in this case.

Other Issues (3–4 Minutes)

Identify any relevant issues related to other discipline areas (counseling and research/assessment) that you think are embedded in this case.

Discuss 1–2 particular theories/concepts that illuminate your understanding of these other issues you identified and specifically explain how they do so.

Application (10–15 Minutes)

Identify which issues and related theories/concepts (from each of the areas you previously discussed) are most salient and have the most utility for considering how to resolve this case. Explain your rationale.

Discuss what the theories/concepts you have identified suggest for effectively resolving this case, and how you would utilize (in an integrated fashion) these theories/concepts in the resolution of this case.

Chapter 3

Resolution of a Case Study

Molly A. Mistretta and Kara Werkmeister

INTRODUCTION

In Chapter 2, the authors presented two different ways to analyze a case study. One approach was to examine issues through a specific content lens (content area by content area). Another approach involved identifying major issues in the case and analyzing that particular issue through several content areas (issue by issue). It does not matter what approach you use; conducting a thorough and robust analysis of a case to connect issues to pertinent theory is the first necessary step prior to developing resolutions to a case study. This chapter will use the analysis produced in the *content by content area* approach in the previous chapter to present how to develop thoughtful resolutions to the environmental problems present in the case entitled, "Student Veteran Support and Discrimination", by Stacy A. Jacob and Kara Werkmeister. The first task in resolving a case study is to generate theory-driven solutions. This chapter will explore how theory guides the development of potential resolutions. The second part of this chapter will present other considerations for practitioners as they shape resolutions that are based in theory, but are also appropriate for the particular contexts and circumstances present in the case.

DEVELOPING A CHAIN OF REASONING

Once at the resolution stage, students often struggle with generating quality responses to case study problems. For instance, consider the plight of two different students as they struggled to resolve a case study. Imagine

Student One. He observed a difficult problem occurring at his internship site. As he described the situation to others, he was asked how he would resolve it if he was the one in charge. He thought for a few moments and proceeded to identify several good steps to take. When asked to share his reasoning behind a few of his resolutions, he appeared to lose all confidence in the decisions he would make. In fact, he said, "Well, maybe . . . I don't know . . . I guess those really aren't good ideas after all". It is hard to feel confident about potential resolutions when they are based purely on personal theory, and are not grounded in the formal theory and research of the student affairs profession. This student was in his second year of a student affairs master's program and would be entering the field as a new professional in less than six months. He should be able to apply theory to problems in the field, and effectively apply and explain those theories as they relate to problems in student affairs to others. Certainly, the supervisors, co-workers, and students he works with in the future would depend upon him to work confidently toward resolving problems.

Now imagine Student Two. During a comprehensive exam case presentation, she provided a strong, thoughtful analysis of a fictionalized annual student life event that erupted into chaos and physical altercations. The student did a great job of exploring the conditions that contributed to this outcome, which included tensions among student groups, lack of appropriate administrative advising, and poorly implemented risk-management protocols. She tied these issues to relevant theory to further explain why and how this situation occurred. However, when she presented her recommendations for resolving the case, they weren't realistic or appropriate given the institutional context and organizational constraints. An under-resourced student affairs division will likely not be able to hire more staff. Bureaucratic structures aren't likely to individualize policies or processes. Also, students and new professionals are often surprised to find that there are few incentives for faculty to engage in activities outside of teaching and research. Theory-driven resolutions are effective only if they are filtered through considerations such as timing, appropriateness, personal philosophy, and ethics.

The above scenarios point toward an important aspect of crafting resolutions to complex problems in student affairs. Good resolutions are not something that one simply makes up or pulls randomly from a menu of possible options. Good resolutions derive from a *chain of reasoning*, which Krathwohl (2009) describes as a series of logical steps used to guide the presentation of findings. This book provides a chain of reasoning as a way to assist emerging and new professionals in working through complex problems in student affairs. The first step in the chain of reasoning requires that you understand the relevant facts and context of any given situation. This step is already done for you if you are presented with a written case study. The second step in the chain was outlined in the preceding chapter, which is to identify issues within the case that should be analyzed through relevant theoretical lenses. The third step in the chain of reasoning is to make logical connections between the analysis of issues in the case and your suggested resolutions. Successful resolutions are based on the identified issues and informed by the theory used to understand the nature of the problems or issues present in the case.

Without connecting potential solutions to the case analysis, emerging and new professionals may miss opportunities to design and implement resolutions that address the full range of issues and concerns embedded in a given situation. This is exactly what happened with Student One. He came up with some good approaches to the problem he was observing in his internship site. However, because he had not done a thorough analysis or connected the issues to theory, he lacked the confidence that his proposed resolutions were appropriate for the situation, or that he had adequately addressed all of the concerns. The fourth step in the chain is to assess your initial solutions to determine if they are ethical, appropriate, and realistic. Student Two did an excellent analysis of the problems. However, her resolutions weren't practical, given the cultural and organizational limitations of the institution. By following the *chain of reasoning*, new and emerging professionals are better able to justify why their proposed resolutions are appropriate responses for the problems they want to address.

RESOLVING A CASE STUDY

For the purpose of this chapter, we will continue to look at how in the previous chapter, co-author Kara Werkmeister developed resolutions for the case, "Student Veteran Support and Discrimination". Kara identified one content area, and using environmental and cultural theory, she analyzed the some of the issues in the case. Notice that Kara began by identifying the primary problems in the case associated with the campus environment. Then, she began to connect theory to each of those problems to better understand the scope of the problem. In the first environment problem Kara addressed, she observed that the physical environment of the Student Veterans Center was not conducive to engaging student veterans. According to the case, the room had "a few couches, an American flag, and no door to separate the room from the rest of the center". This room is not specifically identified as serving student veterans, nor does it have a physical arrangement that supports use by student veterans. In her analysis, Kara draws upon the work of Strange and Banning (2001) to identify the problems inherent in the Student Veterans Center as it currently exists. In doing so, we can also look to Strange and Banning (2001) to imagine what it would take to physically create a more welcoming environment for student veterans. Not only can theory help us understand why certain problems exist, but theory is also valuable in point-ing us toward possible solutions. How can we apply the work of Strange and Banning in this case to create "architectural or environmental probabilism" (p. 14) on the campus of Southeast Community College as it relates to the Student Veterans Center? Tabitha, as the person charged by Dr. Michael Tapeman to take action in this case, could recommend the following short-term steps to address concerns with the physical environment:

- Purchase and install a door to provide privacy for students who use the center. The presence of a door would be a physical indication to student veterans that the room is a "safe space" to privately share their concerns and struggles with others.
- Arrange for the placement of signage outside the Center for Student Success and on the new door to the Student Veterans Center. Besides serving as directional cues to those looking for the Student Veterans Center, the signs also function as symbols of inclusion. The new signs will signify to veteran students that this is a place intentionally cre-ated for their use. The signs may also change the way others view the environment. The addition of signs, which can reflect the campus's values, sends the message to all that student veterans are a welcome presence on campus, and highlights the fact that the institution pro-vides resources to support their success.

The second environmental problem in this case was the person-environment incongruence John Smith experienced as he met resistance in trying to cre-ate veteran-friendly programs on campus. Kara notes in her analysis that John is experiencing *person-environment incongruence* (Strange & Ban-ning, 2015) as he tries to advocate for military-affiliated students on cam-pus. He meets resistance from the Center for Student Success Director, Luke Moore. Kara believes that John represents Astin's (1993) Social Activist type, which according to the case is different from other students on cam-pus, who may be more aligned with Astin's Hedonist type. It may explain why John is struggling in his work with Luke, as Luke may not be used to students at SCC taking such initiative in advocacy work. Strange and Ban-ning (2001) indicate that students experiencing a lack of congruence with their environment will ultimately feel dissatisfaction, which may cause them to seek out a more congruent environment. To resolve this problem, John needs greater congruence (or less incongruence) with the SCC environment. One way for Tabitha to address the problem of environment incongruence is by recommending the following:

- The Veteran Student Center should function as a stand-alone office physically housed in the Center for Student Success. John (and likely his fellow student veterans) represent a student typology different from most SCC students. In order for the Student Veterans Center to develop programming successfully, it will need to function in an environment that supports the Social Activist typology. By giving the center more autonomy, this will minimize conflict with the way the Center for Student Success under the direction of Luke Moore generally functions. Tabitha will suggest to Dr. Tapeman that John should be hired on a part-time basis as a program coordinator for the Student Veterans Center with a budget appropriate to support John's suggested initiatives. This suggestion should be implemented rather quickly to ensure the Student Veterans Center does not lose momentum in the implementation of their planned events. It is also important that the Student Veterans Center continues to thrive as the admissions marketing push by SCC continues to generate attention from prospective students and other campus community members.

The last environment problem Kara identified was John's perception of the culture on campus as being indifferent, and even chilly toward student veterans. He tells Dr. Tapeman that he had been "discriminated against . . . made fun of by classmates" and had never felt more "unsupported, unappreciated, or disrespected" than he had on campus. This indifferent, or even chilly "psychological, or felt climate" describes how John feels about SCC and his experience there (Peterson & Spencer, 1990, p. 13). The two previous problems Kara identified also feed into this third concern. Lack of signage for the Student Veterans Center and the apparent lack of care and attention directed toward creating a physical space that appropriately meets student veteran needs sends the message that the institution does not truly care about student veteran concerns. An institution that is most responsive to the needs and attitudes of the majority student population also makes it difficult for John to navigate the institution, both academically and socially. This may explain why John is having a hard time adjusting to campus, as the transition from "barracks to residence halls" is not something other students or administrators on campus can relate to. Tabitha might respond to this concern by recommending the following long-term resolution:

- Southeast Community College should establish a Student Veteran's Advisory Board. Populated by administration, faculty, and military representatives, this board would have two major responsibilities. The first is to serve as oversight for the Student Veterans Center. The Advisory Board would assist the center in assessing needs among student veterans, developing a center mission, and make recommendations for staffing and resource allocation. Second, the advisory board would also provide SCC with institutional recommendations for proactively working with student veterans across campus.

OTHER CONSIDERATIONS

Students working on a case study often ask, *What other criteria/considerations should I take into account in developing an action plan?* Often, a student will do an excellent job connecting possible resolutions with theory. However, this is not enough. Even the best theory-driven solutions will fail because the solutions do not take into account the context in which they will be implemented. A theory-driven solution may not work because the culture of the office or institution won't support it, or a potential solution is not realistic given the resources available. When you resolve a case, you need to think beyond the immediate needs, determine what is realistic, and examine how the proposed solutions align with ethical and philosophical approaches to work in student affairs.

While there is no right or wrong way to present your solutions to a case study, being able to organize your action plan in a logical, coherent fashion enables you to communicate your thoughts on the situation effectively. After all, you are likely analyzing this situation because you bear some (or all) responsibility for the outcome. Therefore, the outcome of this problem will likely affect you as well as fellow colleagues and students on campus. How well you communicate your proposed solutions will affect the amount of support you can gather for your action plan.

The following are a few issues you will want to consider as you develop resolutions to the problems present in a case study.

Reactive vs. Proactive Responses

Students and new professionals generally find it helpful to organize their responses by thinking of them as either short-term or long-term approaches. What are the things that need to be addressed immediately? Short-term solutions tend to be one-time actions to address a specific set of circumstances or issues. Such solutions are needed to diffuse the current situation and resolve immediate concerns. In Kara's case, one short-term resolution might be for Tabitha to contact Luke Moore to determine how the military connected support group best fits within the organizational structure of the institution. Is this group an activity sponsored by the Student Veterans Center, or should it function as an independent student organization that collaborates with, and supports, the Student Veterans Center? Resolving this issue should also help clarify who is the spokesperson and individual ultimately responsible for the activities of the military connected support group.

Long-term approaches tend to be proactive responses to address broader issues to ensure this type of problem either does not occur again, or if it does, the effects are limited. A long-term approach to the violation of John's privacy is to ensure all adjuncts understand that information about students shared with instructors from the Office of Disability Services is private information, and is not to be revealed to other students or staff unless they have a legitimate educational interest. Education regarding FERPA concerns might be done through an institutional training session, either in person or online, for all faculty and adjuncts. In this case, Tabitha does not have the authority to dictate how adjunct instructors are trained, but she is able to use her relationships with faculty to advance this concern, as well as raise this issue with Dr. Tapeman, who does have influence with his fellow deans to make them aware of the gravity of the situation.

It is important to note that there is no hard and fast rule for what amount of time corresponds to short-term and long-term resolutions. In some cases, short-term issues can be addressed in a matter of days or weeks. Other times, short-term actions may happen over the course of a semester or a year. Long-term approaches tend to extend over a semester and beyond, perhaps even years into the future. It is less a concern about identifying a number to associate with either short or long-term solutions. It is more important to appropriately frame why a resolution might be considered short-term versus one that is long-term in nature.

Important vs. Urgent

These considerations tend to confuse students; while all urgent problems are important, not all important problems are urgent. Put simply, we can assume all proposed solutions are important ones, or you wouldn't be suggesting them. For instance, the long-term solution of ensuring all instructional staff understand the requirements of FERPA is important. Clearly, Southwestern Community College has had an incidence where an adjunct violated a student's right to privacy by revealing information from his student record to an entire psychology class. The adjunct violated school policy and federal law by sharing John's disability with the class without his approval. The institution has an obligation to educate their employees about student privacy policies and laws to ensure this type of situation does not happen again. It is going to take time to for the university to determine when and how they might achieve this goal.

That leaves the solutions to urgent problems. What makes a problem urgent? Sometimes it is helpful to think about problems on university campuses in relation to Maslow's (1943) "Hierarchy of Needs". Problems or issues that affect students' basic needs tend to fall in the "urgent" category. Corresponding with the bottom hierarchical level within the pyramid, student affairs professionals find themselves responding quickly to students' physiological needs, such as ensuring students have appropriate access to shelter, food, water, restroom/bathing facilities, a place to sleep, etc. Also urgent is the second hierarchical level, which corresponds with safety. The second hierarchical level includes providing environments that ensure physical safety and security.

The next levels of Maslow's hierarchy that student affairs practitioners generally consider "urgent" have to do with students' psychological needs. Student psychological needs include having a sense of belonging, either to the larger campus community, or a sense of belonging to a subpopulation of students. The fourth level involves respect from others and recognition as a unique individual. Situations where a student may be bullied, experience prejudice, and/or discrimination can severely undermine a student's sense of psychological security. Those issues are urgent and should be addressed in the short term. Issues associated with general community development and multicultural awareness may be more appropriately addressed through longer-term, on-going initiatives.

The final hierarchical step is self-actualization, which is represented by the realization of personal potential, self-fulfillment, and personal growth. While these are important experiences for students to have while at college, they often do not represent urgent needs for students. In addition, policies and practices that promote student development often take time and planning to implement. Thus, these types of student needs tend to require responses that are best implemented over the longer term.

Appropriate and Realistic

Students and new professionals often struggle in devising responses to problems presented in a case study that are not appropriate or realistic given the facts of the case. For instance, the violation of a student's privacy can have significant consequences. Revealing a student's mental health status to an entire lecture hall of students can be damaging psychologically for the student involved. A violation of FERPA can also open the institution to penalties from the Department of Education, namely the loss of federal funding. So, given the enormity of the adjunct's actions in this case, should she be fired?

Some would argue, that yes, such an action should result in termination. Others might argue it would not be appropriate. The institution could be seen as bearing shared responsibility in this situation, given the instructor received no training in regard to handling confidential information about her students. If it was decided that the adjunct instructor would not be fired, what would be more appropriate steps to take? A formal letter of reprimand in her employment file? Participation in a workshop on FERPA?

Another challenge in determining appropriate and realistic responses lies in examining your role as "decider". Are you a particular character in the case charged with presenting an action plan for resolving the issues in the case? If so, what are your limitations in terms of your own sphere of influence? I encourage students to think about crafting their resolutions in terms of how as the "decider" they might wield enough influence to implement their proposed plan of action. Do they hold enough formal power to implement their proposed plan of action? While establishing an advisory board to raise the level of awareness regarding the needs of military vets on campus might be an appropriate solution for Southwestern Community College, Tabitha Cole, who is a financial aid counselor and the "decider" in this case, might not have the formal power to appoint one.

Nevertheless, Tabitha has two options. One is to seek permission and formal power from those who can confer it upon her to establish an advisory board. She would need to seek permission from the Dean of Students, Dr. Michael Tapeman. Likely, the Dean of Students would also need the provost's support of this initiative to obtain the resources necessary for the advisory board to be effective.

Lacking formal power or permission and support for your action plan, what other sources of power could you rely upon in achieving your goals? Students often overlook this aspect of leadership, but drawing upon one's informal power can yield desired outcomes as well. For example, Kezar and Lester (2011) describe a grassroots leadership strategy to create campus change. Tactics such as collaboration, storytelling, mentoring students, and garnering resources and support can enable academic and administrative staff to challenge current practices and influence campus culture.

Are you a third-party "outsider" who is making recommendations for the actors in the case? This viewpoint gives you the opportunity to act as if you are an outside consultant, hired to clean up a campus problem. In this role, you do not have to worry about your ability to implement your proposed resolutions. As an imaginary, well-paid, highly respected higher education consultant, you can assume the campus would be grateful for your expertise and willing to implement any course of action you suggest. However, you still need to craft resolutions that align with institutional culture and the campus environment. Resolutions should also take into account the organizational limitations and the availability of institutional resources. Last, resolutions to any problem should be crafted to match the abilities and the psychological investment of the individuals involved.

Take, for instance, a possible recommendation that Southeast Community College hire a full-time Student Veteran Support Coordinator. From what we can infer from the case, Southeast Community College appears to be responsive to student needs and interests. There are "lots of clubs and organizations and social events" for the significant number of students who are interested in having a typical collegiate experience while enrolled. That student-centered culture appears to also extend to interactions between administration and students. Despite not having an appointment, John is able to go to the Dean of Students' office and gain access to Dr. Tapeman to speak about his struggles. Dr. Tapeman responds quickly to John's problems by contacting Tabitha and asking her to follow up on John's issues as well as solving "issues for veteran students on campus". Thus, it seems reasonable the culture on campus would support the hiring of an additional staff member if it was warranted.

It may be harder to ascertain whether SCC has the resources to hire a Student Veteran Support Coordinator. While the institution tends to attract affluent, traditionally aged students, community colleges are generally dependent upon a mix of state appropriations, local funding, and tuition revenue. There is a great deal of variation among states regarding community college support, and perhaps SCC resides in a state with low financial support for community colleges. That might help to explain why Luke Moore oversees so many offices and seems stretched too thin.

Speaking of Luke Moore, he would be the person most affected by the addition of a new staff member. Since he is the Director of the Center for Student Success, should he be the supervisor for any new staff person working in the Student Veterans' Center? Luke may appreciate additional staffing to assist with what appears to be a heavy workload. However, Luke comes across as someone who needs to be highly involved in the daily activities of the Student Veterans' Center. Would he have trouble effectively delegating those responsibilities to someone else? Tabitha would need Luke's buy-in and support to help transition any new staff successfully if she or an advisory board were to recommend new staffing for the Student Veterans Center.

Legal vs. Ethical Dimensions

When considering legal and ethical dimensions of a problem in student affairs, it is appropriate to think of law relevant to decisions to be made in higher education as a floor, not a ceiling. In other words, the law represents minimum standards that must be met, rather than the most practitioners should aspire to. Navigating the space between "legal" and "ethical" can be a challenge for student affairs administrators. As legal considerations have proliferated throughout the higher education landscape, it has become too easy to focus on law as the standard to meet in policy, practice, and decision-making.

Responding appropriately to problems in student affairs requires one to have an awareness and appreciation for any legal standards that may exist. Both Tabitha and Dr. Williamson recognized a possible violation of student privacy laws in their discussion about John's experience in class, even though John wasn't lodging a formal complaint. Aware of their professional responsibilities in this area, both Tabitha and Dr. Williamson take initial steps to ensure the situation is not repeated.

If law represents the floor in decision-making on campus, ethical considerations represent the ceiling. It is helpful to think of yourself as a practitioner standing on legal floors while reaching toward moral ceilings. Ethical decision-making can be difficult, especially if two ethical principles conflict. For example, balancing the values of fairness and consistency can be a challenge. Being fair, or just, in regard to a situation involving one student might mean sacrificing consistency in how such situations are handled, or how certain policies are applied, to another student. Each time a student affairs practitioner is confronted with how they might weigh two opposing values, they are facing an ethical dilemma.

Robert Nash (1997) presents a problem-solving approach useful for student affairs practitioners as they analyze and resolve ethical dilemmas. This approach asks decision-makers to answer 10 "essential questions" (p. 3). A few of these questions are worth exploring in depth as it relates to the "Student Veterans" case. Nash's first question in his problem-solving approach asks practitioners to explore the major moral themes in a case. A significant moral theme in this case is the way SCC represents itself to student veterans and the broader community as a "military-friendly" campus, when the actual experiences of student veterans don't live up to this designation. Tabitha recognizes the lack of student veteran support as a problem early on, and encourages John to get involved to improve the experiences of student veterans on the SCC campus.

Nash's ninth essential question asks practitioners to reflect on what the profession's code of ethics might say regarding key moral principles in the case. Is Southeastern Community College acting with veracity (integrity and honesty) and fidelity (honoring commitments made) when advertising itself as a "military-friendly" campus (Council for the Advancement of Standards, 2006)? Could one argue that SCC is guilty of malfeasance by violating Principle II of the CAS Statement of Shared Ethical Principles (2006) in its failure to create environments for student veterans that are "educational and supportive of the growth and development of the whole person" (p. 2). By exploring the ethical implications of this problem, Tabitha will need to address this ethical dimension when presenting her recommendations to Dr. Tapeman.

In working through Nash's essential questions, you may find there is no clear answer. In ethical dilemmas, there rarely are. Hence, the "dilemma" part. Nash (1996) notes that "no solution to an ethical dilemma will ever be fully adequate or fully self-satisfying" (p. 19), but having thoroughly wrestled with the moral implications of a complex problem, one is better positioned to respond to the next ethical dilemma.

Personal Philosophy of Student Affairs Practice

A last consideration for crafting good resolutions to student affairs problems is to examine how potential resolutions square with your own philosophy of student affairs practice. A professional philosophy reflects the way you view your work in the field and how your values influence that work. A professional philosophy helps to keep professionals focused by promoting congruency between what you value and what you do.

It would be difficult to separate decision-making from your own philosophy of student affairs, because its foundation is the values that shape who you are and how you understand the field. Therefore, to name your values and articulate how they shape the ways you react to and respond to problems in student affairs can only help you to better articulate your reasons for arriving at the resolutions you seek to implement.

CONCLUSION

In summary, this chapter walked you through the steps in creating quality resolutions to complex problems in student affairs. As we discovered, crafting quality resolutions for case study problems is an art as well as a science. Using theory to inform possible resolutions is only one part of the process. Student affairs professionals should also consider possible resolutions from several angles to determine if a theory-driven solution will be successful given the contexts and circumstances present in the case. Taking the time to wrestle with case studies and learning to apply a chain of reasoning that connects issues to theory, and theory to resolutions, provides students with the practice necessary to think critically about complex problems. The student affairs field faces new and bigger challenges each day, and it needs practitioners ready and able to resolve them.

The cases in this book are indexed by institutional type, functional area(s), student population(s), salient issues, and theoretical content areas at the end of this book. This index will assist you in finding cases pertaining to a particular topic, student group, or theoretical content area. The remaining chapters consist of 22 robust cases containing complex problems in student affairs. We invite you to engage with these cases, as they represent real problems in the field of student affairs. These cases are designed to challenge your understanding of our students, our institutions, and, most importantly, our work as practitioners.

REFERENCES

Astin, A. W. (1993). An empirical typology of college students. *Journal of College Student Development*, 34, 36–46.

Council for the Advancement of Standards. (2006). *CAS professional standards for higher education* (6th Ed.). Washington, DC: Author.

Kezar, A. & Lester, J. (2011). *Enhancing campus capacity for leadership: An examination of grassroots leaders*. Stanford, CA: Stanford Press.

Krathwohl, D. R. (2009). *Methods of educational & social science research: An integrated approach*. Long Grove, IL: Waveland Press.

Maslow, A. (1943). A theory of human motivation. *Psychological Review*, 50, 370–396.

Nash, R. J. (1996). *"Real world" ethics: Frameworks for educators and human service professionals*. New York: Teachers College Press.

Nash, R. J. (1997). Teaching ethics in the student affairs classroom. *NASPA Journal*, 35, 3–19.

Peterson, M. W. & Spencer, M. G. (1990). Understanding academic culture and climate. In Tierney, W. G. (Ed.), *Assessing academic climates and culture, new directions for institutional research*, No. 68 (pp. 3–18). San Francisco, CA: Jossey Bass.

Strange, C. C. & Banning, J. H. (2001). *Educating by design: Creating campus learning environments that work*. San Francisco: Jossey-Bass.

Strange, C. C. & Banning, J. H. (2015). *Designing for learning: Creating campus environments for student success*. San Francisco, CA: Jossey Bass.

PART II

THE CASES

Chapter 4

Student Veteran Support and Discrimination

Kara Werkmeister and Stacy A. Jacob

In this case, a student veteran tries to fit in and be of practical use to others; however, the student population and college environment do not match the "veteran friendly" marketing the campus uses. As you read the case, think about the environment on the campus and in what ways the main character John does or does not cohere with it. Consider a college and their espoused commitment to providing a certain type of experience. Is John well served and supported at Southeast Community College? How could the players in this case better support and serve John?

CASE

Tabitha Cole has been working as a financial aid counselor at Southeast Community College (SCC) for two years. Southeast Community College is located in an affluent suburb of a major metropolitan city. The majority of the students at SCC are traditional age, wealthy, and attend SCC for a year or two, while they figure out what they want to do in life. SCC is often jokingly referred to as 13th grade. There are numerous clubs, organizations, and social events due to the school's large student population. Students are highly involved in collegiate life. SCC's curriculum is highly focused on academic courses rather than workforce development, and they have a strong articulation agreement with the local research university.

Tabitha's responsibilities include assisting students with various financial aid packages, FASFA completions, loan acquisitions, and scholarship allocations. Tabitha Cole enjoys her job immensely and truly loves helping students.

It is a Tuesday morning, and Tabitha has just finished filing paperwork from a previous student when she hears a knock on her door.

Tabitha: Come in.
John: Thank you, ma'am.

Taking a seat is John Smith; a nontraditional student at SCC. John is 25 years old, but is entering as a first-year student due to his time spent overseas with the military.

Tabitha: What can I help you with today?
John: Well, ma'am, I need some assistance with my GI Bill.
Tabitha: You're a student veteran?
John: Yes, ma'am. Five years in the Marines.
Tabitha: Well, thank you for serving! I'll be happy to help you sort this out. Let's take a look.

As the two look over the extensive document, John makes a statement that catches Tabitha off guard.

John: It's nice to be treated like a regular student. Thanks for helping me!
Tabitha: What do you mean "treated like a regular student"?
John: Oh, sorry, ma'am. I just haven't had the best experience here so far. It's no big deal.
Tabitha: Is everything okay for you here?
John: It's not a big deal, just some of the people on campus here aren't as nice as you, you know, thanking me for my service and such.
Tabitha: [noting John's facial expression] You seem upset.
John: I'm fine, ma'am.
Tabitha: You said that some of the people on campus don't thank you for your service and such, what did you mean by that?
John: It's really just this one class—Intro to Psych. There have been some comments about me being a veteran.
Tabitha: From the students?
John: Not really, it's more the teacher.

Seeing Tabitha's surprised facial expression, John shakes his head, seemingly disappointed.

John: I know. Spend five years overseas only to come back and be asked to "show my battle scars" and explain PTSD to the whole class. I've been overseas, so I "must know how to explain it," right? Anyway, thanks for all of your help. I really appreciate it.

Uncomfortable, John gathers his papers and leaves the office. Tabitha, upset by John's story, decides to look into the matter. She logs on to the SCC system and pulls up John's schedule. Finding the information for his Psychology 101 course, Tabitha calls the professor, Dr. Bob Williams.

Dr. Williams:	Hello.
Tabitha:	Hello, Bob, it's Tabitha from Financial Aid. I was calling in regard to a student, John Smith. He's in a Psychology 101 course at 9:00 a.m. I believe that is section 4 of the class. I am calling you as the Department Chair because John seems to be a bit offended by some comments being made during class and I am not sure what to do.

Dr. Williams asks Tabitha to tell him more and she explains what John has revealed to her. After hanging up with Tabitha, Dr. Williams makes a note to ask Joni Bradford, a new adjunct instructor, about the issue. Joni is a doctoral student in psychology at a local research institution. SCC often uses doctoral students from this university to fill in as adjuncts for popular courses. This is the first semester Joni has taught at SCC and so Dr. Williams does not know her well. Later that day Joni passes by his office.

Dr. Williams:	I had an interesting phone call today. Do you mind coming in and talking with me for a few minutes?
Joni:	Sure, what's going on?
Dr. Williams:	Do you have a John Smith in your Psych 101 course?
Joni:	Yes! He's an older student, a student veteran.
Dr. Williams:	Is he having issues?
Joni:	Well, I mean, when I call on him in class or ask him to give us an example during the discussions he gets weird about it sometimes. But I really think he's a great example and the other students seem to like my teaching so much better when I use real examples. I really want to be a great teacher.
Dr. Williams:	What do you mean, "Ask him to give you an example"?
Joni:	Well, when we were learning about post-traumatic stress disorder, I was having trouble connecting to the students during that discussion, and, you know, sir, he's been in a *war*—so I asked him to explain what it's like.
Dr. Williams:	What war is like?
Joni:	No, I asked him to explain to the class what it's like to have PTSD.
Dr. Williams:	You asked him this during class?
Joni:	The class just always seems to really perk up when I use examples of real-life things and I want to be a good teacher.

	With John there's an *obvious* age difference, and he has a limp, and so when we got his information from The Office of Students with Disabilities saying he was a veteran and that he suffers from PTSD, I thought he would be a great example to use in class!
Dr. Williams:	I understand wanting to be a good teacher, but have you thought about this from John's perspective?
Joni:	Well, no.
Dr. Williams:	What do you think it would feel like to have a personal disability put on display for the entire class?
Joni:	Not good. I didn't even think about that.
Dr. Williams:	One of the hard things about teaching, Joni, is that you have to continually examine what you do from multiple angles. Also you violated FERPA. Do you know what that is?

Joni and Dr. Williams continue their conversation and he learns that the training for adjuncts at SCC consists of a half-day session during which new instructors get their ID, email account, learn how to enter grades and use the Learning Management System, and nothing more.

A week later, Tabitha is working in her office in the Financial Aid Office. She is filing some paperwork when she notices John at her door.

Tabitha:	Hi John, come in, come in! How is everything going?
John:	Hello, ma'am. Fine, thank you. Just here to drop off this form to you.
Tabitha:	How about that class? Any better?
John:	Thank you, ma'am, I'm fine.

Not satisfied with John's response, Mrs. Cole persists.

Tabitha:	John, have you told anyone else about those comments?
John:	Well, ma'am, I'm not quite sure who I would tell. And it's hard to find anyone who would *really* understand what I've been through, you know—someone with the same experience.
Tabitha:	What about our Student Veterans Center? It's in the Center for Student Success?
John:	I didn't know about it, but I'll check it out. Thanks.

Later that day, John stops by the Center for Student Success. He spots it, wanders in, and meets Luke, the Director of the Center for Student Success.

John:	Excuse me, sir. I was hoping someone could help me?
Luke:	Oh, hello! What can I do for you?
John:	I was looking for the Student Veterans Center?
Luke:	Oh, it's right there!

Luke points to a room that is one of the many office-like spaces in the Center for Student Success. It has a few couches, an American flag, and no door to separate the room from the rest of the center.

John: Is there anyone who works there who I can speak to?

Luke: I'm the Director of the entire Center for Student Success and oversee all the offices here—the Student Veterans Center, the Leadership office, Multicultural Connections, and Volunteer Opportunities. Right now, I'm running late for another meeting, so I have to go, but feel free to come and use the Student Veterans Center anytime.

As Luke hurriedly leaves, John looks around at the Student Veterans Center and thinks, "So it's just a room?"

As he leaves the Center for Student Success, John hears his phone ding, signifying he has received an email. Pulling out his iPhone, John sees he has received an email from Tabitha, following up on the paperwork he submitted.

FROM: Tabitha Cole; tabitha.cole@scc.edu
TO: John; jfs1211@scc.edu
SUBJECT: Financial Aid Follow-Up

John,

I am following up to let you know that I have submitted your paperwork that you dropped off this morning, and everything should be updated within the system by Friday at 4:00 p.m. I also wanted to ask if you had a chance to stop in the Center for Student Success and check out the Student Veterans Center? I've never been there myself, but I really hope it's a place you can find support and assistance. If there is ever anything I can do for you, please let me know.

Sincerely,

Tabitha Cole
Financial Aid Counselor
Southeast Community College
Financial Aid Office

John, touched by the gesture, decides to email back.

FROM: John; jfs1211@scc.edu
TO: Tabitha Cole; tabitha.cole@scc.edu
SUBJECT: RE: Financial Aid Follow-Up

Mrs. Cole:

Hello, ma'am. Thanks for the email. I really appreciate all the help and advice you've given me throughout the last few weeks. I actually just left the Center for Student Success. They do have a Student Veterans Center, but it really is just a room.

I was hoping to find someone to talk with about everything that's been happening, someone who may have also been through this whole move from barracks to residence halls. It's been a rough start to the year, and I do appreciate the idea you gave me to come here and check it out. However, it doesn't seem like there is anyone I can meet with so I don't really think it's going to be much of a help. I do appreciate the suggestion though, and thanks again for all the help with my GI Bill.

Have a great week.

John

After receiving John's email response, Tabitha is puzzled. SCC is proudly identified as a "military friendly campus"—so she is surprised to hear John's description of the center. Knowing the Director for the Center for Student Success, Tabitha decides to contact Luke.

FROM: Tabitha Cole; tabitha.cole@scc.edu
TO: Luke Moore; luke.moore@scc.edu
SUBJECT: Student Veterans Center Inquiry

Luke,

I have a general inquiry regarding the Student Veterans Center here at SCC. I've been working with a student here in Financial Aid who's having some issues adjusting to college life after having been in the military for a number of years. I recommended that he reach out to the Student Veterans Center, but he did not seem to find it useful. I was hoping that you might be able to explain to me just what kinds of resources are available for student veterans here, so that I'm more informed and better able to assist students who ask these kinds of questions in the future.

Sincerely,

Tabitha Cole
Financial Aid Counselor
Southeast Community College
Financial Aid Office

FROM: Luke Moore; luke.moore@scc.edu
TO: Tabitha Cole; tabitha.cole@scc.edu
SUBJECT: RE: Student Veterans Center Inquiry

Tabitha,

Thanks you for your email. I do oversee the Student Veterans Center. It offers students a place to meet or work that is a safe space. We have seating available, and the room is always open for students to walk in and utilize at their convenience. If a student needs assistance adjusting, you could send them to the Counseling Center.

Luke Moore
Director for the Center for Student Success
Southeast Community College

Tabitha, unsatisfied and frustrated with the response, decides to email John Brown again with an idea.

FROM: Tabitha Cole; tabitha.cole@scc.edu
TO: John; jfs1211@scc.edu
SUBJECT: Student Veterans Center Idea

John,

I reached out to the Director for the Center for Student Success about the resources available to students in the Student Veterans Center, and it appears as if you were correct in speaking about the lack of materials/resources available there. However, I think that you could utilize this information, as well as the difficulties you are currently facing on this campus, to make a difference. I know I do not know you well, but from what I can see, you are an intelligent young man with confidence and a desire to become socially involved and accepted. That is the making of a fine leader, John. I think that you could really utilize this situation to better the resources for students like yourself here on campus, and I am more than willing to support you in any way possible. I deeply apologize for the problems you have been facing here at SCC.

Please let me know if I can be of further assistance.

Sincerely,

Tabitha Cole
Financial Aid Counselor
Southeast Community College
Financial Aid Office

Reading the email from Tabitha, John furrows his brow. "What could I do?" he thinks; both touched by her kind words and frustrated by his experiences at SCC. John knew that, back on base, they had support groups and resources for military members and families, but he was not sure what was typically offered on a college campus. Over the next few days, John communicated with individuals on his old military base, asking questions and seeking more information about the resources that were offered there. One idea that he was particularly drawn to was the idea of a "military allied students" group, which would be open to student veterans, family members, friends, or even students on campus who just wanted to do service-related projects to support the military. After writing down all of his ideas, John called Luke to set up a meeting. The next day, John arrived for his appointment with Luke.

John: Hello, Mr. Moore [extending his hand] my name is John.
Luke: Hello, John [shaking his hand] what can I do for you? I have you on my calendar under "group-creation request." Are you interested in starting a club here at SCC?
John: Well, sir, I'm not sure. You see, I'm new here, and I just noticed that there isn't really a lot of support for veterans.

Luke: We have a Student Veterans Center, have you seen it? And we host a veterans' reception, each semester—which is a wonderful event that community members also can enjoy. Would you like me to get you a flyer?

John: That sounds great, sir, but do you think we could do more? I have lots of ideas.

Luke: What do you have in mind?

John begins telling Luke all of his ideas including a military connected support group, sending care packages, getting speakers, supporting the ROTC, a mentee program for new student veterans, and some special event at orientation and move in.

Luke: These are great ideas, John! Why don't we start with the support group idea.

After scheduling a date and time for the first meeting, reserving a room, and assigning tasks to be completed (such as advertisements and catering booking), John leaves the Center for Student Success feeling overwhelmed and successful. "This is awesome," he thinks.

John creates advertisements for his military connected support group and has a successful first meeting, which Luke attends. They decide on several events and service projects, and John feels proud of the initiative and support in the group. One of the students who joined the group is a volunteer tour guide in the Admissions Office. While waiting to give a tour, the student tells the person in charge of admission marketing about the new student group. The marketing person contacts John for an interview and the next week the group is featured on a major marketing campaign for SCC. The next week John is featured on the SCC website and billboard and Luke calls John into a meeting.

Luke: John, [sitting down] I saw the website and the billboard, can you tell me about it?

John: [caught off guard and visibly confused] Excuse me, sir?

Luke: The support group, John? No one called to ask me about it. That group is under my supervision; it is now being marketed by SCC, but no one ever called to talk to me about it.

John: Sorry?

Luke: I am concerned that I was not consulted about the marketing and now I am suddenly reading about you and your group everywhere. Can you understand why I am concerned when I am ultimately responsible for the Student Veterans Center's group?

John: I'm sorry, sir. I just got asked a few questions from marketing and responded. I thought it would be good advertising for the

	group. I get you're upset, but I didn't write it, and I did mention the Student Veterans Center working collaboratively with me.
Luke:	I think you see this differently. You are a volunteer but everything that comes out of this office is a representation of me and so I would like to know about these things.
John:	Sir, I apologize, I didn't mean to offend you—I was just trying to get our name out there. I think it's important for the group to include anyone who wants to be in it. That's how it works on base, kind of. There are resources for lots of people, newly engaged, widows, families, veterans. I just thought we should be like that, sir—let any student join who wants to.
Luke:	It sounds like you want this to be a group completely on its own, John, which is fine. But if it is a student group, it won't have the Student Veterans Center's name attached to it.
John:	Umm, okay.

Luke gathers his papers and leaves the meeting room. John also stands, but instead of walking to his residence hall, he heads to an office that he was shown on his initial campus tour.

John:	[Entering office of Dr. Michael Tapeman, Dean of Students, speaking to secretary] Hello, ma'am. I need to speak with Dr. Tapeman.

John waits for a few minutes and is then directed back into Dr. Tapeman's office.

Dr. Tapeman:	Hello! What can I do for you?
John:	Sir, I appreciate you meeting with me, and I apologize for not making an appointment. My name is John. I am a veteran, and I am a student on this campus. I have been discriminated against here countless times. My professor uses me as an example of PTSD, breaching my privacy on a regular basis, asking me to not only relive what it's like to suffer from the service I did, but asking me to speak about it in front of an entire lecture hall. I am made fun of by classmates and peers. And when I sought support and resources here, I found that the Student Veterans Center was just a room. Instead of giving up, I decided to be a leader, sir. I decided to do my best to help other students on campus. I worked with the Director of the Center for Student Success to create a support group for military connected students, in collaboration with the Student Veterans Center. And I was just told that this too will not be

supported, or funded. I have fought for my country, sir. I have fought for you, and for every single person on this campus. I am a Southeast Community College student. I am a veteran, and I have never felt more unsupported, unappreciated, or disrespected than I have on this campus. The only person that has been nice to me is Mrs. Cole in Financial Aid. I want you to tell me what you are going to do to fix this.

Dr. Tapeman asks John questions and listens to his story. Before they part, Dr. Tapeman assures John that he will help him. After John leaves, Dr. Tapeman calls Tabitha Cole.

Dr. Tapeman:	Tabitha, this is Michael Tapeman. How are you today?
Tabitha:	Good. And you?
Dr. Tapeman:	Good. Listen, John Smith just left my office and he is very upset about his experiences here at SCC. He spoke very highly of you and how helpful you have been. So I was thinking, I would like for you to work with John and help solve some of his issues and issues for veteran students on campus. He will be emailing you to make an appointment to do so.

Questions

1. Southeast Community College is marketed as a "military friendly campus." What are a college's responsibilities to live up to their marketing and how far should a college go to do so? What are the ethics of advertising a college?
2. John does not fit in at SCC and in trying to find support reaches out to an unlikely person, Tabitha, the financial aid officer. How do you serve students when you are the not the usual person they reach out to? What tools and theories do you need to effectively do so? How do you help a student that is mismatched to the campus environment?
3. How is diversity defined in this case, and what theory would help you better understand and work with John? What plans would you devise to serve student veterans like John?
4. Who owns a volunteer program in a college when it is conceived by a volunteer? Why? How do you work with and/or supervise student volunteers?

Chapter 5

Black Student Experiences at a Rural Branch Campus

Jordan W. Brooks and Molly A. Mistretta

This case is much more than a story of an African American student's run-in with some local white residents off-campus. It also explores the complex issues that arise between campus and community, whites and people of color, as well as the branch campus and main campus. How do the organizational and environmental issues present at the Donora branch of McKean State University influence what happens in this case?

THE CAMPUS

Located in the second-largest city in the state, McKean State University is a public research institution enrolling approximately 37,000 students. Over the last 50 years, McKean expanded its outreach by adding branch campuses in rural, underserved areas of the state. The branch campuses tend to attract local students and offer enrollment to those who don't meet the selective admissions standards at McKean's main campus. The curricular offerings typically include associate and pre-professional degrees. The McKean Options Program also provides a pathway for students to transfer to the main campus after successfully completing their general studies requirements at one of the branch campuses.

The McKean branch campuses operate rather independently from the main campus, with little coordination or oversight. Each campus has its own provost, who makes decisions based on the unique local needs of each campus. In addition, the six branch campuses exist in the shadow of the main campus, often lacking in resources readily available on the main campus. Faculty and administration are drastically understaffed and struggle to provide basic services to students. Turnover is also a problem. Many faculty and staff start their McKean careers at branch campuses, but soon leave to pursue positions at the main campus when openings occur, or depart to more prestigious institutions.

About 500 students attend McKean University at Donora, a rural town of 15,000, mostly white residents. Like the other McKean branch campuses, approximately one-third of the students at McKean-Donora are students of color, and most are African American students from urban areas. Most McKean-Donora students live on campus.

Jamal Williams, the Coordinator for Residence Life, is African American; as is Resident Assistant Eboni Cole and fellow students Shane Thomas and Zhané Peterson. Officer Alan Jennings, Police Chief Drummond, Director of Residence Life, Edward Williams, and the new Vice President of Student Affairs, Dr. Angela Booker, are white.

THE INCIDENT

It is 1:00 a.m. on Wednesday morning at Hatcher Hall. The Coordinator for Residence Life, Jamal Williams, just finished accompanying Eboni, a Resident Assistant (RA), with her final duty round of the night. As Jamal heads back to his apartment, he gets a call from one of the campus police officers, Alan Jennings. Officer Jennings informs him that a student is being taken to the hospital. The student, an African American sophomore named Shane Thomas, reported that he was walking around just off campus and was physically assaulted by four white men from the town. One or two of the assailants were carrying weapons.

Jamal asked how bad Shane looked and whether he was walking alone. Officer Jennings told him that the student was indeed walking alone and had a few visible bruises and cuts on his body. After hanging up the phone, Jamal proceeded to call the Director of Residence Life, Edward Williams, to inform him about the situation. Edward told Jamal to meet with him in the morning so they could discuss the details from the police report. However, Jamal decided to go to the hospital to check on Shane, provide him support, and gather more information about his condition and the assailants, if possible.

When Jamal arrived at the hospital, the emergency room physician was in the process of examining Shane. The doctor asked Shane whether he felt any pain in his head or neck, or if he experienced any limited range of motion. Shane said, "No, I think I'm okay." The doctor began examining his wounds. Shane had many small cuts and scrapes across his arms and chest and he had a few large bruises. While the doctor was examining him, she asked him what happened.

Shane said, "I was walking to the gas station and cut through the back alley behind the university print shop as a shortcut. As I was walking through the alley, I looked ahead and noticed four white guys hanging out in front of the gas station watching me. As I got closer, they all started walking toward me. I wanted to avoid them, and not make eye contact, but there really wasn't another way to go. Two of them were as big as me and the other two were short. Then one of them pulled out a knife and said, 'You don't belong here, and let me show you what we do to those who don't belong here.' While I was facing him, another guy pushed me to the ground. I tried to get up but they just kept kicking me and dragging me up the alley. They eventually stopped and ran off. So I ran off."

The doctor, while finishing her exam, tells Shane, "Well, I'm glad you weren't hurt worse. Just to be sure, I want to take some X-rays in case there is damage that we can't see."

After the doctor has left, a white Donora police officer came in to take Shane's statement and file a report. The McKean Police Department often works closely with local law enforcement. Many McKean police officers are from the local area and enjoy friendly relationships with the police force in the town of Donora. In fact, the Donora Police Department often hires McKean officers when openings occur.

The Donora police officer asked Shane what happened. Shane responded, "I was on my way to the convenience store when these four white guys jumped me. I cut through an alley, and as I was getting closer to the gas station, they surrounded me." The Donora police officer asked, "Did you try to run away?" Shane said, "I tried, but one of them pulled out a knife, and I didn't know what to do then. He said to me, 'You don't belong here, and I'm going to show you what happens to people who don't belong here.'"

The Donora police officer asked, "What were the other guys doing at the time?" Shane replied that he didn't know. But, he said, "One guy came and hit me, and knocked me to the ground," Shane motioned the strike to the back of his head. "They just kept kicking me and dragging me back up the alley. When they stopped I ran off as fast as I could."

When the Donora police officer asked Shane if he could describe the assailants, Shane really couldn't give good descriptions. When the officer kept pressing Shane about what they looked like, Shane got frustrated and said, "I don't know! I really didn't get a good look! I was more focused on the knife. It was dark and, most of the time, I was on the ground trying not to get kicked in the face."

Later that night, Jamal ran into Officer Jennings as he was patrolling the residential area of campus. Jamal asked, "So what is going to happen from your end?" Jennings responded, "Because the details of the case are vague, it is hard to identify the attackers. There is not enough credible evidence for us to draw from to make a case. The local police we spoke with wonder if this was a conflict between friends and Shane doesn't want to get his friends in trouble."

"So you mean to tell me a student who was jumped, and probably too shaken up from the event to remember all the details, isn't going to be taken seriously? Why can't the campus police investigate this further?" Jamal asked.

Jennings shared that there wasn't anything else the police could do at this point. "A report has been filed, and if something like that happens again, they have that report to consider. But I don't think something like this will happen again. Things like that don't happen here. Maybe Shane did something to provoke a fight."

Jamal walked away shocked by the response. He hoped that in the morning, his supervisors would be able to influence the university and city police to investigate this case further.

That next morning, Dr. Booker, the new Vice President of Student Affairs, called a meeting with the Student Life staff to discuss the incident. The Director of Student Life, Edward Williams, Jamal, and the Chief Drummond of McKean-Donora's campus police were invited to discuss the situation and prepare a plan of action. Chief Drummond opened the meeting with his take on reports from Officer Jennings, as well as the status of the investigation with the city police.

Drummond began by stating, "There is not enough evidence for the university police to perform a formal investigation. Shane's story was too vague to give us much to go on. I also wonder if the beating was as serious as he claimed. Looking at him, he appears to only have some minor cuts and bruises. Since Shane told us the event happened with members outside of our campus community, it is really up to the city police, and they are not investigating it further."

Dr. Booker asked, "So what will you do now?"

"I believe our hands are tied. It would require more information for any further action to be taken. Plus, I talked with Sherry Proctor, the Director of Counseling and Health Services. She looked up his student records and noted from his admissions application that Shane enrolled here after being released from juvenile probation. I was able to access his juvenile record. He experienced domestic violence at home and often stole and lied to get what he needed. He's not exactly the most credible victim," Chief Drummond replied.

Dr. Booker was unsure what to make of the situation, so she asked the group, "We should still inform the community either way and warn students of possible danger . . . right?"

Chief Drummond was adamant about not issuing a statement. "I say that no statement should be made unless we have some credible evidence that this was more than a fight among a group of teenage boys. I don't want to start a panic on campus with the black kids, and we shouldn't be so quick to accuse the townspeople of being racist. We have good town-grown relations, I'd like to keep it that way."

Edward Williams spoke up, "The Chief has a point. We really can't describe the alleged assailants better than they were white and 'two were short and two were tall.' That doesn't help students protect themselves. I understand why local police can't take further action without more information. Last thing we need is to cause panic among the students."

Jamal found himself uncomfortable about the direction the meeting was taking. He was the first to see Shane after the assault and found his story to be credible. Jamal felt that students had the right to know that *something* happened to a fellow student while he was off campus. This would be particularly important for African American students, since they are a visible minority within the Donora community, and since the injured student is black. But he also understood that the lack of information the police had to go on made this a difficult case to solve. Most of all, he was disappointed that the investigation was being dropped so soon.

Jamal couldn't help but wonder if the investigation would have gone further had the victim been a white student. He decided to speak up. "I'm just concerned that if we do nothing, we may not be warning students of a potentially dangerous situation. The men who attacked Shane could feel like they got away with it and might do it again."

Chief Drummond disagreed. "There is no history of events like this. We should focus our efforts on assuring the campus that Shane is okay and getting the help he needs. Any tension around the situation will just fade."

Dr. Booker took Chief Drummond's advice and decided not to make a formal campus statement from her office. Neither did the Department of Student Life, nor campus police. Dr. Booker instructed that the events be recorded in the public campus police blog. She recommended Chief Drummond to use the following wording: *A student suffered injury off campus and was transported to the hospital for evaluation. Details surrounding the incident are still being gathered at this time.*

AFTERMATH

Shortly after that meeting, Jamal returned to his office in Hatcher Hall. A black female student entered his office to talk about rumors she had heard about Shane. Zhané Peterson asked, "I heard that some white guys jumped Shane right in the alley across from the gas station."

Eboni Cole, walking into the office to check her staff mailbox, overheard the conversation. She added, "Yeah, the boys on the third floor were talking about how these four guys followed Shane and jumped him when he was by himself off campus. Is it true?"

Jamal struggled with how he would answer the question. He wanted to be forthcoming with the students, but he also felt the expectation that as an administrator, he should support the plan established in the meeting earlier. So he said, "I have heard the rumors and I did check on Shane last night. We aren't certain about everything that took place, but information is still being gathered."

Zhané was exasperated by his answer. "And not telling me that some racist white people are out here jumping us is okay while the university goes through its proper steps and procedures? I mean why hasn't anyone told us? There is just some small bit on the McKean-Donora police website saying a student went to the hospital. Are they scared to tell us? Why? What are they hiding?"

Jamal sighed. "Zhané I see how you can feel that way, but I think there is a difference between hiding information and taking time to make an appropriate response. It's just like last semester when BSU's Black Heritage Month banner was stolen. You all got the group together and asked me to attend the meeting to help decide the appropriate action to take. This is a larger issue with a lot of variables and a lot of people both inside and outside of the university are involved."

Zhané thought about that for a moment. "I guess . . . I can see that . . . but I think the police should be searching for these people. Students need to get together and protect each other from this. I feel like the Black Student Union should get people together like our own neighborhood watch. And if the school and town are taking too long to get justice for Shane, we need to protest. Our concerns should be taken seriously."

Jamal became frustrated because this was exactly how he thought students would feel. He wanted to be able to give clear details to Zhané, and he was not confident about how the administration was handling the situation. He ended the conversation by promising to share all he can, as more information became available. The students left feeling unsatisfied and so did Jamal. Similar conversations took place with other students over the course of the next day and a half. Jamal picked up on a growing sense of frustration among students, and he was concerned that at some point, it might boil over.

Jamal headed back to the Residence Life Office to get some feedback on how to better respond to students about this incident. As Jamal entered the office, he noticed a large group of students and staff gathered around the TV in the corner. On one of the local channels, Shane was being interviewed by reporters about the assault. Shane described the incident in detail and was quick to point out the lack of response by McKean State University-Donora and the local police.

Knocking on Edward Williams' office door, Shane stuck his head in. "Hey, mind if we talk?" Jamal got right to the point, "Edward, this isn't going well. Did you just see Shane on the news? Students are asking me what is going on, and they are frustrated by the lack of information. They think the campus isn't doing anything because the university doesn't take crimes against black students seriously. This could spill over into something bigger."

Edward grimaced. "Yeah, I caught it at the noon newscast. Look, these are college students we are dealing with. They always overreact to stuff. Last week, we had a group of students protesting the lack of gluten-free options in the dining hall. We have fewer than 400 residential students. How many different things can the dining hall staff cook every day?"

Jamal pressed harder with his point, "Edward, we need to take this seriously. Black students tell me stuff that they don't share with the rest of the staff on campus. There isn't anyone else for them to talk to. At best, they feel uneasy about the environment here at Donora. It's not what they are used to, and they don't feel welcome in the community. They joke that there is probably a KKK group in town, but now they are starting to think that is true. That is why they drive to Elliotville, rather than spend time off campus in Donora."

Edward thought about this for a moment, "I didn't realize. But it makes sense they would share that with you. But I don't know what to tell you. I don't think Chief Drummond or the Donora police are racist. In my experience, they take *all* reports seriously. It just so happens that there isn't much to go on with this one."

Jamal asked, "Are you going to talk to Dr. Booker about this? At least make her aware that the students are unhappy?"

Edward responded, "I don't see the point. She made her decision about it, and she rarely budges once she makes a decision. I'm not going to rock the boat. I'll need her reference if I want to make a move up to the main campus someday. It's her responsibility to manage this. Don't worry! It's not on you! And in a few days, there will be something else to grab students' attention. You know . . . drama on social media, lack of parking, or tuition increases. Any of those will do."

Later that evening, the McKean-Donora Black Student Union led a loud, but peaceful protest about the handling of this matter though the walkways of campus. Local and regional media outlets interviewed several students in the protest. Jamal was proud of the students for taking action, but felt as if he had let them down in this matter. He also noticed that few students sought him out about this or any concerns since Shane did his initial news interview.

Soon after the protests were aired on the eleven o'clock news, Jamal was notified that the Vice-President for Student Affairs from the McKean main campus would be at Donora at 10:00 a.m. the next morning to lead an emergency meeting with all of the McKean-Donora Student Life staff. Jamal realized this was his opportunity to speak up about his concerns regarding how the Donora campus and local police handled Shane's assault.

Questions

1. Jamal wants to share his concerns about how the Donora campus police and the local police handled Shane's assault. Where should he first direct those concerns, and how should he go about doing this?
2. What should Jamal say about how the matter was handled?
3. How might Jamal address the fact that he disagreed with his superiors about notifying students? What are the potential consequences he may face for doing so?
4. What suggestions might Jamal make for improving the current situation?
5. What are the environmental/cultural issues that negatively affect the experience of students of color at the Donora campus? What could be done to make this a more welcoming environment for these students?

Chapter 6

Student Athlete Struggles to Find Footing on Campus

Kerri Butler and Molly A. Mistretta

Large universities are complex institutions that sometimes struggle to manage competing expectations and interests. This struggle is often apparent through the management of competitive athletics. In this case, we can see how the university struggles to balance academic vs. athletic missions. What are the pressures experienced by institutions with large athletic programs and how can these institutions best ensure their student athletes are treated ethically?

St. Royal University is a large, private institution that enrolls around 30,000 students. The university is located in the central part of the state in a largely rural area, and the town that shares that same name is a typical small college town. When the students are gone for breaks, it is a rather quiet place to be. However, the population of St. Royal swells considerably whenever there is an athletic event occurring on campus.

St. Royal is well known for their intercollegiate Division I athletics. All of their athletic teams are successful in their conference, and many are nationally recognized. The students, alumni, and the larger campus community are supportive of the athletic programs at St. Royal. Their school pride is reflected in the attendance and enthusiasm displayed at games. With a large national alumni base, St. Royal has a tremendous following of fans at away games, too. Athletics are the heart and soul of university life at St. Royal.

One sport in particular that does well and has great support from the campus is the women's soccer team. The women's soccer team is the most successful athletic program at the university. They won their conference three out of the last five years and made it to the quarterfinals in the NCAA tournament 15 times. Many players have gone on to play professional soccer and several have represented the United States on the women's national team. The attention the women's soccer team receives is reflected in its new training facility. The facility consists of a new practice field and a large, new building housing an indoor field, locker rooms, coaches' offices, weight room, athletic training rooms, and meeting rooms. There is also a common room with televisions, couches, and a kitchen.

Charlotte is a first-year member of the women's soccer team and is excited to be at St. Royal. Soccer is a huge part of Charlotte's life; she has been playing the sport she loves since she was four years old. Charlotte is a quiet, caring, friendly young woman with a fierce drive to succeed. Charlotte comes from a working-class family that lives in a suburban area in Maryland. Charlotte's full athletic scholarship covers all of her tuition, housing, meal plan, and books. With one of the highest tuition rates in the country, Charlotte could never have afforded St. Royal on her own.

Charlotte's new roommate, Miranda, is also on the women's soccer team. Miranda and Charlotte realized after a short time that they have a lot in common besides soccer and have become good friends. Miranda enjoys a lot of the same television shows that Charlotte does, they are both middle children, and they also share a great love for animals. Neither Miranda nor Charlotte are really into the party scene.

On the soccer field Charlotte is a midfielder. She is strong, good in the air, and wins tackles often. One of Charlotte's limitations, however, is that she is not quite as quick and agile as her coach would like her to be. Vicki Carlson is considered one of the best soccer coaches in the sport; she consistently produces championship teams and players who eventually play Olympic and World Cup soccer. Vicki's teams are successful because she has high standards for her athletes and she pushes them to work hard. She is a demanding coach who oversees the women's soccer program with military precision.

The season has started out well for Charlotte. She worked hard in the preseason, and felt that work rewarded when she was named a starter in the team's first scrimmage. Playing at this level, Charlotte realizes that the deficiencies in her game can't be compensated for by her size and strength. She is going to have to keep working on her speed and agility. This was reinforced in her first individual player's meeting with Vicki, who told Charlotte she was too slow for the midfield. Charlotte wasn't sure how to respond.

Charlotte: I am not really sure what you are asking of me. I know I need to get quicker, but how? I am willing to do anything to improve my individual performance so I can help the team.

Vicki:	You need to spend another hour every day doing agility work and improving your speed of play with the ball. We don't have time in practice to help everyone with their individual weaknesses. Fixing those is something that you need to take care of on your own if you want to continue to start and play on this team. Frankly, right now Charlotte, you are hurting the team.
Charlotte:	Yes, coach. I promise I'll do what I need to do to improve. I'm sorry that I haven't been performing up to your standards and I will work hard to change that.
Vicki:	Well, that is good to hear. Don't do this for me though, do this for yourself and your teammates. I can always find someone else with all the skills a midfield position requires. You must have the will and self-discipline to become quicker. Great athletes demonstrate high levels of determination and drive to reach their goals.

After leaving the coach's office, all Charlotte wants to do is cry. She wasn't prepared for Vicki to say she could lose her position on the team. She could lose her scholarship! Charlotte is concerned about how she would find the time to fit in the extra work. How was she supposed to practice another hour a day on her own, as well as participate in the two and a half hour team practices? Now that the semester has started, she has class and homework as well. Charlotte feels completely overwhelmed.

That evening Charlotte tells Miranda what happened in her meeting with Vicki. Charlotte divulges to Miranda that she is stressed about the pressure that is involved with the extra training. Miranda tries to comfort Charlotte. She hugs her and tells Charlotte if she needs to talk that she is there to listen.

The next morning Charlotte contacts the team's strength coach to see if he is willing to help her improve her quickness. The coach tells her to come to practice an hour early and he will work with her. Charlotte works hard in those one-hour sessions, but finds it distracting when Vicki comes out of her office to watch. Charlotte struggles to not get upset when Vicki yells comments like, "Come on, Charlotte, you can do better than that! Push yourself!"

Two weeks go by and Charlotte continues to train an extra hour before every practice. Her strength coach tries to reassure her that it takes longer than a couple of weeks to see improvements, but Charlotte is frustrated. All the while Vicki continues to tell Charlotte how slow on the field she is, and that she must be "the slowest player in the conference". Vicki also tells Charlotte she should be getting quicker by now, and wonders if maybe Charlotte doesn't want her starting spot bad enough. Charlotte is having a tough time handling the criticism from her head coach. Charlotte has never had a coach yell at her like Vicki does, and it is beginning to affect her ability to concentrate on the ball.

Over the past two weeks, Charlotte was starting to find it difficult to make time for everything. She has class all day, and then has to run from class to the athletic training room to get treatment for her sore muscles. She does her extra training, participates in team practice, and after all of that, goes back to her room or the library to study. The hurried schedule is starting to affect her eating habits. Charlotte begins skipping meals and eating small snacks on the go. Charlotte is so exhausted from all of her responsibilities pulling her in different directions that she finds herself crying often. One night, Miranda walks in on her crying.

Miranda: Are you okay, Charlotte? What's wrong?

Charlotte: I'm okay, I just think I'm really tired and really stressed out. Classes and soccer have been super stressful and I haven't really been sleeping all that well lately.

Miranda: You need to take it easier on yourself! You've been running yourself into the ground, Charlotte. Have you been eating? Sometimes when I don't eat a lot I get really tired and don't feel like doing anything.

Charlotte: I know, I know, but if I don't get quicker, I don't play. Yes, I've been eating! And it doesn't help that Vicki is just making me nervous all of the time now! I'm so afraid that I'm going to do something wrong! She's always on my case! She's really hard on me and I just can't take it anymore!

Miranda: I understand Charlotte. Coach *is* really hard on you, and sometimes it seems unfair. Maybe you should talk to someone about it.

Charlotte: Yeah maybe. Thanks, Miranda.

Although she knows she should be eating properly, Charlotte wonders if she is getting a little quicker because she is leaner. Charlotte thinks about what Miranda said, but does not know who to talk to or what to do about her situation. Charlotte doesn't want to talk to her parents about it, because she doesn't want them to think she can't handle being at St. Royal. They are so proud that she is attending a great school and playing soccer there.

She considers speaking to her athletic academic advisor, Samantha, as they have developed a good relationship. All of her meetings with Samantha have been helpful so far. Usually Samantha and Charlotte talk about her grades, and how she is doing in her classes. Charlotte isn't sure that Samantha can help her with her stress, but she decides to bring it up at their next meeting.

Samantha: How are you doing, Charlotte?

Charlotte: I am doing all right. I have been a little busy this week with midterms so I haven't gotten much sleep. Other than that though, I am doing well.

Samantha: How are classes going?

Charlotte: They are going all right.

Samantha: Well Charlotte, it has come to my attention from some of your professors that you have been absent from class a lot recently. Why haven't you been going to class?

Charlotte: I have been going to class! Those absences were probably because of soccer.

Samantha: I checked on that, and yes, some of them are because you were traveling with the team. But quite a few of your absences haven't been team-related. Your midterm grades are posted, and you have two Ds, two Cs, and a B.

Charlotte: Well, I haven't been feeling very well lately so I missed a few classes to rest and feel better.

Samantha: Why have you not been feeling well?

Charlotte: I don't know.

Samantha: You can tell me, Charlotte. Whatever you tell me stays here.

Charlotte: Well, I have been working really hard recently. I haven't been sleeping because I've been studying at all hours of the night. I have been training extra hard every day and that is starting to wear on me. I don't know, I guess I am just having a hard time handling all of the pressure of soccer and school, and I don't know what to do. Coach has been really tough on me, and I am afraid to make a mistake or play poorly because I don't want to get yelled at or let the team down. And then of course, there is my scholarship to think about. If coach wants to, she could just pull my scholarship and then I won't be able to go school here anymore because my parents can't afford this school. Right now, I just feel like I don't have control over anything in my life. I feel like I am just being pulled in all sorts of directions by so many different people! (Charlotte begins to cry.)

Samantha: I'm sorry that you feel like you are being stretched too thin. College is tough by itself without also competing in a Division I sport. I know it is difficult right now, but you have a lot of people around you who are willing to help you succeed. First, we need to make sure you keep your grades up. We can get tutors to work with you during study tables. They can help you understand the material better and hopefully you won't be up really late at night studying. But, you have to attend your classes because I can't help you unless you make the effort to be at class and listen and take notes.

Charlotte: Yes. I promise I will go to class unless I have a game. I'm sorry that I haven't been, and that I'm crying now.

Samantha: I understand Charlotte, don't worry about it. It is tough trying to juggle both soccer and academics. But, you have to make time for yourself too, and make sure you are taking care of yourself, like eating and sleeping. May I ask you something? Are you eating properly? I know you are not sleeping well and getting enough rest at night, but it is important to eat too.

Charlotte: I'm eating! Why do people keep asking me that? I swear I have been eating, but I've got to be quicker on the field, and dropping weight helps with that. My eating is not a problem.

Samantha: Okay, I believe you. Is there anything else you want to talk about?

Charlotte: No, not really. Thank you for listening to me.

Samantha: Anytime you need to talk my door is always open.

Charlotte leaves her conversation with Samantha upset and confused. She knows she is doing poorly in her classes, which is causing her a lot of stress and discomfort. Charlotte has always been a straight-A student, so Ds and Cs are really making her worry. She also does not understand why everyone keeps asking her if she is eating. Charlotte likes her leaner body. Not only has losing weight helped her to get quicker and do better in practices and games, but she also feels that she looks better.

Samantha is not really sure how she feels about the meeting with Charlotte. She hopes she got her point across to Charlotte about her class attendance. She is concerned about how Charlotte feels she is being treated by Vicki. Samantha does not know what to do about this issue. Over the years, several players from the women's soccer team have complained about Vicki's coaching style. Samantha is aware that there is a fine line between coaching and verbal harassment. Samantha wonders if she should report Vicki's behavior to someone. But she fears that if she speaks with anyone about it, Vicki may take it out on Charlotte.

Most important, though, Samantha knows Charlotte is not telling the truth about her eating habits because her weight loss is quite noticeable. Samantha fears that Charlotte is not eating as much as she should be, especially since she burns a lot of calories in practice. Samantha thinks she needs to know more about Charlotte's eating habits and Vicki's alleged verbal abuse before she mentions it to anyone else.

Samantha begins attending Charlotte's home games, and watches a few practices in hopes of getting a better understanding of Vicki's coaching style. Samantha did witness Vicki yelling at Charlotte and some other younger players using derogatory terms such as "lazy", "worthless", and "fat". Once, Vicki threw soccer balls at players when she wanted to get their attention for play correction during an inter-squad scrimmage.

Samantha decided that she needed to speak with someone about Charlotte. Samantha took the few steps over to the athletic director's office and asked to speak with him. It is not typical for an athletic academic advisor to speak with the head athletic director.

The athletic director at St. Royal University, Charles Morris, is a busy administrator, overseeing a $110 million athletic program. In particular, the revenue-generating sports of football and men's basketball get most of his time and attention. Charles is under incredible pressure to produce winning seasons in all sports year after year. Based on what Samantha knows about Charles, she realizes that her conversation with him may not go the way she hopes.

Charlie:	Hi, Samantha. How are you? What can I do for you?
Samantha:	I am doing well, thank you. I came in to talk to you about Charlotte Peters, an athlete on the women's soccer team.
Charlie:	Okay, what about her? Is she struggling academically? Because if so, you know you really should be talking with the compliance director.
Samantha:	Well, yes she is, and I have already spoken with him about it. But I want you to know that Vicki is requiring her to do extra training, which is putting a lot of stress on Charlotte. I even witnessed Vicki yelling at Charlotte in practice. Vicki can be pretty harsh. Charlotte tells me it is affecting her eating and sleeping habits, and she is having problems concentrating on her academics.
Charlie:	I appreciate your concern for Charlotte, but Vicki has high standards and a good women's soccer program. Vicki is tough on her athletes because they are a competitive team. Maybe this university just isn't a good fit for Charlotte. It sounds like she just can't handle the pressure of a top Division I program with a coach who has a winning record and wants to keep it that way. I know Vicki gets excited at times and raises her voice, but let's be honest, what college coach doesn't?
Samantha:	I understand that Vicki wants to win, but . . .
Charlie:	No, Vicki *has* to win, Samantha. If Vicki doesn't produce winning seasons, then she loses her job. Unfortunately, that is the world of college and university athletics. Vicki is under lot of pressure to have successful seasons, and in order for her to do that, she has to put a little pressure on her athletes to get better. That is what being a part of a top Division I program is all about, winning.
	I appreciate your care for Charlotte's well-being. That is why we hired you. If you think she would benefit from counseling,

I'm happy to help make a referral so we can get her into someone quickly. It sounds to me that she might need help figuring out some better coping strategies.

Samantha: Well, I appreciate that, and I'll talk to Charlotte about that. But, I think her problems start with the coach.

Charlie: Samantha, I've told you where I stand on this. I need to end this conversation because I've got other responsibilities and I can't micromanage how every coach runs their team. I hope Charlotte is able to succeed here, I truly do. But we can't expect each coach to bend over backward to make sure their players are happy with their coaching style.

Samantha feels like she had no real solutions to Charlotte's situation. She does call Charlotte and offers to make an appointment for her with one of the university counselors. However, Samantha does not respond to her message. The following Monday, Samantha receives a phone call from Dr. Estelle Simon, the chair of the St. Royal Student Intervention Team (SIT). Dr. Simon reports that Charlotte passed out in the residence hall the previous evening and was taken to the hospital. Dr. Simon is following up with Samantha, asking for information regarding Charlotte's experience so far at St. Royal University.

Questions

1. What information should Samantha share with the Student Intervention Team?
2. What action(s) should the Student Intervention Team take to address Charlotte's issues?
3. Is Vicki's behavior acceptable as a Division I coach? Why or why not?
4. How well do you think St. Royal University balances the needs of its academic mission with that of its athletic programs? What is the institution's responsibility toward the well-being of its student athletes?

Chapter 7

An Alcohol Incident During Orientation

Anne C. Cassin and Melissa A. Rychener

As you read this case, consider the developmental needs of the students as well as the need to provide consequences. Think about the extent to which a lean student staff contributed to the sequence of events and what steps would be needed to get orientation back on track.

SETTING

The University of Southwest at Lake Bonito (USLB) is the second largest of the nine universities in the University of Southwest system. USLB has been around for fewer than 40 years, and it continues to grow both in terms of student population and campus size. Students of color make up 57% of USLB's population, and about 37% of the total student population is Latino. Institutions enrolling more than 25% Latino students are considered Hispanic Serving Institutions (HSI). As an HSI, USLB works hard to recruit and retain Latino students. Because many Latino students, especially first-generation students, retain strong ties to their families and communities during their college years, reaching out to Latino families and opening up programs and events to this community has become a priority at USLB.

Orientation at USLB is a three-day overnight program designed to assist new students and their families with their transition to USLB through a combination of academic, informational, and social sessions. For the students, the program concludes with a final informational session, advising, and registration. Families attend a separate final informational session.

The Assistant Director of Orientation, a Summer Hall Director/Family Orientation Coordinator, and 30 to 45 student staff stay in on-campus housing during orientation so that they are easily accessible to the orientation students and their families. During orientation, there are Orientation Leaders who are bilingual in Spanish and English to work with the families who have non-English-speaking members so that they may fully participate in the family orientation. The new Assistant Director of Orientation, Sonia Delgado, recently graduated from a Student Affairs M.A. program. Although she had significant experience in orientation as an undergraduate and as an intern during her graduate studies, this is her first professional position.

CASE

"The calm before the storm" is usually how the weather is described right before a major thunderstorm, tornado, or hurricane. The first three weeks of orientation at the University of the Southwest at Lake Bonito (USLB) also fit that description. There were fewer incidents than in other years, and all relevant campus departments were working together— orientation, residence life, academic affairs, and campus police—to address any minor issues that arose. The orientation staff was grateful for the relative calm of the initial orientation weeks of because they had fewer student workers than expected. Despite heavy recruiting, the orientation program had only managed to hire 30 student staff instead of the anticipated 45. During each of the 14 weeks of orientation programs, 300–400 first-year students and their families arrived on campus and, during some weeks, there were programs for transfer students as well. At 4:10 a.m. on Thursday June 23, the calm of the first three weeks broke and the storm came barreling in.

The new Assistant Director of Orientation, Sonia Delgado, received a call from the Summer Hall Director and Family Orientation Coordinator, Dawn McNeil. Dawn notified Sonia of an alcohol incident involving orientation student staff. Sonia asked, "What do you mean 'involved'?" The student staff caught orientation participants drinking?" Dawn responded, "No, some orientation student staff members were drinking with the participants." "You've got to be kidding me," Sonia sighed. Sonia got out of bed, threw on her clothes, and headed to the building where the incident took place.

As she approached the scene, she muttered a quiet, "Oh my gosh." She was not prepared for the sight of one of their student staff members, Andres Guzman, standing in handcuffs with a campus police officer. Sonia joined Dawn and the campus police. Dawn said she had been contacted by Officer Anderson, who informed her that there was an alcohol incident involving both orientation participants and orientation student staff. Dawn gave

Sonia the names of the four orientation participants (Felipe Garcia, Lana Livingston, Eric Price, and Cesar Martinez) and three orientation leaders (Andres Guzman, Brandon Reynolds, and Marcus Jenkins). Knowing the Orientation Leads needed his statement for their reports, Officer Warren began to describe how campus police became involved.

Officer Warren: I was walking inside of the building on my rounds, heard some loud noises, looked up, saw the lights go out. Heard another noise that sounded like bottles falling so I came up to check things out. I knocked on the door several times before Brandon opened it. I could smell beer and saw several students gathered in the apartment. I called for the other officers on duty and began to question the students. I took down their names and student identification numbers. When Officer Anderson and Officer Ortiz arrived, Officer Anderson notified Dawn while Officer Ortiz assisted in collecting information.

Officer Anderson informed the professional staff that all persons present—orientation student staff as well as orientation participants—were issued "minor consumption" citations. Additionally, the two orientation student staff members, Andres and Marcus, were arrested for furnishing alcohol to minors. The orientation participants were waiting for further instructions in the apartment where the incident took place. Dawn confirmed that two of the students had family members participating in family orientation. Just then, Sonia got a call from Ana Maria, the Director of Orientation and Family Programs, who had been brought up to speed about the situation. Ana Maria needed to tell Sonia what would happen with all of the students involved.

Ana Maria: The orientation student staff members are immediately released from their positions. Orientation participants need to meet you and Dawn at the front of the residence hall at 7:00 a.m. Bring them to my office where I will meet with them along with either you or Dawn, to be formally released from the orientation program and given further instructions. Normally, incidents with drugs or alcohol result in students being immediately removed from on-campus housing, but because of the hour and the fact that they have been drinking, see if it's okay with Residence Life if the students remain there until 2:00 p.m. tomorrow. I need to call the Vice President of Student Affairs and let him know what's happening now, but call me if you need anything.

Sonia told Dawn about Ana Maria's request that the prospective students be given until 2:00 p.m. the next day to move out, and Dawn agreed to allow this. Sonia went to the apartment to repeat Ana Maria's instructions to the orientation students. One of the orientation students, Felipe, asked, "What will happen with Andres and Marcus?" and the others chimed in saying, "Yeah, what's going to happen to them? Where did they take them?" Sonia replied, "I'm not sure, but at this point you need to think about yourselves. Unless you have other questions, head back to your rooms and try to get some sleep because you will have a meeting at the main office in less than three hours."

The orientation students went back to their rooms, but Sonia remained behind to check on Brandon, one of the orientation leaders, and hear his version of what happened.

Sonia:	Okay. We know what we were told by the police, but can you tell me your side of what happened?
Brandon:	[*sighs*] I didn't do anything. I was in my room. So stupid. I should have left.
Sonia:	Who invited everyone over?
Brandon:	[*frustrated*] Andres and Marcus. I had no idea they were planning on drinking and having people over until I got back into the room after the pool party!
Sonia:	Now, I don't want you to think I am accusing you of anything, but did you guys have the alcohol in here already or did someone go purchase it recently?
Brandon:	No, we didn't have any before tonight. I don't really drink and when I do, it's definitely not here. You know Marcus turned 21 last week, so he bought it. I don't even know when he had time to do it! We have been working all day. Guess he cut out after our last session since he didn't have to work the pool party.
Sonia:	Okay. Tell me what happened after the pool party.
Brandon:	[*shaking his head*] I got back here and went to change, and Andres was in his room already. The door was cracked, and he had music going. Marcus was in there too, but I didn't know it. I was messing around in my room on social media and after a little while I hear the two of them joking and laughing and stuff. I come out of my room and start talking with them. Marcus tells me that they got people coming over in a bit. I was like "All right, cool. Just don't be too loud because I gotta work the early session tomorrow." I went back to my room. Not too much later Andres gets a phone call and right after that he goes to open the door and people come in. I heard cans open and stuck my head out the door to see what was going on. They asked me

if I wanted one and I was like, "Nah, I'm good" and went back to my room. A little later they started getting loud and somebody spilled something. They tried to get quiet real fast, but I guess campus police heard them already. There was a knock on the door and none of them were going to open it. I was like, "Dude, y'all need to get the door." None of them moved. So I left my room, climbed over all of them, and opened it. I should have just stayed in my room and acted like I was asleep. They took names and called Dawn and you. You know the rest.

Sonia: [*softly*] Brandon, why didn't you call us when you saw they had alcohol?

Brandon: [*leaning forward and putting his hands on the sides of his head*] I didn't want to be a rat. I wasn't drinking. They chose to, but. . .I guess I didn't think they would be so stupid about it. We're friends. I didn't want to get them in trouble, and I didn't think they would get me in trouble. My mom's gonna kill me.

After reassuring Brandon that she would continue to support him as much as she could, Sonia told him that Ana Maria wanted to see him at 2:00 p.m. tomorrow in her office. Sonia returned to her apartment and immediately began writing her reports so that she would have it done in time for their meeting with the students at 7:00 a.m.

A little while later, Sonia and Dawn met the students and walked them to the Residence Life Office. It was an uncomfortably quiet walk. Sonia and Dawn were rather exhausted and didn't speak more than was necessary, which apparently increased the anxiety for some of the orientation students, because one of them started to cry. When the group arrived at the orientation office, Sonia went to Ana Maria to let her know. Ana Maria told Sonia and Dawn that they would sit in with her for the meetings, and then she gave them an overview of how the meetings would proceed.

Ana Maria: As the students come into the office one by one, I will present them with the signed Housing Contract and go over each policy they broke: Alcoholic Beverages, Compliance with Staff, and Quiet Hours. I will tell them that Judicial Affairs will be in contact with them by mail with notice of the allegations against them and the date and time of their hearing. During the hearing, their version of what happened will be discussed and any further sanctions will be given. Until the hearing, students are required to leave campus, which means that they will not finish orientation or register for classes. Because attending orientation is a prerequisite for registration, and because they will miss part of the orientation, they will need to attend part of another orientation session. After this explanation, I will invite the students to ask any questions they have. I will have them contact whoever is listed as their emergency contact to notify them that the student will be leaving orientation early, and then I will dismiss the student to return to their rooms and pack their things.

It was decided that Dawn would sit in on the first two meetings. After they wrapped up, she left to get back to her duties with the family orientation—which was especially important since they were now down two orientation student staff members. On her way out, she told Sonia to be ready if it got a little out of control in the meeting. Sonia asked why. Dawn said that when Ana Maria dialed the number of the students' emergency contacts on speakerphone, she gave the students the option of explaining why they were going home early. When Cesar told mother what had happened, she began to yell at him.

Mrs. Sanchez: How could you do this to your family? What were you thinking? You weren't. Eres estúpido! (*You are stupid.*) No caring for how hard we have worked to get you to school! Mijo! I am so disappointed in you. You are the first one to go to college, we were so proud of you. What will your father say? You need to tell him when you get home. How could you do this?

Dawn said Mrs. Sanchez spoke so loudly and quickly that it was impossible for Ana Maria to intervene and end the conversation before Cesar started to tear up. When Mrs. Sanchez had finished, Cesar just said he would call her when he left campus.

Before Sonia went into Ana Maria's office for the next meeting, yelling ensued in the lobby outside the main office. Eric Price's mother was upset with her son, and confronted him heatedly about how he was ruining his college career, before it even started. Once she realized she was making a scene, Mrs. Price got quiet. Ana Maria came out of her office and asked if Mrs. Price had any concerns she would like to discuss. Once in Ana Maria's office Mrs. Price began her argument as Eric sat there silently staring at the ground.

Mrs. Price: What Eric did was wrong, but if it wasn't for your staff, he never would have done what he did. And now, because of your staff, my son is not allowed to register for classes and might not be able to live in housing here. How is that fair?

Ana Maria: Mrs. Price, I do understand that you are upset about your son facing consequences for his actions last night and not being able to register for classes today. Please keep in mind that he will be allowed to register once he repeats orientation. I can assure you that those staff members are already being dealt with for their role in all of this. However, Eric still chose to stay in the room knowing what activities were taking place, and not only did he stay, he chose to participate in the activities as well. This morning we have heard that there were other students who had been invited, saw what was going on, and made the decision to leave. Eric could have made that decision too.

Mrs. Price: [*Trying not to yell*] But Eric should never have been put in a position to make that kind of decision. These students were supposed to be role models. One of them was even my orientation leader! I trusted him.

Ana Maria: We trust our staff to be role models for these students as well, but not all incidents can be prevented. Those student staff members will be held responsible for their actions. What is important in relation to Eric, is that he signed this form [holds up the Orientation Housing Contract], like all of the other students and staff who stay in the residence halls at any point during the summer. He was found in an on-campus housing unit while underage drinking was taking place. He broke four of the seven rules on this contract violating it, the rules outlined in the Resident Handbook, the Student Code of Conduct, and also the law. I will be referring this matter to Judicial Affairs, and you can contact them directly with any additional questions.

Mrs. Price said she was overwhelmed but would be in touch if any questions did come up, and she thanked Ana Maria for her time. The rest of the meetings were much calmer and shorter. There was some time before Brandon's meeting, so Sonia and Dawn finally had some time to talk.

Sonia: I just can't believe it was these guys. There are a few on our staff I could see doing this, but not them.

Dawn: Nah. I don't know about Brandon, but for the family orientation staff, we probably could have called Andres and Marcus being involved. So, if Brandon was hanging out with them, it was just a matter of time.

Sonia: Why's that?

Dawn: Well, those two have been starting to go downhill a little lately. Showing up late, poor attitude, that kind of thing. We kind of suspected they were doing some shady stuff, but they were there and doing their jobs.

Sonia: Really? What kind of "shady stuff" are you talking about?

Dawn: Marijuana. Their eyes were red a lot in the mornings.

Sonia: Did anybody say anything to them? Cause it sounds like it wasn't just a one-time thing. Did anyone else see them like that?

Dawn: No, we didn't say anything to them. They showed up, and we needed people. I don't think anyone else noticed. If they did, they didn't say anything about it.

Sonia was stunned. All she could think about was what if Andres and Marcus had been pulled aside earlier about their tardiness and suspected drug use? Maybe this situation could have been prevented. Why didn't her colleagues think those were critical issues to address? However, this wasn't all that Sonia had to think about. When orientation resumed the following week, how should they deal with the fallout that this incident was likely to create?

Questions

1. How would you advise Sonia to address Dawn's decision not to confront Andres and Marcus about her suspicions? How might Sonia go about trying to change the culture of the orientation team so that holding staff accountable as well as providing them support would become the norm?
2. What kind of response is this incident likely to elicit from the rest of the student staff? If you were advising Sonia, how would you suggest the orientation team address this incident with the rest of the staff?
3. How could the orientation programs have been modified to account for a smaller staff?
4. What are the benefits and drawbacks of involving parents in orientation? By involving parents in orientation, does this better serve populations of students who have historically been excluded from higher education in a culturally appropriate manner? Or does it increase the incidence of unhealthy interference of parents?

Chapter 8

Supporting LGBT Students at a Religiously Affiliated College

Renee K. (Austin) Coyne and Michael G. Ignelzi

While reading this case, think about the interaction of campus context and cultural traditions with revised institutional goals and changing student demographics. What challenges or limitations to change do strong cultures present? Also, consider issues of institutional fit for both students and staff highlighted by this case.

SETTING

Holy Cathedral College is a small, private, Catholic institution located on the outskirts of a medium-size metropolitan city. Holy Cathedral boasts a beautiful, quiet campus for students even though it is only 20 minutes from the city. Stepping onto the campus grounds feels like stepping into a retreat. The modest campus buildings are well kept, despite their age, and many are tucked under the immense span of enormous oak and maple trees. The natural beauty of Holy Cathedral's campus draws students looking for a contemplative and serene college experience.

The college opened in 1858 as a seminary for young Catholic men focused on teacher training and religious studies. Holy Cathedral still holds tight to its Catholic roots, but has transitioned into a liberal arts institution for men and women with three academic subdivisions—the School of Business, Arts and Humanities and the School of Science & Environmental Studies. Holy Cathedral's mission states:

> Holy Cathedral is committed to being a comprehensive Catholic institution of higher learning, faithful to the teachings of Jesus Christ as handed down by the Church. Dedicated to advancing the dialogue between faith and reason, Holy Cathedral seeks to explore and impart truth through excellence in teaching and research, all in service to the Church, the nation, and the world.

Five years ago, Holy Cathedral's strategic plan was revised to focus on increasing the number of students receiving an education at the institution. This initiative was created by the Board of Trustees after assessing the long-term financial health of the institution. Although Holy Cathedral was not in immediate financial danger, the Board believed that more updated facilities would lead to larger enrollment, which would secure the institution's financial position and offer a more appealing academic environment for its students. This plan led to constructing new residential suites, expanding the current dining hall, and updating student amenities such as recreation facilities and the student union.

Student enrollment increased, which led to some diversification of the student body, particularly in relation to religious beliefs and values. Although traditionally a conservative Catholic institution, the admissions staff at Holy Cathedral no longer preferences admission to students of the Catholic faith. Students are not required to profess the Catholic faith, but they are required to abide by the values and traditions of Holy Cathedral, which are based upon the Catholic faith. This change has produced some concerns among many staff and faculty members, but most see the value in opening the environment to all students who wish to learn in a faith-based, nurturing environment. Holy Cathedral's alumni have not been as supportive of the changes to campus and the student body. Many alumni have sent angry letters to the Director of Alumni and Development, the President's Office, and the Board of Trustees. A few high-level alumni donors have threatened to stop contributing and take their money to an institution "that more strictly follows the Catholic faith's teachings".

The Holy Cathedral community is welcoming its largest first-year class this fall. The students in the first-year class are primarily Caucasian, middle-class, traditional-aged, and from the surrounding area and states—similar to the makeup of the rest of Holy Cathedral's student body. The percentage of students from ethnic and/or racial minorities is currently at 5%. The student body has become more diversified in the past five years regarding religious beliefs with 60% currently identifying as Catholic, 25% as other Christian denominations, 5% as nondenominational Christian, and 10% with no religious affiliation.

There is another change creating excitement and anxiety on campus. A new president has been hired and is beginning his tenure at Holy Cathedral. He has a strong reputation of leading with authority, respect, and humility.

CHARACTERS

Anthony White: President of Holy Cathedral College. He comes to Holy Cathedral with experience in small, private college leadership. He professes a Catholic faith, but struggles to determine where the line is between faithful obedience to Church doctrine and acceptance of alternate views.

Henry Phillips: Provost of Holy Cathedral College. He is a devout Catholic and firm in his conservative beliefs. He attended Holy Cathedral as an undergraduate and returned after he finished his doctoral degree to join the faculty. He taught in the Chemistry Department for 20 years, previously served as Department Chair, and has been Provost for four years. For many at Holy Cathedral, he is a prime example of the college's successful legacy and commitment to tradition.

Rita Longwell: Director of Alumni and Development. Rita has created a strong and proud alumni network. The active alumni database has grown immensely under her leadership, along with the number of alumni who give annually to the institution. She is strongly committed to the teachings and rituals of conservative Catholicism.

Dave Brown: Dean of Students. Dave has been at Holy Cathedral for three years. He has both an M.A. and Ph.D. in Student Affairs. He has been pushing for the Office of Student Life and the larger campus to incorporate a more educational/developmental approach in the co-curriculum.

CASE

The beginning of the fall semester held excitement and energy that Holy Cathedral had not seen in years. The new residential suites were now open and student enrollment had risen from 2,100 students to 2,500. The residence life team has been working diligently since last year to hire and train more RAs. The Student Life division is putting in long hours and busily creating welcome events and programming for the students arriving at Holy Cathedral.

The shift to a more inclusive admissions approach in relation to religious diversity has created some tension within the Holy Cathedral community. This tension lay just under the surface, dormant, until Holy Allies presented the opportunity for emotions to surface. Holy Allies is the name of an organization that is seeking recognition as an official, university-sponsored group. Holy Allies mission is "to provide a safe, open environment for students who are gay, lesbian, bisexual, or transsexual; students who are questioning their sexual identity; and heterosexual students who want to support and learn more about the LGBT community". The group has completed all of the necessary paperwork for campus recognition and found a faculty advisor.

For the Office of Student Life, approving this group for official recognition would be a controversial decision given the strong Catholic tradition of the college. Dave Brown, Dean of Students, is encouraged by the student body's desire to create a support and conversation space on campus around issues of sexual orientation and identity. He believes that the ability to dialogue openly and to respectfully disagree is underdeveloped in students and many faculty of Holy Cathedral. He sees the current situation as an opportunity to promote needed support and valuable learning around a challenging issue for persons of faith. Additionally, through his position and observation of the campus, he is aware of the transformation taking place in the student body and that some students at Holy Cathedral are gay or lesbian or questioning their sexuality. Dave is also aware that there are many students, staff, faculty, and alumni who would strongly oppose a LGBT support/information group on Holy Cathedral's campus. He has an idea of how he would like to move forward, but because of the sensitivity of this situation, he thinks he should first consult the new president, Anthony White.

The conversation begins with Dave explaining what Holy Allies has expressed as their mission and goals, as well as the typical procedure for becoming a recognized group on campus.

Anthony: Well this is certainly a situation I was not expecting to see early on at Holy Cathedral. My previous institution went through some of these growing pains as well, but our ties to Catholic traditions were not as strong and consistent as I've seen at Holy Cathedral. So these students want to create, essentially, a gay/straight support and alliance group on campus? Hmm. And how do they align their group with the mission of the institution?

Dave: The students shared that this group would allow them to meet in open conversation regarding issues of sexuality in a manner similar to how Jesus met and interacted with all of his people. They expressed their desire to explore these issues and how they intermingle with their own personal faith. It is their belief that these conversations will help to strengthen their faith. They believe this group will serve the students at Holy Cathedral who are currently marginalized, and students who know a friend or family member who is gay or questioning their sexuality.

Anthony: Well, being a private, Catholic institution, we have the ability to say "no" to this request based on the teachings of the Church. But I assume you already know that with your time and history here, so I'm guessing that you see this from another angle.

Dave: Yes, from my own interactions with students and the information that gets passed along to me from my staff, there is a small population of students struggling with sexual identity and faith on this campus. Based on the traditions here, I think they are afraid to speak out or ask questions which might identify or label them. They are struggling to find their way, explore their faith, and balance their academics. The fact that a few students on campus have recognized the need to offer support and a respectful conversation around the issue is, I believe, a good thing.

Anthony: I can see what you are saying, but you must understand the difficulty in allowing this group to be recognized by the institution?

Dave: Of course, that's a problem. As a collective community, we are responsible for upholding the mission and values of Holy Cathedral, which align with the teachings of the Catholic Church. However, we are also responsible for creating an environment that supports the needs of all of our students.

Anthony: How will this group meet the needs of all students on campus when many might be adamantly opposed?

Dave: All students at Holy Cathedral have or will encounter issues related to sexual orientation and identity in their workplace, families, and/or friend groups. Avoiding this conversation sets our students up for failure in their professional, social, and personal lives. It is our role as an institution focused on students to create an environment where these issues are discussed and students can wrestle through society's beliefs, the beliefs of the Catholic Church, and their own beliefs. If they can't question, affirm, or evaluate in a safe environment, then how will they be able to when the risks of hiring, job loss, promotion, losing/gaining relationships, et cetera are greater?

Anthony: Dave, I understand your reasoning. I see what this organization might add to the conversation. One of my concerns is the precedent that recognizing this organization could set. Are we ready to extend organization status to students wishing to explore atheism, polytheism, abortion? I know that sounds extreme, but micro decisions can lead to macro changes over time.

Dave: As a private, Catholic institution, we still have the opportunity to evaluate and decline submissions which do not align with our mission or vision. But in this case, I feel that a quick "no" doesn't offer the students a chance to dialogue and explore. These students are responding to a need that has been seen in our community, but has not been adequately addressed by staff or faculty. Allowing these students to begin a conversation with others on campus would be consistent with supporting the process of discernment, which is a core value of Catholic faith. I'm requesting your support in offering these students the opportunity to operate as a student organization with Developmental Status. This would allow them a chance to meet and offer some open dialogue sessions on campus. They would not be able to use the Holy Cathedral name, receive student organization funding, or host large group events. But it would allow them to begin the process of becoming a viable group that could serve an important need on campus.

Anthony: Still, even this level of recognition by the university could cause anxiety and upset within much of the community. How would you address this possible outcome?

Dave: This trial period would allow my staff team to assess this. It would also hold the students in Holy Allies accountable to reflect on their own beliefs and actions in relation to the larger community. We can't be certain of the response from the community or the positive effect such a group could have unless we allow this.

Anthony: I see your passion and your perspective on this situation. While I do maintain some concerns, I am supportive of providing students opportunities to expand their understanding of their faith and themselves. I will support your decision to offer Developmental Status to Holy Allies.

The students involved in Holy Allies are excited to begin some programming and open dialogue sessions. To begin branding and advertising their organization, they create an emblem of a rainbow-colored scarf wrapped around a cross. They use the emblem on posters, table tents, and in emails; and members and supporters of the group begin wearing the emblem on their purses, backpacks, and persons.

As the number of crosses wrapped in a rainbow scarf increases on campus, the voices of students, staff, and faculty, against the group and their purpose, begin. Other student organizations on campus express their upset that Holly Allies had been granted Developmental Status, and speak adamantly of their beliefs in the sin of homosexuality. The larger campus community differs greatly regarding their views on this new student group.

A collection of students opposed to the Holy Allies group design and distribute a counter-emblem. It also uses a cross in the background but highlights the phrase, "One Body, One Blood, One Sexuality". Conversation and dialogue are clearly occurring on campus, but much of it is not constructive.

The tipping point begins with someone defacing the Holy Allies materials posted on campus. The picturesque campus is now tagged with phrases of

"Fags", "You're not wanted here", "Gays suck", and "Homo = Hell". The Office of Student Life sends e-mails condemning these acts of harassment, but without knowing who is doing these things, it is difficult to prevent.

In response to the defacing of the Holy Allies materials, members of the group encourage supporters to wear their emblem to the All-Campus Homecoming Mass. As word of this arrangement spreads around campus, students in opposition to Holy Allies plan to wear the "One Body, One Blood, One Sexuality" emblem to the service. At the October all-campus mass, many students arrive wearing one or the other emblem—even some faculty, staff, and alumni show their support for one side or the other. As Father Patrick, one of the campus priests, moves through the liturgies of the mass, he becomes increasingly uncomfortable with the outward displays and palpable tension among attendees. He decides to withhold Holy Communion and instead only offer a blessing to members of the congregation wearing either emblem. The students, staff, faculty, and alumni on both sides are outraged. Father Patrick makes a single statement when he announces his decision during the Mass, saying, "Coming to the communion table and partaking in the Body and Blood of Christ is the most sacred part of our faith. Although these emblems represent important faith questions, wearing them today as part of a larger group demonstrates an act of protest, and active protests have no place in this ceremony of faith."

The next day, the college newspaper reports, "College Denies Holy Communion to Protestors". The article quotes students and alumni on both sides of the issue. Those supporting Holy Allies indicate the college is a closed, unsafe environment. Those opposed to Holly Allies are offended they were denied Holy Communion, as they are devout supporters of the Church and the traditional mission of the college.

President Anthony White calls his senior staff together for an emergency meeting. His office phone and e-mail is inundated with concerns and angry campus constituent messages about the situation. He knows that he will soon need to respond to Board members, the campus, and the press about the incident. President White is saddened by how quickly the situation escalated. He supported Dave in his request to give Developmental Status to Holy Allies, but perhaps he should have paid more attention to his reservations. It is too late for that now; a clear plan is needed to address this mess. He opens the meeting with his staff by asking them to share their reactions to the recent events.

Rita: Based on this problem with Holy Allies, I'm dealing with hundreds of alumni concerned about the direction of Holy Cathedral. Many have indicated that they will cancel their planned donations and any future support if we don't address this immediately. We just need to get rid of Holy Allies. Holy Allies started this mess that led to the protesting, and, if you ask me, they created a target for themselves. And, let's be honest, a student shouldn't come to a Catholic institution if they think they might be homosexual.

Dave: I understand your concern and position as liaison between the college and alumni community, Rita, but your interpretation of the situation and what we should do is not helpful. Every student attending Holy Cathedral may be struggling through some of their own faith decisions. We should be an institution that is welcoming and supportive of any student who wants to learn and explore their faith.

Rita: Let's not forget about our responsibility to support our alumni as well. The alumni that I've spoken with feel hurt and angry that this institution would support and encourage homosexuality. Moving forward, this institution needs to show it still follows the values of the Catholic Church.

Henry: Dave, I want students to learn from their experiences at Holy Cathedral, but faculty members don't feel equipped to be dealing with these types of issues. Some have tried to have conversations with students, but they end up in heated arguments and wasted class time. Faculty members are under a tight timeline to cover course content, and students need to be primarily focused on their academic studies. Also, if we are a Catholic institution, then shouldn't we follow Catholic Church teachings and traditions? That worked well for us in the past.

Dave: Ignoring this issue doesn't make it go away or help our students. We are now admitting a larger and more diverse student population to Holy Cathedral, as part of the Board's strategic plan, who have or are exploring differing perspectives on their faith.

Henry: Perhaps that plan was ill conceived. I'm concerned about losing the Catholic faith traditions that have made Holy Cathedral a respected institution.

Anthony: While I appreciate your differing views on this situation, we need to turn our attention to designing a response plan that addresses the immediate incident and longer-term challenges that this situation has uncovered. I made a judgment call in supporting Dave's request to give Developmental Status to Holy Allies, and I take responsibility for that. I realize that there are personal disagreements and tensions among us about this, but we now have a responsibility to respond collaboratively in the interest of this college and its constituents. I need your best thinking, consultation, and support.

Questions

1. Did President White make a wise decision in supporting Dave's request to give Developmental Status to Holy Allies? What other options or additional steps to Dave's request might President White have suggested?
2. What could Dave Brown and/or his Student Life staff done to better anticipate and help manage the problems that occurred because of Holy Allies' introduction to campus?
3. Was it realistic to expect that Holy Allies and LGBT students could be effectively supported at an institution where sincerely held religious views marginalize individuals with such identities? As student affairs professionals, what are the limits to our abilities to effectively support certain groups of students within particular institutional cultures?
4. What could the institution have done to better prepare for the increase in student diversity resulting from the changes in their recruitment efforts and admissions policies?

Chapter 9

Provisional Admissions Decisions at a Branch Campus

Correy Dandoy and Stacy A. Jacob

The following case examines the ethics of admitting underprepared students at an under-resourced, under-enrolled branch campus. The main character, Cara, is trying to balance the need for more students with the ethics of admitting students who could possibly fail out. As you read the case, think about the various lenses the people in the case view the problem through and why they think they are doing the right thing for students. What pressures contribute to the problem and how does the organization operate in the face of this problem? Also, consider the main campus's responsibility to its branch campus.

MAIN CHARACTERS

- **Cara** is a 28-year-old white female and the Director of Academic Advising at JSU-Hodgetown. This is her second job in student affairs.
- **Judy** is the Assistant Director of Admissions at JSU-Hodgetown. She is a 29-year-old white female, who received her MBA from the JSU main campus three years ago.
- **Donna** is the Director of Admissions at JSU-Hodgetown. She is a 43-year-old white female.
- **Janet** is the Dean of Academic Affairs at JSU-Hodgetown and Cara's supervisor.

CASE STUDY

Cara has been the Director of Academic Advising at the Hodgetown campus of June State University (JSU) for a year and two months. JSU is a public research university in the Midwest region of the country. JSU's main campus enrolls approximately 46,000 students each year. It has several branch campuses that operate all over the state, with varying enrollments and budgets. Hodgetown is a small rural town in the northwest corner of the state. JSU-Hodgetown (JSUH) is a small, non-residential campus with a total enrollment of around 1,000 students; and the student population at the campus is not diverse.

Ten years ago, in an attempt to improve the campus's academic reputation, JSUH instituted minimum admission standards. Previously, the campus had open enrollment. All students, after achieving junior status and at least a 2.5 GPA, can transfer to the JSU-Main Campus. Currently, the acceptance rate at JSUH is approximately 87%. The number of applications from students of color is extremely low. Last year, of the 843 applications received, 92 were from African American students, 39 of these students were accepted to JSUH, and 19 African American students enrolled.

The JSUH campus has been having trouble meeting enrollment numbers for the past five years, and a team of researchers concluded that the main reasons are that the campus is not residential and the campus has a negative image in the surrounding region. JSUH is known as a school of last resort for students who are not accepted anywhere else, instead of a lower-cost alternative for well-prepared students to begin their education.

The campus struggles with decreased funding, and many offices are understaffed. The Student Success Center houses a career services office with one full-time staff member, an academic advisement center with one full-time advisor, and a tutoring center, which is overseen by a faculty member teaching several courses each semester while supervising five part-time student tutors.

Cara feels fortunate to hold her position as Director of Academic Advising. She graduated with her master's degree in Student Affairs in Higher Education and then worked as an academic advisor for two years at a large, public institution in another state before coming to JSUH. Her role is to be the academic advisor for all incoming and second-year students before they declare a major and are assigned a faculty advisor. Although Cara reports to the Dean of Academic Affairs, she is highly autonomous and only sees her supervisor every other week or so. Students are required to meet with their advisor before starting their first semester at JSUH, after that they are able to self-advise and register. Cara encourages her students to meet with her at least once each semester; while many do, most do not.

Cara also serves as the chair of the Admissions Committee. This committee is charged with the task of determining which students will be permitted to attend JSUH as provisional admits. Provisional students do not meet all the requirements for admission and possess at least one (but not more than two) of the following deficiencies:

- Did not take the SATs or ACTs.
- Have not taken at least two years of math involving trigonometry (Algebra II, Calculus, etc.).
- Have not been enrolled in school for four or more years.
- Do not meet the high school 2.25 GPA requirement.

When a student falls into one or two of these categories, the JSUH Admissions Committee can admit the student based on an interview. Cara serves as the final decision maker on the admission of provisional students. Generally, the Admissions Committee meets, discusses, and makes recommendations for provisional students; however, Cara can decide to not call the committee if she feels she can make an appropriate admission decision without their input. The Admissions Committee is made up of the Director and Assistant Director of Admissions, Judy and Donna, respectively, and seven faculty members from various departments.

Donna and Cara became friends fast when Cara started her job in April. At the time, Cara needed to make admission decisions or call committee meetings for several students who applied for admission the following semester. Donna let Cara know that Cara's predecessor called committee meetings for every provisional student and that it was rare for him deny a student admission. Donna also explained that due to enrollment and budgetary issues, it would be best for Cara to admit as many provisional students as possible.

In her first year, Cara called together the Admissions Committee for 23 provisional students during four separate meetings throughout the summer. At each meeting, Cara, Judy, and Donna were all present, but only one out of the seven faculty members attended the meetings, and it was a different member every time. Cara admitted all of the students the committee discussed. These decisions seemed to please Judy and Donna. Cara believed that she was giving students with potential a chance. Eight of the students evaluated by Cara and the committee identified as either African American or Latino. Cara also believed giving this diverse group of students a chance at JSUH would be beneficial to the students as well as the university.

During her first year at JSUH, Cara came to know 11 of the students she had helped to admit. She especially encouraged provisional students to come see her when they were scheduling their courses. Eight of the provisional students that Cara got to know well succeeded in finishing their first year with the minimum 2.0 GPA needed to remain enrolled in the university. Cara was disheartened over the three who left—she had done everything she could to help those students!

One of the students Cara knew was Sidney, a 19-year-old African American woman. Sidney stopped by to see Cara at least once a week, sometimes just to say hello, or at other times with an appointment to talk for an hour. Cara knew Sidney was putting a lot of effort into her courses, but she was still struggling, especially in her math course. Sidney complained to Cara about the hours of the tutoring center and that her math professor was unavailable at times that Sidney wanted to ask questions. On a few occasions, Sidney talked to Cara about the lack of diversity at JSUH, saying, "I am the only black student in three of my five classes. In the other two, there are two other black kids. The same two in both classes! I feel like people look at me differently. I feel like the professors don't know what to do with me. I wish there was a group, or somewhere I could go to talk about that side of things". Cara tried to help Sidney, and she looked for resources designed to support students of color on campus. Unfortunately, JSU-Hodgetown has no multicultural office and Cara knew only one African American staff member who worked in Financial Aid.

Joanna, another provisional student who met with Cara regularly and was dismissed from the university due to her GPA, came to see Cara a few weeks after the spring semester ended.

Cara: Joanna, this situation really is so tough for me. I really wanted you to be here next year. Tell me how you're feeling about this past year.

Joanna: It really sucks. I tried really hard. My mom says this just wasn't the right place for me.

Cara: I know it does. Why do you think your mom said it wasn't the right place for you?

Joanna: I don't know. She says I wasn't ready to be here.

Cara: What do you think?

Joanna: I think I wasn't ready to be here. When I got accepted I was so happy. My mom was too, but then I got here and did the math placement test and that was hard, and I started to get scared. My math class just moved too quickly, ya know?

Cara: What would you have done differently?

Joanna: Made my schedule work with the tutoring hours. Not been so anxious about math that I forgot to study for history and write my term paper for English. It all happened really fast. And now, my mom is ticked. I'm going to have to start paying back my loans right away.

Cara: [thinking, *this is so heartbreaking.*] I know this is so difficult for you but you're a very motivated young woman, and I know you will be successful wherever you go.

Joanna: I feel like I'm starting over but even more behind. I guess I'll look into community college for next semester.

Cara: I think that's a good idea.

Joanna: I wish someone had told me that last year.

Cara: Joanna, try not to think of this whole year as a waste. You made some great friends. You loved your art class. You're not leaving here today the same woman you were when I first met you.

Joanna: I guess you're right.

Following her meeting with Joanna, Cara was drained. She decided to check on the other provisional students that had been admitted, most of whom she saw at their advising orientation session and then never again. Seven were students of color. Using the JSU degree audit system, Cara discovered that 11 of the 12 students had lower than a 2.0 GPA for their first year, and were leaving the institution. Fourteen students she had admitted to the university did not successfully complete their first year and only one of those students who did not meet with her regularly succeeded. Comparatively, the retention rate at the campus for non-provisional students from the first to second year was 90%.

Cara began examining the situation to figure out what she had done wrong. She thought she should have given the students more support, or found them more support on campus. There was not a strong tutoring center on campus, particularly for math, which is the subject that students seemed to struggle with the most. After much contemplation, she began to wonder about the decision to admit the students in the first place. Perhaps admitting them all had been a mistake. Cara wanted to find out more about provisional student admission, her committee, and what the process should look like from a source other than the Admissions office personnel. She asked for a meeting with her supervisor, Janet, the Dean of Academic Affairs.

Cara: For the most part, I feel really great about my position here at JSUH. I really enjoy the students I get to work with, and I truly appreciate the trust and autonomy you've given me.

Janet: That's great, Cara. I'm really glad you are enjoying your position.

Cara: The one area that I am struggling with is the provisional student piece. Part of my job, as I understood it from you when I was hired, was to head the committee to decide on students who didn't meet admission requirements. Last fall, I admitted all 23 students that I took to the committee. Fourteen of them are not coming back this year because of poor grades.

Janet: Hmm. Provisional students are tough, Cara. We want to give students a chance, but sometimes they just aren't ready for the demands of the classroom here. Why did you admit all of the students who came your way?

Cara: I had a conversation with Donna and Judy, who told me that those students always end up getting admitted because our enrollment numbers have been down for several years, and admitting them helps us meet our goals. It seemed like a good enough reason to admit these students, but now I'm not so sure anymore.

Janet: So, what do you think now?

Cara: That I was wrong to not look deeper into these cases. I want to give students with potential a chance here, but I feel like I took part in lying to those students, encouraging them to try a JSUH education when they were not ready.

Janet: Cara, you didn't lie to the students. You did your job and thought you were genuinely giving them a chance. But, as you've seen, it's problematic if we admit too many freshmen who need academic support. This campus is just not equipped to provide the services they need.

Cara: I am learning that the hard way.

Janet: It's unfortunate, but we just can't accommodate the needs of all the students who would benefit from additional academic support. The person in your position before you successfully fought for the power to make these decisions. You know what students need. We can't give *every* student a chance here. Donna and Judy have one thing in mind: enrollment numbers. They only see numbers. I trust that you will use what you know to make the right decisions this year.

After thinking more about her meeting with Janet, Cara decided that in her second summer as Director of Academic Advising, she would not be so naïve. She knew more about the university and its lack of resources, and she was ready to make more informed decisions. Cara also felt that she wanted to hear faculty members' opinions on the provisional student policies, and she wondered why those who were invited to be part of the Admissions Committee did not attend meetings. Cara reached out to all seven faculty members, and three of them agreed to commit to attending the first meeting of the summer.

Before the end of May, Admissions sent Cara six provisional student applications to be reviewed for admission. Cara called a meeting to review these files, and she, Judy, Donna, and three full-time faculty members were present: Dr. Amy Peluso from Engineering, Dr. Michael Hanzlik from English, and Mr. Stanley Thomson from Business. Cara began the meeting by discussing the first student: an adult learner who had been out of school for nearly a decade. According to the records, the student, Lori, had not completed an algebra class in high school, and had taken and failed two community college courses immediately after graduation.

Judy:	One of our admissions counselors spoke to Lori on three separate occasions. She has been working as an administrative assistant in a manufacturing company for eight years. She has a lot of potential, and I think she'd do well here.
Cara:	Although I have not spoken to Lori, I am not sure about her potential. She has never taken an algebra course, and she tried, and failed, two community college courses after high school.
Donna:	[taken aback] Yes, but since those attempted community college credits, Lori has been working. In our experience, working adults gain a lot on the job that allows them to succeed in courses here.
Cara:	I understand what you are saying, and it may be true, but I find it hard to blindly admit this student to JSUH when her academic record shows that she is not likely to be able to do well in classes here.
Judy:	So you are suggesting that we do not admit this student?
Dr. Peluso:	If I could speak up—I agree that adult learners do show more willingness to learn than traditional-aged students, but I also see Cara's point that Lori's academic record doesn't necessarily bode well for her success here.
Judy:	This student wants to get her bachelor's degree in English.

Cara:	She will still need to be able to pass the required math course in order to succeed and the tutoring center is always overwhelmed.
Judy:	What happened to giving students a chance? Letting these students prove themselves?
Cara:	My job is to make the best admissions decision about provisional students. I believe in giving students a chance, too, but not if we can't support what could be their academic struggle. If a student is seriously underprepared, giving them a chance with little to no resources is not enough or right.

The committee discusses the next few students and Cara comes to the same decision: to not admit the student. Judy and Donna argue that each student has potential to be successful. After a few more students are discussed, Donna gets angry and says that Cara is taking advantage of her power in the situation and suggests that they end the meeting.

Dr. Hanzlik:	What good would it be to end this meeting? At least we are all discussing the issue at hand here, which is that we need students to fill our seats, but qualified students don't seem to be the applying.
Cara:	Right, and my goal is to give students a chance who truly have a possibility to succeed here at JSU.
Donna:	May I remind everyone that the Chancellor has made clear goals about where our enrollment needs to stand to keep our doors open.
Dr. Peluso:	I know that enrollment numbers are important, and I want my classes to be filled next semester. But like Dr. Hanzlik said, I want to help students who can succeed not just admit them to fail them.

Cara can tell this meeting is getting out of hand, but she is pleased with the discussion that is taking place, and pleased that the faculty members agree with her. She is not sure how productive the committee will be. She decides to discuss the remaining students at a meeting she schedules for the next week. In the meantime, Cara wants to devise some sort of plan of action to take to Janet. Cara feels troubled but proud that she stood her ground this year.

Questions

1. During Cara's first two years at JSUH, the institution is in the middle of an attempt to change its reputation through an admissions policy. This policy change has cultural, behavioral, and, possibly, mission ramifications. What are the various institutional consequences for this policy change and how are they playing out?
2. JSUH is severely understaffed and this is creating hardships for underprepared students. What kinds of programs could Cara create, with her limited time and resources, to help these students?
3. In Cara's conversation with the student Joanna, student development theory could be used to better understand Joanna. What theories would you use to understand Joanna and how could those theories be used to help both the student and the overall situation for underprepared students?
4. Identify a university's various ethical responsibilities to their students, employees, and the bottom line. What responsibilities have been violated in this case and why? Construct an argument for the violated responsibility that is most important to you and propose a solution.

Chapter 10

Rigid Academic Policy Within a Changing Institution

Caitlin Barbour Ginter and Molly A. Mistretta

Institutions of higher education tend to be more complex than many imagine. In this case, we can see how despite a university president advocating for increased participation in study abroad programs, barriers from within the institution are preventing the achievement of this goal. How do organizational and environmental issues in this case influence possible outcomes?

THE SETTING

Rogers University is a regional, mid-sized private institution in a suburban community adjacent to a large metropolitan area in the Northeast. Of the 4,000 undergraduate students, the majority are middle-class and white. Although Rogers is a moderately selective institution, it has struggled to attract a diverse body of students. Recently, Rogers welcomed a new president, Dr. Benedict Harrison, who considers addressing the university's struggle with diversity a priority. He would like to see modest gains in diversity among the student body, and also a greater understanding of and appreciation for diversity throughout the academic curriculum and within co-curricular activities.

One area the new president has addressed is the number of students who take advantage of study abroad opportunities. He views study abroad opportunities as transformational experiences that promote cultural awareness and a broader worldview. With greater numbers of students studying abroad, the president anticipates that students will be able to demonstrate greater multicultural competence, thus creating a more welcoming place on campus for diverse and underrepresented student populations.

The university's student abroad programs are developed and housed within the Office of International Students, which reports to the Vice President for Student Affairs at Rogers. Alex Harlow is Rogers' only study abroad advisor and has been charged with increasing efforts to encourage students to study abroad. The new emphasis on study abroad is a challenge that Alex welcomes. In response to the president's new initiative, Alex managed to develop several creative programs for marketing study abroad opportunities on campus. She also hosted several representatives from overseas partner universities and developed a team of Study Abroad Ambassadors. This team consists of students who have studied abroad previously and who work with Alex to serve as on-campus recruiters and as sources of information for their peers who may be considering an educational experience abroad. Alex considers them her best source of firsthand information for interested students.

Thus far, her efforts have been fairly well received by the campus community. While it is too soon to compare study abroad participation to that of previous years, she has seen a large increase in foot traffic in her office as students inquire about many of the international educational opportunities available through her office.

THE CASE

Alex Harlow knew that expanding the study abroad program at Rogers would be challenging when she took the job. She did not, however, expect to encounter resistance from the academic side of the institution. Although she was prepared to encourage students to consider going abroad in spite of financial issues, worried parents, and health concerns, she had not expected to encounter a student whose academic department prevented him from going abroad.

In the beginning of the spring semester, Alex met with Jeffrey Banner. Jeff is a sophomore interested in spending the upcoming fall semester abroad. Fall semester works best for Jeff because he anticipates doing an internship the following spring semester. Alex also realizes that Jeff needs to be on campus his senior year to take several upper-level courses in his major, including his Senior Capstone, which is a graduation requirement.

Alex met Jeffrey last fall when he attended an informational session for students who were interested in participating in Rogers' study abroad programs. She understood him to be a good student who is generally respectful and well liked on campus. Therefore, she is surprised when he walks into their appointment that morning noticeably frustrated and angry.

Alex: Hi Jeff! How was your weekend?

Jeffrey: Awful! Seriously, the worst!

Alex: You seem really upset about something. What's up?

Jeffrey: I am! Apparently my advisor in Exercise Science won't let me go abroad. At all. Ever. It's ridiculous!

Alex: Okay, take a deep breath and let's start from the beginning. Why don't you tell me what's going on.

Jeffery: Well, remember that info session last fall? That got me so excited about going abroad, so I spent the entire break researching the different programs you guys offer, and I found one that I was really interested in; it's the one in Germany, with the really great Exercise Science program. I also talked with my roommate, who went abroad last year, and said it was the best experience of his life. That sold me on going! I want to go next fall, so last Friday I went to my advisor, Dr. Harper, to talk to him about the courses I would need to take and stuff, and he told me it's not possible, that the department has some stupid requirements, and that if I want to graduate on time, I can't spend a semester abroad. I don't get it. Why can't they just make an exception? This is an incredible experience and one that I think would really help me in my field. I mean, Dr. Harper's been abroad, and now he's being a hypocrite telling me I can't go.

Alex: Okay, let me just make sure I am hearing you correctly. You met with your advisor, but from what you understand, he's telling you that because of course requirements in the department, it isn't possible for you to spend a semester abroad and still graduate on time. Is that right?

Jeffrey: Yes! See, it really doesn't make sense! I mean, the university acts like it wants us to study abroad, the president has been talking about the benefits of doing it, you see the posters and programs about it on campus, but the university keeps us from actually experiencing it. I just don't get that! Why don't Dr. Harper and the rest of the faculty tell us about these stupid restrictions earlier? If he had, maybe I would have been able to go last year or something.

Alex gives Jeff a moment to calm down, and then suggests that she contact Dr. Harper to better understand the situation. She explains to Jeffrey that she just wants to be sure that she understands the entire conversation as well as the department regulations before deciding how to proceed. Alex knows of Dr. Harper's reputation on campus, and since he has had international teaching experience, she is hopeful that he will be open to clarifying and discussing the situation with her. Jeff agrees to let Alex handle it and schedules a meeting with her for later in the week to follow up.

After Jeff leaves, Alex calls Dr. Harper's office to discuss Jeff's situation. Dr. Harper explains that Jeff's only option for a study abroad experience is the coming fall semester, but he is also required to take a prerequisite course during the fall semester to be eligible to do the spring semester internship.

Dr. Harper says that he personally sympathizes with Jeffrey's frustration, especially since the German university also offers a course that is academically and structurally the same as the required course. Dr. Harper is of the opinion that if students can take the same or similar course, there is no reason why they should not be allowed to take advantage of the opportunity to study abroad. Alex asks who she could contact in the department to pursue this further. Dr. Harper suggests that she discuss the matter with Dr. Kathleen McMannis, the Department Chair, to see if an exception can be made. He says that he would be willing to support Alex's request.

A few days later, and after many attempts to contact her, Alex succeeds in scheduling a meeting with Dr. McMannis to discuss Jeffrey's situation.

Alex:	Thank you so much for meeting with me. I know you must have a busy schedule and I appreciate your time.
Dr. McMannis:	Of course. What can I help you with?
Alex:	Well, I'd like to discuss with you a situation that came across my desk the other day. I have a student who would like to study abroad next semester, but he is unable to because of department policies. [Alex explains the predicament and elaborates on Jeffrey's desire to gain a more global knowledge of his discipline. She presents Dr. McMannis with information on the Exercise Science program at the institution in Germany, as well as a copy of the course that Dr. Harper believes would match the prerequisite offered at Rogers.]
Alex:	So you see, since the course content is nearly identical to what students would be required to take here on campus, we were hoping that it might be possible to allow him to take the course abroad and still get the credit needed to continue with his internship and degree. I believe the international experience would be a great benefit to him and would fit nicely with both his degree and the goals that the President is pursuing to increase study abroad opportunities for students at Rogers.
Dr. McMannis:	Ms. Harlow, I understand what you are saying, but I simply cannot allow it. Our department's policies are very clear, and I believe that I have a much better understanding of what is best for the students in our department than you. Regardless of whether or not the course abroad is

the same as ours, we feel that students are best prepared for their internships by taking the course here on campus. We have good relationships with all of the sites where our student are placed, and we can ensure their experience in this class best prepares them for their internship placement. Why should I give a student permission to take this course abroad when I know they can get a much better education here?

I know that President Harrison has been promoting the study abroad experience around campus, but he really should have checked with the faculty about this first. The faculty work hard to develop quality academic programs for our students. If students take their major seriously, they need to commit to being heavily engaged in the course-work. We can't have them taking off whenever they want because a semester in Italy, or wherever, sounds fun.

Later that afternoon, Alex relays to Jeffrey what has transpired between Dr. Harper, Dr. McMannis, and herself. Although he is clearly not happy, Jeffrey remains calm and thoughtful. Alex provides him with information about alternative short-term trips abroad over the summer or during spring break. The programs are offered through Rogers University, and although only a few are directly relevant to his degree, he will be able to take courses that would serve as electives. Jeffrey replies that he does not think that going abroad for only seven days over spring break will allow him the international experience he is seeking, and he cannot go during the summer because he has to work. He thanks Alex for her time and effort and leaves.

Alex is frustrated with the entire situation. She had anticipated that Dr. McMannis would be more supportive of the President's emphasis on study abroad opportunities. Alex also feels bad that she was unable to help Jeffrey resolve this problem, and had not looked forward to informing him of Dr. McMannis's response. However, she realizes that she did everything she could with the knowledge she had, and the outcome was not her fault.

Alex considers going to her supervisor for guidance, but decides against it. Her supervisor, Dr. Mona Burnett, is generally quite busy with overseeing Rogers' Student Affairs Division and is often knee-deep in budgetary and student conduct matters. While supportive, Dr. Burnett hasn't spent much time involving herself in the study abroad program. Alex is aware her office is unlike others in Student Affairs, and she gets the sense that Dr. Burnett is more comfortable letting Alex set the direction for the program. Therefore, Alex feels that she would like to reflect on this matter for a couple of days to think of some possible solutions before broaching the subject with her supervisor.

Early the following week, Jeffrey appears in Alex's office without an appointment. He mentions that he needs to discuss something that he feels she should be aware of. Jeffrey has approached students in other programs within the School of Education and has conducted an informal assessment of those students' views on study abroad opportunities. He explains that while not all students express an interest, many do and would take advantage of a semester abroad if the academic limitations were not so restrictive. Jeffrey points out that most students in the School of Education are required to take a similar prerequisite course before they can begin their teaching observations in their junior year. Thus, those students have no real options for studying abroad in their junior year, either. Jeffrey said it would be interesting to know how many other majors on campus have similar restrictions. Alex agrees and begins to wonder if Jeffrey's situation is more common than she thought.

Alex realizes that not many students are able to prepare for a study abroad opportunity as freshmen and go abroad during their sophomore year. The pressure most first-year students face when transitioning to the university environment makes it unlikely that they would be ready to plan for a study abroad opportunity that early. She also believes that many students are developmentally ready to go abroad as juniors and seniors, once they have had a chance to determine which course of study they would like to pursue.

Jeffrey has spent some time thinking about President Harrison's goals for Rogers, and it is his opinion that academic departments are preventing students from having the type of transformational experience that Rogers' new president has been promoting. He notes that there are conflicting interests between the institution helping students develop greater cultural understanding and academic departments that seem to prevent study abroad. After talking with other students who have studied abroad, Jeffrey is convinced that it is a life-changing experience that would forever influence how he views the world.

After expressing his beliefs, Jeffrey tells Alex that he is working together with several other students to protest the department's obstacles to study abroad, and to build a case to present to Dr. McMannis in an effort to persuade her to enact a policy change that would allow students to take certain required courses abroad. The group has already scheduled a meeting with her for next Monday. They intend to argue the need for a more global perspective for all students within the Exercise Science program. The group has researched several other foreign universities included in Rogers' list of approved overseas programs that offer courses similar in content to the prerequisite course. They hope to convince Dr. McMannis that since a number of foreign universities offer the same or similar course, students should be allowed to take it while abroad as long as it meets the academic criteria laid out by Rogers.

Jeffrey explains that they have already spoken with Dr. Harper about their plan in the hope that he would join them. However, while Dr. Harper supports the students in their efforts, he is unwilling to be a physical presence. As a junior faculty member, Dr. Harper does not wish to disrupt the good professional relationship he has with Dr. McMannis. Jeffrey is hoping that Alex will agree to be there to show support for the students and for expanding the study abroad program on campus.

This is something Alex was not expecting, and she feels unprepared to respond immediately to her student's request. On the one hand, she would like to support her students and go with them to meet with Dr. McMannis. It would enable her to better connect with her students, and they would see in her an advocate for their study abroad concerns. Such an action would also allow her to advocate for the study abroad program in a meaningful way, and a strong show of student interest and support might help her expand the study abroad program as expected by Rogers' new president, Dr. Harrison, and her supervisor, Dr. Burnett. She considers the possibility that this type of action may in fact be exactly what the President is looking for.

On the other hand, she is unsure if it would be wise so early in her career at Rogers to participate in such a bold action. If she were to join the students, she could risk either alienating herself from members of the faculty and staff or developing a reputation as a troublemaker. What should Alex do?

Questions

1. Where should Alex's loyalties lie? To her students? To the institution? To her faculty and staff colleagues?
2. Should Alex participate in the meeting with Dr. McMannis, where students are protesting the current departmental policy regarding study abroad? Is it likely to be effective? Would Alex's presence at the meeting make it more effective? Are the risks to her career that she mentions worth taking so that she can show her support to her students?
3. Other than joining the students in their protest, how else could Alex advocate for giving more students the opportunity to study abroad? What steps could she take to garner support at Rogers?
4. Where else should Alex seek help or guidance in making this decision?
5. Who holds the power to provide the outcome that students are seeking?

Chapter 11

From Foster Care to the Ivory Tower
A Homeless Student's Struggle
Sara Gould and Molly A. Mistretta

What types of support should colleges provide for students? In this case, a student who grew up in the foster care system struggles to succeed in college without traditional systems of support. Despite a caring environment, the college she attends is unable to meet her needs. As you work through this case, think about the socioeconomic lenses that institutions of higher education operate out of and what corresponding assumptions institutions make about their students.

IN THE CAREER SERVICES OFFICE

In her second year as a career counselor at Grandbard College, Kate is excited to start a new year. She is the newest career counselor on staff and spent last year developing great relationships with students as they explored their postgraduation options. Students liked her because she was friendly and went out of her way to help them. Kate didn't mind going the extra mile because she could relate to what her students were experiencing as they approached the "real world".

Kate is also really happy to be at Grandbard. It is an elite liberal arts college with approximately 2,000 students. Known nationally for its rigorous academic curriculum, about 70% of its alumni pursue graduate studies. Although the students she works with are smart and driven, many newer students assume they don't need the Career Services Office until their junior or senior years. What they don't realize is that leadership positions on campus often require the need for a resume or polished interviewing skills. Off-campus internship opportunities also catch younger students unprepared. Kate and her supervisor, Barbara, recognize this issue and work diligently to market services at the Career Services Office to all students.

Over the summer, they brainstormed ideas about how to raise the profile of Career Services among first-year students, who upon matriculating to Grandbard tend to be more interested in the offices of Student Activities, Greek Affairs, and Intramurals and Recreation. Kate and Barbara jumped at the chance to work with faculty coordinating this year's Inquiry Program, which is a three-credit interdisciplinary course that all first-year students take. While the course features a common reading, all sections also have a specific thematic focus and service-learning project. Kate and Barbara volunteered to assist faculty by coordinating the course's service-learning projects. They created presentations that explain the details of each course's service-learning project, as well as outline what other services their office provides to first- and second-year students on campus. Kate did the majority of these presentations and completed them all by the end of September.

One day, Elizabeth, a first-year student at Grandbard, showed up to the Career Services Office for a 15-minute resume drop-in appointment. Kate was available, and took Elizabeth back into her office to talk.

Kate: Hi, Elizabeth! I'm Kate. My understanding is that this is your first time in the office. We are so happy to have you here and love when we see first-year students taking the initiative to come in.

Elizabeth: Yes, it's my first time! I remember you speaking to my Inquiry class about resumes. I don't have a resume, so I wanted to come in for an appointment and get some guidance.

Kate: Well, you're in the right place. So, what exactly do you want to use your resume for?

Elizabeth: I hope that by the end of next semester I can begin looking for an internship. Right now, I just want to get something on paper.

Kate: That won't be a problem at all. We only have 15 minutes for a drop-in appointment; so let's get started. My understanding is we are starting a resume from scratch?

Elizabeth: Correct.

Kate: I am going to give you some resources [handing over some brochures and sample resumes from a rack in the office]. Take these home and look through them. They describe some possible resume formats and will help you get started. Remember, your resume is supposed to be a snapshot of your life and experiences. As a freshman, it is perfectly fine for you to list high school experiences as well.

Elizabeth: [Shifts awkwardly in her seat] Um, okay. That might be a little difficult for me.

Kate: Don't worry, most students struggle with the first draft. For now, just worry about getting your thoughts and ideas on paper. We will work through it and talk out the rest later. How do you feel about getting started this way?

Elizabeth: [Looking through the printed resources] This seems to make sense. I can work on creating something, and I'll bring it back. Thanks for all of your help.

Kate: Anytime, I look forward to meeting with you again! Here is my business card. My contact information is on here; if you need anything in the meantime, feel free to contact me.

About two weeks have passed since Elizabeth's initial appointment. Kate has been trying to manage the influx of appointments and the office as a whole is still extremely busy. Kate checks her calendar and notices that Elizabeth scheduled a resume review appointment the next day for a half hour. For some reason, Kate distinctly remembers Elizabeth, despite all of her other appointments that have occurred in between their meeting. Kate remembers Elizabeth as being uniquely mature for her age, and is pleased to see that she has been working on what they discussed.

Kate: Hi, Elizabeth! It's great to see you again. How have you been?

Elizabeth: Hi, I've been doing well. School is really overwhelming so far. I've never had to deal with so much work.

Kate: I understand it can be a lot. We have a lot of resources on campus to help you if you ever feel like you need it.

Elizabeth: Thanks, I appreciate that. I brought you my resume. I'm not really sure how I feel about it.

Kate: Well let's take a look at this. I'm going to look over your resume quietly and then we will discuss after, just because I can't always talk and think at the same time! Help yourself to the candy dish. [Reviews resume] Wow, Elizabeth. You actually have a lot of great experiences on here. This will be good.

Elizabeth: I've always really thrown myself into school. It's always been sort of like a safe space for me so I tried to get involved. I'm glad I have some good information to hopefully get an on-campus job. After being around all these people here, I'm starting to think I may need one to keep up.

Kate realizes that Elizabeth has listed every single high school she has ever attended. Her resume showed seven high schools located in different cities. Elizabeth had even attended three different high schools in the same school year. This intrigues her, as during her entire time at Grandbard she has never seen a student that bounced around so much.

Kate: If I may ask, why are there so many high schools listed?

Elizabeth: Oh, well, I've spent my entire life in foster care. I moved around a lot.

Kate: Thank you for sharing that with me. How has your experience been so far at Grandbard? Are you doing all right?

Elizabeth: You're the first person to actually ask me that question since I've been here. Just like in high school, I'm trying to throw myself into my work and to be successful that way. I'm nervous with Thanksgiving break coming up because I'm not sure they will let me stay in the residence halls. I really don't have a home to go to. My caseworker has been trying to set up something for me, and my roommate keeps bugging me about what I'm doing over break. I don't feel comfortable sharing the details of my life with her. She's so different from me. She sees college as a time to have fun and do lots of stuff. I can't keep up with the way she is able to spend money. Her parents pay for everything, and she has lots of pretty clothes and goes on vacations to cool places. It seems like everyone here is like her. I wish I had a normal life.

Kate: Look, I can see that you are struggling. It sometimes helps to know that people care. There isn't much I can do during this appointment, but here's this [Kate writes down her cell phone number on a sticky note and gives it to Elizabeth].

Elizabeth: What am I supposed to do with this?

Kate: Give me a call. If you ever need anything, I'm here for you. I know you don't have a huge support system, but you have one in me.

Kate has not been able to stop thinking about Elizabeth, especially with Thanksgiving break coming up. Kate had reached out to the Office of Residence Life to see if Elizabeth could stay on campus over the break. The Director of Residence Life was sympathetic, but explained that with no staff scheduled to work in the residence halls over the break, it would be a liability to have Elizabeth staying there by herself.

Later that week, Kate and the Director of Career Services, Barbara, have a supervision meeting. They discuss upcoming office events and the various issues that popped up during career counseling appointments. Kate brought up the topic of Elizabeth with Barbara.

Kate: I'm wondering about a student I've met with a couple of times. She's really sweet, but I am worried about her. She comes to us

from the foster care system and has no one. She's doing fine academically, but she's struggling socially and financially. On top of
that, she doesn't have anywhere to go for Thanksgiving.

Barbara: Wow, I've never heard of a foster care student here at Grandbard.
I'm glad you've connected with her! Staff and faculty connections
with students are an important part of the Grandbard experience.

Kate: I gave her my cell phone number. Is that okay?

Barbara: Sure! Faculty give their home phone numbers to students all the
time. I've given students my number a few times when I thought a
student might need some extra career coaching while on a jobsite
for an interview or so they could reach me ask me a question as
they negotiate a job offer.

Kate: Well, what do you think I could do for Elizabeth?

Barbara: Check with the Multicultural Affairs Office. They coordinate
holiday break plans for international students. I know they have
a network of local families that international students stay with
during breaks. Maybe they can find a place for Elizabeth.

Kate: Thanks! I didn't even think of that!

After the meeting, Kate contacted the Multicultural Office on campus.
After explaining Elizabeth's situation, Kate asked if they had any way to
place Elizabeth with a host family over the break. Unfortunately, the office
had arranged a travel experience for international students over the short
break instead. It was a bus trip to New York City. The students would stay
in a hotel, watch the Thanksgiving Day Parade, visit Ellis Island, attend a
Broadway play, and eat a traditional Thanksgiving dinner catered by their
hotel. The cost of the trip was $500, which Kate thought was a reasonable
price. However, she knew it might as well be a million dollars because there
was no way that Elizabeth could afford it.

Kate was disappointed to find that there really wasn't any help on campus for students lacking traditional support systems. As an expensive, highly
selective private college, Grandbard didn't attract many students like Elizabeth. It really was a testament to Elizabeth's tenacity and hard work that
she was even at Grandbard. While Grandbard pledged to minimize student
loans, and the subsequent debt burdens for financially disadvantaged students, there weren't any other institutional efforts or policies to address the
needs of students like Elizabeth.

MEANWHILE IN THE RESIDENCE HALLS

Elizabeth was overwhelmed with her coursework. It terrified her that if she
couldn't make it at Grandbard academically, she would have nowhere else
to go. While she had worked hard in high school to get good grades, she

realized that all of the moving around had left her with gaps in her education. The expectations in college were much higher than she encountered in any of her high schools, which didn't offer AP or Honors courses. She could do the work, but it was a struggle to do it well. It seemed to take her so much more time and effort than her peers to complete assignments and prepare for exams. On top of it, she felt that sometimes her professors and the other students were speaking another language as she struggled to understand references used in even the most casual of conversations. She realized her own experiences growing up made her different from her classmates.

Elizabeth struggled with her anxiety. Even though she made a few casual friends, she felt lonely and isolated. Elizabeth remembered from Orientation that the Counseling Center could help students with a multitude of issues. However, she was disappointed to find that she couldn't get an appointment for a month because they were so busy. Elizabeth remembered how nice Kate from Career Services was and thought she would be easy to talk to. Elizabeth called Kate that evening using the number Kate gave her.

Kate: Elizabeth, hi! It's great to hear from you. How are things going?

Elizabeth: Hi, Kate. I was actually wondering if I could talk to you about some things?

Kate: Sure, of course.

Elizabeth begins to disclose everything that she has been feeling throughout the semester, such as her homesickness for a home she doesn't even have, feeling unsupported, and feeling overwhelmed by being surrounded by people with lots of money and the ability to be carefree.

Elizabeth: I don't fit in here. I've never fit in anywhere. I'm so confused. I don't even understand what I'm doing in college half the time. College is so much harder than I thought it would be. It feels like every time I take a step forward, I take two back. I thought things would be better once I got to college. Like, I made it! But it's not okay, and I don't see it improving.

Kate's heartstrings are tugged because she has a soft spot for Elizabeth. She wants to help her in the best way that she can, but she really doesn't know what she can do.

Kate: Oh, Elizabeth. I am so sorry that you are going through all of this. I wish I could help you in the way that you need it.

Elizabeth: [crying] But . . . but . . . I thought you were a counselor?

Kate: I mean, technically, I am a counselor. I am a career counselor, which means I can help you with professional development and achieving your career goals.

Elizabeth: [crying] I don't know what I am going to do. My RA said I can't stay in my room over the break and I have nowhere to go. I hardly have any money because this semester has been more expensive than I thought it would be. My loan money won't come in until after the holidays.

Kate feels caught. After all, she did give Elizabeth her phone number and invited her to contact her if she needed to. Kate was also frustrated and angry that Grandbard would admit a student like Elizabeth and not provide any support given her unique background. Not knowing what else to do to help Elizabeth, Kate makes an impulsive offer.

Kate: Why don't you stay with me for Thanksgiving? You can come with me to my mom and dad's for Thanksgiving dinner. I'm sure my parents would be glad to have you join us.

Elizabeth: [stunned silence] Are you serious? Are you sure? Oh, Kate . . . thank you! Thank you! I won't be any problem. You'll hardly know I am there, I promise.

As the reality of what Kate had done set in, she began to have second thoughts. But then Kate wondered, *why not?* Faculty invite students into to their homes all the time for meals. She even knew of faculty and staff at the college who hired students to babysit and even house-sit when they went on vacation. Was this much different?

KATE'S SECOND THOUGHTS

Thanksgiving weekend went off without a hitch and Kate enjoyed being able to help Elizabeth out of a difficult situation. As the winter holidays approached, Kate became more caught up in Elizabeth's situation. Elizabeth had run out of money and the Financial Aid Office couldn't advance her student loan funds until after the New Year. Kate gave Elizabeth money to purchase toiletries and collected food from friends for Elizabeth to keep in her room. Kate again invited Elizabeth stay with her when the residence halls closed for winter break and she couldn't stay on campus.

Over time, the situation began to take a toll on Kate as she realized that by inviting Elizabeth to stay with her, she created a dynamic in which Elizabeth turned to her for almost every need. Kate was not only fulfilling Elizabeth's physical needs for food and shelter over breaks, but she often provided a comforting ear as Elizabeth shared her anxieties and concerns about her situation. It was clear that Elizabeth had some issues from her difficult childhood, but she resisted contacting Counseling Services on campus because "she felt so comfortable talking to Kate".

Kate started the spring semester stressed and exhausted. Kate soon realized that this could continue until Elizabeth graduated. Elizabeth was having a hard time finding a job because of Grandbard's rural location. The little college town was small and had few businesses. Elizabeth was able to secure an on-campus work-study position, but it didn't completely cover her expenses. Kate simply couldn't continue to help Elizabeth financially. Her own student loans didn't leave much after she paid rent, utilities, and groceries.

As the situation continued, Kate felt much of her time and energy was being directed toward supporting Elizabeth. She was less focused and enthusiastic about her work, and Barbara noticed. At Kate's annual evaluation in the spring, Barbara pointed out some areas where Kate's performance was lacking. She told Kate she sensed that she was struggling with something and asked Kate if she was okay. Kate wanted to unburden herself, but knew she had let things with Elizabeth spin far beyond her own abilities to help. Should she share with Barbara the full extent of her involvement with Elizabeth?

Questions

1. How does the culture of a school like Grandbard College contribute to the issues in this case?
2. Kate struggles to identify appropriate boundaries in her relationship with Elizabeth. What decisions did Kate make that you agree with? Which decisions of Kate's would you make differently?
3. What are some needs of students from foster care and low socioeconomic status (SES) backgrounds while enrolled in college? How can college and universities better serve this population to promote matriculation and retention?
4. How can supervisors assist new professionals to navigate the culture and expectations of their work environment?

Chapter 12

Hazing in the Band

Kristin M. Gregory and Stacy A. Jacob

In this case, a female student is selected to join an all-male section of the band and faces extreme hazing. As you read the case, consider the student's desire to be a part of the organization and how the environment of the campus influences student behavior. Also, think about leadership and how it influences the behavior of the members in the band.

It is marching band audition day at Eastern State University (ESU), a large research institution with a reputation for its enthusiastic school spirit, and soon to be first-year students are each awaiting their turn to try out for one of the most prestigious marching bands in the country. The ESU Marching Band, known for the drum corps marching style and exciting half-time shows, draw as much attention and excitement from fans at the football games as the game itself. In addition to their recognition on campus, the marching band has performed for various films, television shows, and music videos. Because of their acclaim, ESU holds auditions each summer for the marching band, and approximately one-third of auditioning students are cut.

Students, alumni, and members of the local community are highly committed to upholding the many and rich campus traditions, which often seem antiquated to outsiders. One of the long-standing, but informal, traditions of the marching band is their all-male sousaphone (tuba) line. Each year they receive a featured section of the halftime performance that is demanding both physically and musically. For years, female students have tried to successfully audition into the section, but have been turned down for a variety of "reasons" by the marching band staff, including poor marching technique, difficulty holding the instrument up for long periods of time, and poor musicianship.

There is a strict chain of command in the ESU Marching Band's leadership that starts with the band director and proceeds down to the assistant band directors, specialty music faculty, and then down to student leadership such as the drum major and section leaders. The student leadership of the band relies heavily on hazing rituals to initiate new members before their first performance. Band members are reluctant to question this practice for two reasons. First, members generally come from high-preforming high school band programs where hazing is the norm, and second, they fear retribution in the form of hazing.

Nervously waiting among the hopefuls is Hannah Sloan. Hannah is a nationally recognized tuba player within the music community and has won many solo awards and competitions. To expand her musical repertoire and prepare herself for a career as a music educator, Hannah auditioned for and was selected to perform in a world-class drum corps for two summers prior to enrolling in ESU. Hannah was not socially accepted throughout high school because of her interest and success in music and is nervous about making friends and fitting in at ESU.

After the conclusion of the ESU marching band auditions, Dr. Jack Bates meets with Dr. Sarah Jones, a new music professor at ESU who specializes in low brass (including tuba/sousaphone). Dr. Jones has volunteered to assist with the audition portion of the marching band, and she and Dr. Bates are discussing an outstanding freshman sousaphone player—the only woman to try out for a coveted place on the all-male sousaphone line.

Dr. Bates: Well, we only had one girl audition for the sousaphone line this year, but this one was in a class of her own. Hannah Sloan was exceptional but doesn't meet our "requirements."

Dr. Jones: You have to be kidding if you don't think she is qualified to be on this line, female or not! She has twice the credentials as some of the senior members who auditioned. She could run circles around these guys!

Dr. Bates: I understand that, but we like to keep our sousaphone line strictly male. They usually have the stamina that it takes to perform the feature.

Dr. Jones: This young woman has the same stamina, if not more! She marched in a drum corps for goodness sake! You know Hannah is well known throughout the music community, right?

Dr. Bates: Yes, I know. But she doesn't fit my requirements.

Dr. Jones: The reality is that you have never disclosed on any audition materials that you are only looking for male sousaphone players. Can you imagine if she goes public with your decision?

Dr. Bates: I just don't know if the band and ESU are ready for this. Perhaps we should call in the girl and let her know what she may be up against.

Later that evening, Dr. Bates and Dr. Jones speak with Hannah in the band office.

Dr. Bates: Hannah, we need to have a conversation before I post the official band roster.

Hannah: Yes, sir?

Dr. Bates: We have decided to break tradition for the first time in the 30 years I have been here, and it involves you. We would like you to be part of our sousaphone line—

Hannah: [interrupting with excitement] Yes, I would love to!

Dr. Bates: Let me finish. This is not going to be easy for you, and I am still not completely convinced this is a good idea. There are going to be a lot of people, especially returning members of the band, who are not going to like this decision. You are going to have to work twice as hard as everyone else to be successful. Is this something you are willing to do? You are talented, and I am willing to put you in a different section if you'd like.

Hannah: No, Dr. Bates. I love the sousaphone.

Dr. Bates: [frustrated, hoping she would back out] All right, Hannah. If you are willing to do this, then we are. Just know, I won't help you after today, and I can't protect you from the backlash that will come of this. Understood?

Hannah: Of course. I think I can handle it.

As Hannah leaves, Dr. Jones pulls her aside and says, "Hannah, if you run into any problems, you let me know. I will be away at a conference this week, but you have my cell phone number in the welcome packet I sent to the entire studio."

The evening went even worse than Dr. Bates expected. After the final band roster was posted and the first band meeting was over, he spent an hour with the returning sousaphone players who were livid with the decision and threatened to quit. After getting them to the point that they were willing to stay, he asked to speak privately with the section leader, Mark, and said, "I know Hannah is a girl and you are upset. You are the section leader; do whatever you need to get them ready—including Hannah. Treat her no differently than anyone else. Whatever the section does, she does. If you have any problems, you know the chain of command."

The first day of rehearsal was difficult for Hannah. None of the members of her section would address her unless it was to correct her or call her awful names. One of the most difficult encounters Hannah faced on the first day was with her section leader, Mark, who was responsible for helping the new students learn their drill spots. Mark was from a high school with an award-winning band that used hazing to promote excellence. He chose ESU because the band reminded him of his high school band.

Mark:	[directly to Hannah] You are in the wrong spot.
Hannah:	[innocently] I don't think so. I followed my directions, and I am pretty sure this is where I am supposed to be. I can check it again though.
Mark:	I don't think you get me, you idiot. YOU are in the WRONG spot.
Hannah:	[genuinely confused] But I checked my spot three times. This is where my sheet says I should be. Do you want to see it?
Mark:	I know your flipping sheet is right! What I am saying is that you shouldn't even be in this section, you bitch! Quit while you still have a chance.
Senior Sousaphone Player:	No one wants you here, so don't expect us to be bending over backward to make you feel at home here!

Frustrated and upset by band practice, Hannah returns to her residence hall and runs into her Resident Director, Julia. Julia has approximately three years of experience post her master's degree in residence life.

Julia:	[makes eye contact with Hannah] Hannah, how was the first day?
Hannah:	Awful. Just awful. My section won't speak to me, the band won't speak to me, and Dr. Bates won't do anything about it. Plus, my studio teacher, Dr. Jones, is out of town, and even if I called her, she wouldn't be able do anything. My section leader basically told me to quit while I still could!
Julia:	[maintains eye contact throughout the conversation and speaks in an understanding tone] It does sound like you had a terrible day. Hannah, I think it's Dr. Bates's job to make sure you are having a good experience in marching band. He shouldn't let this stuff happen. Have you considered approaching him about it?
Hannah:	No. He said that he couldn't help me when I met with him yesterday to talk about joining the section. And we were told during

the band meeting that if we had any problems, we were supposed to follow the chain of command, which means talking to
my section leader. I was excited about being the first female in the
sousaphone line, and knew it was going to be hard, but not this
hard. This is just like high school all over again.

Julia: It seems as though you were hoping for things to be different in
your life at ESU. Can you tell me about that?

Hannah: Yeah, I really had a hard time with high school and feeling good
about myself. I love music and would do just about anything to
keep it a part of my life. In my high school, it was really hard
to enjoy something that wasn't "cool." Because so many people
thought I was strange, it really made it difficult for me to like
myself.

Julia: How did you see college being different for you, Hannah?

Hannah: I figured that it would be easier to fit in.

Julia: You've had an awful day and it sounds like this isn't what you
envisioned for your experience at college. And yet, at the same
time, it seems like you dare to be different; you chose to be brave
and break a long-standing tradition around here. It seems to me
that you have to decide who you want to please here: yourself or
your new peers.

Hannah: I guess you're right, Julia.

Julia: It's going to get better, Hannah. And you are right; quitting won't
solve any problems. Try giving everyone, including you, a few
days to adjust. I'm here if you ever need someone to talk with.

Hannah: Thanks, Julia. I appreciate it. Hopefully tomorrow will be better.

The next three days were not much different from Monday for Hannah.
Although she felt that she was catching onto the music and the routine, Mark
was being particularly hard on her and the rest of the first-year sousaphone
players for no reason. During the afternoon, the marching band separated
for sectional rehearsals across campus. Hannah was shocked by the intensity
of the rehearsal, even compared to her drum corps experience. Mark had
each of the new sousaphone players practice their marching techniques in
front of the veteran members. Each time they made a mistake, Mark would
hit them with a stick to correct them. He continually called Hannah a bitch,
hit her with the yardstick, worked her to the point she fell down, and said
over and over, "I'm gonna make sure you quit."

At the end of rehearsal Mark said, "You newbies suck. Tonight, I am
calling a section meeting at my place. 7:00 p.m. All of you must be there!
Bring your mouthpiece."

It is the end of the day and Julia is sitting in her office at the residence hall
when she notices Hannah stumbling into the hall, looking upset and hurt.

She goes out into the lobby to see what is wrong, and notices bruising all over Hannah's body and a cut on her face.

Julia: Hannah! What happened? How did you get hurt? Are you all right?

Hannah: I'm fine—just an accident at band. I tripped over a rock while I was marching and fell on the band field.

Julia: [Looking at Hannah better, she realizes that a simple fall could not have produced such bruises. She makes eye contact with Hannah and keeps it.] Are you sure? It certainly doesn't look like you fell.

Hannah: [tearing up] Um—

Julia: Hannah, come on. Let's go into my office so we can talk privately.

Hannah: Okay.

Julia: Now what's really going on?

Hannah: Nothing. I told you, I fell.

Julia: I can tell that it wasn't just a fall, Hannah. I am concerned. Is there anything you want to share with me?

Hannah: [starts sobbing] Yes. You're right. It wasn't a fall. My section leader did this to me and to all the other freshmen. He was watching our marching skills and kept hitting us with a stick every time we screwed up.

Julia: Hannah you need to go to the health center and get checked out! You could be seriously hurt.

Hannah: I don't want to. Maybe I deserved it. They were right, when they called me a stupid bitch. I am ruining things for the section, and need to get my act together.

Julia: That's ridiculous! Beating someone with a stick will not make them a better sousaphone player in the marching band; nor will calling them stupid. I have to report what you told me to the Vice President of Student Affairs, Dr. Potter. What happened to you is against ESU policy and you were hurt. This is serious, Hannah.

Hannah: No, please don't! Getting them in trouble is only going to make it worse for me!

Julia: I don't have a choice. It's my job to make sure you are safe here at ESU. Right now, you are not. I would like to try to help you fix this.

Hannah: Do whatever you have to do, I guess. But we have a sousaphone rehearsal tonight at Mark's house. Mark called it and Dr. Bates said we're obligated to attend every rehearsal, full band or sectional.

Julia: [shocked] Hannah! You are in no condition to go there! You've just shared with me that the individuals at this meeting hurt you, and now you are thinking about seeing them again this evening. I am going to go talk to Dr. Potter now about this entire situation. We can help you deal with Dr. Bates in the morning.

Hannah: [half-heartedly] I don't know—

Julia: Based on your condition, I think you should stay here. I can't force you to do that, but I think it's something you need to strongly consider. I am going to go speak to Dr. Potter about this now, all right?

Hannah: Okay. [Hannah leaves the office and walks upstairs.]

Julia rushes to call Dr. Potter to report what has just happened. He answers his cell phone and Julia explains the situation and her concerns about hazing in the band. Dr. Potter tells Julia that he is 45 minutes away at a meeting in the city but will meet her in her office when he returns. In the meantime, Julia goes to Hannah's room to let her know what is going on. She tells Hannah that she will either be in her office, Dr. Potter's office, or her apartment so Hannah can find her if she needs anything. When Dr. Potter arrives, he looks concerned.

Julia: I really appreciate you coming back to campus to handle this situation. I am concerned for this student.

Dr. Potter: There was no question if I was coming or not. This is a serious claim.

Julia: Thank you. I really do believe we have a serious situation on our hands. My resident is the first female sousaphone player at ESU. She came into the residence hall after rehearsal bruised and upset, claiming that her bandmates were verbally and physically assaulted during an unsupervised portion of today's rehearsal. I worry that they are abusing her emotionally as well.

Dr. Potter: I heard about this student at the beginning of the week. Let's call Jack Bates now to hear what he has to say about any of this. I find it hard to imagine he would condone hazing of any kind.

Julia: I don't think she is making this up. I saw the bruises. She was a wreck. The story she told is disturbing.

Dr. Potter: We will call Jack Bates and find out what is going on.

Dr. Bates: Hello?

Dr. Potter: Hello, Jack? This is Sam Potter and one of my Resident Coordinators, Julia. You are on speakerphone. Julia is concerned about one of your band members.

Dr. Bates: What's going on?

Dr. Potter: Julia is concerned about hazing. Have you seen any instances of this happening within the band?

Dr. Bates: I know many of the new students think that their section leaders are especially rough on them and treat them poorly. Many times the problem is simply that the new students are not used to the intense culture and attention to detail we look for here.

Dr. Potter: Understandable, Jack. But why would we see a student bruised quite badly after one of your rehearsals?

Dr. Bates: You'd be surprised how often students get bruised at camp. They bang themselves with their instruments, trip in holes on the practice field, you know.

Once it is clear to Dr. Potter that Jack Bates seems unconcerned, he wraps up the conversation and says to Julia, "I don't know what is going on, but we need to investigate further. Where is Hannah right now? I would like to speak to her."

They both head to Hannah's room but she is not there. Hannah, despite the advice of Julia, is on her way to Mark's house.

Mark: [slightly slurring his words] Oh, look who finally showed up! You're late! We will have to keep that in mind when it's your turn to prove to us why you should be here. You will never be one of us, you stupid whore.

Hannah: [a bit frustrated and angry] I'm sorry. I got lost getting here.

Mark: I didn't want you in this section at all. Apparently we all don't get what we want! [He turns his attention to the other freshmen sousaphone players.] We're taking each of you upstairs to test if you really deserve to be here.

Mark turns on the stereo, and then he and the rest of the senior section members and one of the new first year sousaphone players head upstairs.

Hannah is the last person left in the room downstairs. The long wait has made her more anxious about what is to come. She considers leaving, but knows she will never be accepted by the sousaphone section if she leaves at this point.

Senior Section Member: [walks over to Hannah and grabs her by the arm] You're next. Get up!

Hannah: Okay.

They head upstairs to what seems to be Mark's bedroom. Mark and rest of the senior section members stand around the room muttering slurred words and laughing with one another.

Mark: Saved the best for last. Those other guys think they got it rough? Well that's nothing compared to what you are getting. Guys, hold her.

Hannah: Wait! What? Please stop!

Mark: Hell no, bitch! You want to be part of this section? Guess what. You never will because you are a girl. And we're going to prove that tonight.

Julia decided to wait for Hannah to return and is working in her office. At 10 p.m., she hears someone furiously banging on her office door. She goes to the door and finds Hannah bloody and bruised and sobbing.

Julia: What happened?
Hannah: I went to my sectional tonight.
Julia: What happened? Did someone attack you again?
Hannah: I, I, they beat me. They—they—[begins crying] raped me.

Questions

1. The band directors in this case made a decision to accept a female student into the sousaphone section knowing that her presence would disrupt the culture and tradition that her bandmates were familiar with. How could they have eased this transition? What things could they have done?
2. If you were in Julia's place, what would your first action be after Hannah revealed what happened at her sectional meeting? Outline a plan for what Julia should do to help Hannah.
3. Why might Mark and the other upperclassmen have engaged in hazing? What conditions can create an opportunity for hazing and how can college officials mitigate them?
4. Hazing is generally seen to be an issue in Greek Life. Where else can hazing arise? How can we educate all students on hazing? What other forms can hazing take? Why is hazing so problematic? Are there any forms of hazing that aren't problematic? When does an initiation practice become hazing?

Chapter 13

Controversial Speech in the Student Newspaper

Deron T. Jackson and Melissa A. Rychener

In the following case, a student writer uses racist language in an article about underage drinking. What kind of response will satisfy students' calls for justice while supporting the development and safety needs of all concerned?

Anthony Lewis, the new Director of Multicultural Programs, picked up *The Crimson*, to catch up on campus news. Since he arrived at Sawyer University six months ago, reading the student newspaper has connected him to campus events and to his students. After working in student affairs at larger state universities in urban areas for the past 25 years, this is his first time at a small rural state institution, and his first time in multicultural affairs. Serving students of color was always part of his "unofficial" role, but now he is ready to fully and formally embrace his role as the Director of Multicultural Affairs. Flipping through the paper, he came to an article with the jarring headline, "Underage and Still Drinking," and he decided to dig in.

After the first two or three paragraphs, Anthony noticed the name one of his students, Trina Sanchez, a junior education major with an impressive community service background. Rather than outlining her many achievements or presenting a more complete view of who she is, the article had a stark characterization of Trina. "Trina was drunk as a skunk, and, no, this is not a reference to her being black at a white party." Anthony sat up, concerned about this public, racialized portrayal of Trina as a drunk. He wondered if Trina had consented to being named in this article. Wouldn't standards of journalistic ethics dictate that students should not be identified in an article of this nature connecting them to illegal behavior? Furthermore, what did "being black at a white party" have to do with being drunk? Why was her ethnicity mentioned at all? He sighed and kept reading. Trina's appearance was characterized as "ghetto," and her clothing was "like a hip-hop video girl"—both cultural attributions that had nothing to do with the topic of the article. Anthony knew that Trina would be upset by the way she was portrayed in the article, and he anticipated that many other students would be outraged as well. He looked at the byline and wondered about Peter Brookings, the article's writer. Anthony guessed, based on what he had read so far, that Peter Brookings had limited experience within a diverse community. He probably had no idea how offensive his words were to students of color—or perhaps Peter used them to intentionally incite a reaction. He kept reading.

In the next paragraph, the name of another student appeared, Tyler Walker. Anthony knew Tyler, a sophomore, through his involvement as a mentor for new students. In sharp contrast, the version of Tyler reflected in this article was a one-dimensional stereotype. The author wrote, "Tyler was drunk, with bottles in his hand, and chains all over his neck. He appeared to be impersonating his favorite rapper." If Tyler had attended the party and consumed too much alcohol, this was a poor decision and one that merited discussion and possible consequences. However, the writer's portrayal of Tyler as a hip-hop cultural icon made Anthony wonder if the student writer's only experience with people of color was in music videos. How sad that the editors didn't work with this student to improve his sloppy writing and reliance on stereotypes.

Unfortunately, as Anthony continued reading, the article became even worse. The writer went on to say, "Several students were scared Tyler was going to pull out a gun, but that didn't happen." "What's this?" thought Anthony. Now in addition to a racialized description of his appearance, the writer claimed that students were afraid Tyler would become violent? Based on what? Did Tyler make some kind of threat? Knowing Tyler, Anthony thought that was highly unlikely—though he would certainly check it out. Far more likely, in his experience, was that Tyler was suspected of being violent simply because he was black and not because of anything that he did or said at the party. Unfortunately, Anthony had seen this scenario far too many times. He wished that the advisor to the student newspaper took a more active role in discussing editorial choices with his student staff. Students who have little experience with diversity might hold stereotypes that interfere with their ability to be objective.

Anthony sat at his desk for a moment, letting the article sink in, and trying to decide what to do next. There was no doubt in his mind that this article would do far-reaching damage among students of color and especially to Trina and Tyler. Outside of his door, he heard a group of students speaking rapidly in distressed tones. Anthony opened his door to see what was going on.

Several students were standing in the student lounge outside of his office with *The Crimson* in their hands. The students were emotional, and a student he didn't know turned to ask him, "How can they print stuff like this in the paper?" Another student chimed in, outraged, "How can they get away with this?" And finally, a woman he recognized as Trina's roommate said with tears streaming down her face, "They are so racist. They don't even know Trina." Anthony told the students that he shared their sadness and their outrage. He asked them to support each other and try to think of ways to help the community come together so that nobody would feel isolated. He encouraged them to help get word out that the multicultural center would be a gathering place throughout the day for connection and support. He asked one of the student workers to order snacks. He stayed and talked with the students about this event and others that had made them feel unwelcome at Sawyer. At one point, he stepped away to contact Trina and Tyler and asked them to come to his office that afternoon.

When Trina and Tyler came to the office later that afternoon, the following dialogue took place:

Anthony: I have read the article in *The Crimson* and am concerned about the way that you are portrayed and how it is affecting you. I am here first as your advocate and wish to offer you my support. I also want to know more about the extent to which you consented to being featured in this article. I would like to hear from both of you.

Trina: Well, when I first read the article I was shocked. I couldn't believe my friend would write this about me. I felt stabbed in the back! When he was asking me questions at the party, I just thought he was curious. I had no idea he was writing an article. Some of the things yes, I will admit to, but he definitely twisted my words and even made some things up!

Tyler: I have worked so hard building a good reputation on campus with my peers, faculty, and staff, and now this? What will people think of me now? These are stereotypes [pointing to the newspaper article]—not me! Now I think Peter is a racist. I never thought he would want to ruin me! Most of the stuff in this article is false. I swear I am trying to keep my cool, but part of me is pissed.

Anthony: So it sounds like you were at the party in the article and talked with Peter as a friend. However, you did not consent to be included in an article he was writing about binge drinking. Is that correct?

Both: Yes.

Anthony: I'd like to discuss some of the particular claims he made in the article. Tyler, what did you think when you saw the comment about you pulling out a gun?

Tyler: Seriously? Do I look like the type to have a gun? Do I look like a thug? I am a college student, and I represent myself with class everywhere I go. I don't need a gun to feel like a man. Yes, I was at the party in question, and yes I had some drinks, and I apologize for that, but why would Peter write this in the paper? I am not a violent drunk, and I've never had a gun. I'm hurt, I am offended, and I feel like the comments are racist.

Anthony: I understand your perspective, Tyler. Nobody wants to be misrepresented, especially in a way that relies on stereotypes. The fact that this came from a friend must be particularly hard. I appreciate your honesty about drinking, and I'd like to follow up with you about that at a later date. Trina what about you?

Trina: Ghetto? Are you serious? I have been on the Dean's List every semester since coming here. I hate when people judge me because my style is different and, even worse, because of the color of my skin. I am proud of who I am! Peter is just uneducated, judgmental, and uncaring. Sometimes I get so angry I don't know what to do!

Anthony: Trina, I am so glad to hear you say you are proud of who you are. Just think about the people in your life who love and support you and want you to succeed. What would you like to see happen in terms of a response?

Trina: I want Peter suspended; I want an apology and a public announcement that he was wrong. He needs to see that what he did was wrong.

Tyler: I just want to know why. Yes, I am upset about this and I want an apology, but in the end, it is what it is, I guess. I think the editors are more responsible than Peter anyway.

Anthony: Why is that?

Tyler: Let's be honest. The editors are responsible for publishing the article, and you can't be a good editor and accept an article with all this hateful content.

Anthony: You both express an interest in hearing from the newspaper staff in one way or another. I will take your concerns to the advisor of *The Crimson*. I will also talk with the leadership of the multicultural organizations about crafting a community response. Before you leave today, I would like you each to schedule separate meetings with me to discuss your decision-making around alcohol and also to brainstorm about helping you refocus your energy on your academic goals. Will you do that please?

Both students agreed to schedule follow-up appointments, and Anthony mulled over his options. Trina, Tyler, and other students said they wanted a response from Peter and the newspaper staff, and Anthony shared this desire to make sense of why the article was published. However, he knew that this was not an isolated event. He decided that his goal was to redirect the conversation to create a supportive environment for students' expression and inclusion, as well as help students notice and interrupt racism in all of its forms.

Before he could do anything, he received a phone call from the secretary of the Vice President of Student Affairs, Bethany Thomas. Bethany requested Anthony's presence at a meeting in her office in one hour with John Hausman, advisor to *The Crimson*, and Elizabeth Silver, the student editor. Anthony agreed to meet them and began to prepare. How would they deal with the author of the article, Peter Brookings, while not making him the scapegoat for a failed editorial process? He was interested to see how the student editor would explain her rationale for choosing to publish the article. He also hoped to have a better understanding of how the advisor to *The Crimson* viewed his role. Understanding the editorial process seemed to be a necessary part of the discussion, as did addressing the hurt and outrage generated by the article. He made some notes and headed over.

After everyone arrived at the conference room, Bethany opened the meeting and explained that she had been receiving calls from the president, the local newspaper, and even the local news stations over this article in *The Crimson*. She said this is the third year in a row that a controversy related to racism in the student newspaper had occurred, and this time she was going to see that something was done about it. John Hausman, advisor to *The Crimson*, told everyone in the room that he met with the writer, Peter, earlier in the day. Peter had come to his office visibly shaken because students were confronting him in person and through social media. Peter said that his article was his best work, and he did not feel that he'd said anything wrong. When pressed, he admitted that some of what he wrote was "over the top" and may not have been 100% true. "Before I could explore this further," John explained, "I had to run to class."

Bethany: Elizabeth, were you aware that the article contained inaccuracies?
Elizabeth: When I first saw it, I thought it might be controversial, but I trust the writer's judgment. Of course, I thought the descriptions of Trina and Tyler were exaggerated, but they were funny! I thought that they would be able to laugh at themselves—obviously, I was mistaken.
Anthony: Hackneyed stereotypes aren't funny. They are damaging and evidence of a lack of judgment—both on the writer's part as well as yours. Furthermore, your writer made up several of the

	details and exaggerated others. He did not ask for or gain consent from either Tyler or Trina. They had no idea that they were being interviewed for an article. Are these not basic components of journalistic integrity?
Elizabeth:	[looking sheepish] I didn't think about it that way. Also, I didn't know that Peter made anything up, and I assumed he got their consent before interviewing them.
John:	I have to admit it's partially my fault for giving my editors so much freedom to make these decision, but Elizabeth, you should have known better. After the last few years of missteps around issues of race at *The Crimson*, we talked numerous times about how careful we need to look at these articles. If you were not sure, you should have come to me.
Elizabeth:	Well I figured it was freedom of speech, and for the past three years, Peter has been one of the best writers on staff. I never thought he would write made-up things. Again, I partly get why everyone is upset.
Bethany:	We need to be more attentive about what articles might cause conflict and, more important, are offensive to others in the university community.
Anthony:	I want to underscore here that this isn't a matter of restricting content to protect the sensibilities of a particular group of students. This is a matter of teaching the basics of journalistic ethics. I have never advocated for sweeping issues under the rug to protect students' feelings. What I am saying is that interview participants need to give consent to be interviewed. Student writers and editors need to be trained to recognize stereotypes and taught to stick to the facts and not conjecture based on prejudice.

[The others shift uncomfortably in their seats.]

Bethany:	Yes, Anthony, I understand that you are questioning the editorial process. But I also think we need to deal with the issues of racism in the community and creating a safe space for students of color.
Anthony:	I agree that we need to deal with *both* issues of racism *and* journalistic ethics.
John:	I give my students the green light to write whatever their hearts desire, but they have to be smart in their choice of words.
Anthony:	I think this goes far beyond word choice—[trails off]
Bethany:	John, why didn't you review the article to make sure it was okay to publish?
John:	I have been the advisor for *The Crimson* for 10 years and to my understanding my job is to have a meeting with the student editor about the paper, sign some papers, and then give the student editor the green light to get it printed.

Elizabeth: When I met with Dr. Hausman, I gave him a snippet of the articles that were being published. As I stated before I didn't see an issue with what Peter wrote so I didn't feel I needed to show Dr. Hausman the article.

John: I understand that, Elizabeth, but now do you see why it's important to ask questions when you are the least bit unsure? We have been having this problem since you took over as student editor. I'm not placing all of the blame on you, but you need to understand that this is serious.

Bethany: John, what training have you provided for the students on journalistic ethics? How have you addressed the historic incidences of racism in *The Crimson*?

John: We should probably do some more training of our student writers and editors.

Bethany: Noticing that this has been a recurring theme with *The Crimson*, don't you think you should have taken the initiative to take a look at all articles being published just so something like this would not happen again?

John: You are right I should have, but I trust my students are doing their job. I teach classes as well so the last thing I thought I needed to do is micromanage my students.

The conversation continued to go back and forth. John Hausman advocated for his students, Elizabeth and Peter, but he also acknowledged that they had made mistakes. Bethany told John that she was appreciative of him being willing to help not only fix the problem but wanted him to educate Elizabeth in the process. Bethany explained that mistakes like this that negatively affect the whole campus community would no longer be tolerated. She looked to Elizabeth and John and said, "I am sorry that Peter has to be the one, but we have to set a precedent for more responsible reporting. This lack of journalistic ethics can no longer be tolerated on this campus. On this basis, I would like you to ask him to resign from his position at *The Crimson*."

Bethany announced that the university was calling a campus-wide town hall meeting as soon as possible for the students and staff to discuss this incident and how it affects not only the campus but also the local community. She announced that *The Crimson* was suspended until further notice to ensure that no other racist or inaccurate articles would be published until their editorial process had improved. She asked John to contact the appropriate professional journalism organization to schedule training for all student newspaper staff on journalistic ethics. She then brought the meeting to a close.

As he was leaving the meeting, Anthony was lost in thought. He looked forward to continuing to work with Tyler and Trina to make sure that they had the support they needed to get past this difficult situation. He was glad that Bethany was taking such a firm stance for journalistic integrity as well as healing the community. Given the seriousness of the misinformation in Peter's story, he understood Bethany's decision to ask Peter to resign. However, Anthony hoped that Peter and Elizabeth would learn from this experience. He was concerned about whether John Hausman would take a more proactive role in educating the staff of *The Crimson*, and he was also worried that the administration would use this incident as an excuse for clamping down on student expression. Finally, he thought about freedom of speech. At its best, speech can illuminate understanding. At its worst, speech can be a weapon. How to help students to manage this important right with integrity seemed to be at the heart of his new job. He hoped that he had the wisdom and skills to do justice to this responsibility.

Questions

1. In the debate that follows, who is ultimately responsible for this content—the student writer, student editor, or the faculty advisor?
2. What responsibilities does the university have to the developmental needs of the student writer and student editor?
3. What steps can be taken to address the unjust, racist, and inaccurate portrayal of Trina and Tyler in the student newspaper?
4. How can a university community heal after such an event? Consider the needs of all constituents—students, faculty, and staff.

Chapter 14

Student Conduct

Inclusion for Student Organizations and Students With Disabilities

Todd E. Kamenash and Michael G. Ignelzi

This case highlights the dilemma presented when disabilities and behavioral problems join. In reading this case, think about how student affairs professionals and higher education institutions can accommodate behavioral-related disabilities, balancing the needs of the individual and of student groups affected, while also fairly administering student conduct policies and processes.

CHARACTERS

Jeremy Blaylock—Jeremy is a 24-year-old white male. He is a junior at Western State University (Western). He carries a 3.4 GPA in his major of computer programming. He is an active member of the Western Gamers Club (WGC). Jeremy is registered with Student Disability Services for Pervasive Developmental Disorder (PDD; part of the Autism Spectrum Disorder umbrella).

Eddie Blaylock—Eddie is a 20-year-old Asian American male. He is Jeremy's adopted brother. He is a sophomore at Western State University, and a member of the WGC.

Tyreke Nettles—Tyreke is a 22-year-old African American male. He is a senior at Western and is the outgoing president of the WGC.

Zelda Johnson—Zelda is a 19-year-old white female. She is a sophomore at Western and a member of the WGC.

Madelyn Bryce—Madelyn is a 29-year-old white female. She is the Assistant Director of Student Rights and Responsibilities at Western. Madelyn completed her undergraduate and student affairs graduate studies at the same small, private institution. She worked there full-time for five years in Residence Life and Student Rights and Responsibilities. She has been in her current role at Western for two years.

SETTING

Western State University (Western) is a suburban institution with 30,000 enrolled students. In 1895 Western was established as a normal school, training teachers in curriculum development, pedagogy, and finishing (etiquette). To present day, the teacher education program is highly rated regionally and nationally. In the 1990s, technical fields supporting education flourished at Western resulting in marked increases in faculty and student talent for progressive majors including entrepreneurial business, computer science, assistive technologies, creative arts, and architecture. All Western students have a required core of diverse general education offerings for first-and second-year students. Common classroom and experiential service programs are featured.

Western has a moderately sized student affairs operation. The Vice President for Student Affairs and Dean of Students (two separate jobs and people) share supervision of all departments, including Counseling Services, Dining Services, First-Year Experience and Orientation, Health and Wellness Services, Residence Services, Student Activities, Student Disability Services, Student Rights and Responsibilities, Student Union, and Veteran Services.

Staffing in Student Disability Services and Student Rights and Responsibilities consists of a director, assistant director, and a graduate assistant in each office. Staffing in Student Activities consists of a director, one assistant director and one graduate assistant for student clubs, and one assistant director and one graduate assistant for Fraternity and Sorority Life. Currently there is an ongoing search for the director position, with the assistant director for student clubs serving the role of interim director.

Western's Student Activities oversees and provides support for more than 250 student clubs and 12 Greek letter organizations (social, service, and multicultural). Each club is required to have minimal standards for executive positions and leadership succession processes that are maintained by Student Activities. Some clubs are highly organized and meet regularly. Other clubs are less organized, sporadically gathering at events with little direction. Each year several new clubs are founded, and several existing clubs drop out of existence due to student interest and leadership.

The Western Gamers Club (WGC) was formed in 2005. Since its inception, the club has averaged 50 students at weekly meetings on Friday nights in the Student Union. The executive leadership uses a quasi-democratic approach for selecting a wide-ranging array of featured games to play and compete with each week. Most games are online, but some require audio/visual equipment. Some members bring board games and fantasy card games to play.

The atmosphere of the WGC is highly dependent on how inclusive the president allows the game selection process to be. In some years, membership has dwindled because the president limited the types of games played; in other years, the club was highly successful when the process for game selection yielded a variety of games that were popular at the time.

Elections for the WGC President are held on the second Friday in April, so the outgoing president can mentor the incoming president. This year membership grew, and 75 or more students were showing up to each weekly meeting.

CASE

During last Friday's WGC meeting, elections for next year's officers were held. Eddie and Zelda, the two candidates for President, each shared their goals and visions for the club. Both are friendly with each other and well liked by most club members. The election was run by Tyreke, the current President, and the winner is determined by a simple majority of raised hands. If the hand vote is tied, a simple written ballot is used until the tie is broken. In the hand vote, Zelda won over Eddie, 43–35. Eddie was disappointed that he did not win, but he started to walk over to Zelda to congratulate her.

Jeremy, a three-year member of WGC and Eddie's brother, began to pound the table with clenched fists. He went on a profanity laden tirade demanding a vote recount and that the paper ballot process be used. Jeremy accused Tyreke of having a crush on Zelda, which made the election unfair, and then called Tyreke a racist. Jeremy said that his brother Eddie was the best candidate by far and he (Jeremy) wouldn't be a part of WGC unless Eddie was in charge.

Some members agreed with Jeremy and vocally supported him. Eddie and other members tried to calm Jeremy down. Jeremy continued his tirade, and the meeting became an all-out screaming match. About half of the members left the Student Union. Jeremy started banging his head on the wall to the point where he needed medical attention. Police were called and two officers responded within minutes. An ambulance followed shortly thereafter and Emergency Medical Technicians (EMTs) attempted to evaluate Jeremy's injuries. Jeremy refused medical assistance. He kicked and bit one of the police officers.

After this episode, Jeremy went on Twitter and WGC's Facebook page and continued verbally disparaging several members of the WGC.

When the Western Police Department investigates a criminal action, there is a strict chain of evidence protocol and procedures designed to accommodate state and local laws. The police investigation often takes weeks to months and is submitted to a prosecutor. Eventually, summaries are publicly available. To reach a more timely resolution, Student Activities requested a school-run independent investigation. The Dean of Students coordinates with the Student Rights and Standards staff to train a pool of investigators who work in various student services units. To avoid any potential conflict of interest for a potential future hearing, no Student Rights and Standards staff participates in such investigations. The Dean of Students assigned two trained investigators to interview the relevant persons involved and provide a written report including relevant facts and disputed information.

The investigative report included the following notes after interviews were conducted with several individuals involved in the incident:

Tyreke Nettles

Tyreke initially did not mind Jeremy's outburst regarding the election results, but when race and his supposed relationship Zelda became involved, he took it personally and became defensive. He said that at first he tried to calmly reason with Jeremy, but when that didn't work, he began to yell. He stopped once Jeremy started banging his head on the wall and asked that someone call the police for help. Tyreke shared that Jeremy has been a polarizing person in the WGC. Some members want him removed from the club because of his behavior since he joined the WGC. According to Tyreke, when Jeremy gets what he wants, he is participatory and a positive and supportive member. But when he does not get what he wants, he is difficult to deal with. Tyreke said that once Jeremy mentioned on multiple occasions through social media that he really wanted to play a certain game. When Jeremy showed up late to the next WGC meeting and the group had selected another primary game, Jeremy became loud and agitated. He physically got in the way of the monitors of the people playing and eventually pulled the wires to the game controllers out. The meeting abruptly ended. Another time Jeremy caught a male student using a game cheat-code and berated him in front of the whole club, demanding that he be banished.

Tyreke also mentioned that at times Jeremey demonstrates he has "great heart." He can be a likable person, and has recruited many people to the club. He is generally well liked and many members have learned a great deal about PDD because of Jeremy.

However, Tyreke said that in this situation, Jeremy crossed the line by making false accusations against him of racism and of lobbying for Zelda. Tyreke said that he has a partner and he doesn't have a crush on Zelda. He said that in his role as president, it is normal to ask people for their opinions on who they are voting for, and it is not out of bounds to share his opinion with them. His opinion is that having an "attractive woman" in charge, like Zelda, will "obviously" lead to an increase in membership.

Jeremy Blaylock

Jeremy openly admitted that he behaved poorly, but only because he knows that his brother should have won the election. Jeremy said that he asked most of the WGC members who they would vote for and 67 people told him "Eddie." He said that there was no possible way, with that many members voting for Eddie, that Zelda could have won the election. Jeremy said that he likes Zelda, but his brother is far superior in planning, game selection, and ideas for the future of the club. He also claimed that Tyreke and Zelda have a romantic relationship and conspired to influence the vote.

Jeremy said he has always had physical reactions to people touching him, and he didn't mean to kick or bite the police. He claimed that he couldn't always control his actions due to his disability. He reported that he is registered with Student Disabilities Services, and they are great about giving accommodations for classes. Jeremy said that a representative from Student Disability Services, with his permission, previously spoke with the WGC leadership about being sensitive to Jeremy's issues. Jeremy is aware of at least three other members in the WGC that have non-visible disabilities, but unlike him they are shy. He is proud that they have found a home with him in the WGC.

The WGC is Jeremy's only non-academic activity at Western, and he said that he would probably not be a student if not for being a member of the club.

Jeremy said that he uses social media as a way to cope with what's going on. He admits that some people do not understand that he is just venting, but those that do, absolutely agree with him.

Zelda Johnson

Zelda feels confident that she fairly won the election. She feels that the WGC has been greatly improved under Tyreke's leadership and she plans to continue his good work. She is proud that the WGC includes people like her, a self-proclaimed female nerd and geek. She has learned a great deal from Jeremy, but she is uncomfortable with him when he does not agree, and she does not feel she has the skills to deal with his outbursts.

Zelda admitted that she and Tyreke have "hooked up" on occasion and continue to be "friends with benefits," but that has nothing to do with the election. She likes Eddie and Jeremy, but believes she won the election fair and square. She is really looking forward to leading the WGC.

Eddie Blaylock

Eddie said he told the members that he wanted to make the WGC more inclusive with game selection, and that he would consider adding a second gaming night in the week to allow for different types of games. He wanted to create additional leadership positions to manage more gaming events and give other members experience to advance the club. His perspective is that Zelda is interested in continuing what was currently in place, which would not make the club any better. Eddie is disappointed that he did not win. He reports that he started to walk over to Zelda to congratulate her, and that is when Jeremy started his outburst. Eddie tried to comfort Jeremy, but he was aware from previous situations that his brother would take a while to cool down. Eddie did try to tell the police officers and EMTs about Jeremy's PDD, but they ignored his request that they let Jeremy continue to take out his frustrations. Eddie said he has seen Jeremy behave similarly in the past, and it usually lasts about thirty minutes before fatigue sets in and he stops. Eddie said his family would pay for any property damage.

Eddie is touched by Jeremy's loyalty and does not believe that his PDD should be held against him. Eddie is proud of how smart Jeremy is and the progress he's seen in his emotional maturation. He believes that there are still several people in the WGC that do not have patience for or understanding of Jeremy's PDD, and they are making an easy target out of him for their twisted entertainment, not realizing the damage it is doing to Jeremy.

Other WGC Members

Several other members of the WGC, who were interviewed, shared that they are sensitive to Jeremy's PDD and believe that he is mostly harmless. They do not take Jeremy's behavior personally. They think that Jeremy is a productive and important member of their club who has successfully recruited numerous new members.

Some members, however, said that they don't know how to deal with Jeremy when he doesn't get his way, so when he asked who they were voting for they said "Eddie" to not upset him. Some of these members indicated, based on the election incident, if Jeremy were allowed to stay in WGC, they would either quit or create a new club. They shared that while at first they were receptive and then tolerant of his behavior, this time it has gone too far.

OFFICE OF STUDENT RIGHTS AND RESPONSIBILITIES

For any case referred to the Office of Student Rights and Responsibilities, Madelyn is required to determine if the issue can be resolved informally through mediation, conflict coaching, or other negotiation tactics. If not, Madelyn will send the case to a hearing panel for formal review. If there is a preponderance of evidence that violence is involved or that an outcome may be a suspension or expulsion from Western, the case must automatically be assigned to a hearing panel.

Madelyn oversees the training for a pool of volunteer hearing officers, with each hearing containing up to five panelists. Hearing officers include faculty, staff, and students who are required to attend a three-hour training session prior to serving on a panel. The training focuses on the Student Code of Conduct policies, definitions of terms used, hearing processes, guidelines for questioning, decision-making, decision-writing, and tips for being trauma informed. One hour of the training is dedicated to the university's sexual misconduct policy and expectations. Each semester, an optional session with a one-hour mock hearing case is presented. The case is created around a sexual misconduct focus. Roughly half of the hearing officers participate in the optional training. In Madelyn's two years at Western, the only time Student Disability Services has been addressed in the required or optional training sessions is when a trainee asks a question about it. When a case is referred to the Student Rights and Responsibilities office and it is known that the respondent has a disability, guidance from Student Disability Services is sought. In Madelyn's experience, only behavioral guidance has been provided; no accommodations have been made by Student Disability Services related to co-curricular activities.

To complete the investigation for this case, Madelyn reviews the investigative report and speaks with the police and EMTs. She comes to the conclusion that it was more likely than not that Jeremy had kicked and bitten a police officer, which requires her to convene a hearing panel. Madelyn assigns charges of disorderly conduct, assault, and discrimination against Jeremy. Madelyn asks Tyreke, Jeremy, Eddie, Zelda, Officer Ament, and Officer McReady to participate in the hearing due to their direct involvement. Each party is allowed to bring one advisor (who cannot represent them) and up to three witnesses.

OFFICE OF STUDENT DISABILITY SERVICES

With permission from Jeremy, the Office of Disability Services verifies that Jeremy is registered, and that he receives academic classroom accommodations. Student Disability Services indicates that they do not authorize accommodations outside of the academic classroom. However, they do offer suggestions for events based on awareness and addressing students with disabilities. They offer an optional workshop for student organizations when requested. Shortly after Jeremy joined WGC about three years ago, the (then) current president of WGC asked Student Disability Services to provide a workshop. After communicating with several leaders in the WGC, it was determined that giving a workshop to all members might inappropriately alienate Jeremy and others with non-visible disabilities. Student Disability Services did convene a workshop with current WGC leaders. No WGC leaders since that time have asked Student Disability Services for follow-up or any other workshops. None of the students involved in the current situation reached out to Student Disability Services for guidance in any way.

Student Disability Services does not serve as advocates for students in the adjudication process, and as a matter of routine practice informs students that they should expect to be subject to the same accountability and standards as all other students regarding their behavior.

WESTERN POLICE DEPARTMENT

The Western Police Department determined they could not ignore the physical assault on their officer and the damage to the wall, and supplied a criminal report. The local prosecutor declined to move the case forward officially stating there was insignificant harm done to the police officer. An anonymous op-ed in the local newspaper suggests that the prosecutor's teenage daughter with autism may have influenced his decision, but regardless, no criminal prosecution will ensue. The Western Police Department forwards the incident to Student Rights and Responsibilities for adjudication. They provide the following incident report:

> On April 9 at 21:17 hours, Officer McReady and Officer Ament responded to a call for assistance in the Student Union open-rec room. There was a large crowd of students, most attempting to leave the area. Officer Ament observed student Jeremy Blaylock yelling profanities and banging his head into the north wall. A small amount of blood was on Blaylock's head and the wall. Officer Ament approached Blaylock and attempted de-escalation techniques. He warned Blaylock that if he did not respond or cease hitting the wall, he would be cited for disorderly conduct. Blaylock spat toward Officer Ament.

At that time, Officer Ament attempted to subdue Blaylock. Blaylock resisted. Officer McReady assisted and was able to pin Blaylock so that Officer Ament could apply handcuffs. Blaylock kicked Officer Ament in the legs three times. Officer Ament helped Blaylock stand, and Blaylock then bit him on his left wrist. Photos were taken of Officer Ament's injured wrist.

TASK FORCE

Based on the investigation and regardless of the hearing panel outcome, the Dean of Students assigns Alexandra and Madelyn to lead a task force in reviewing student organization policies and sensitivity training pertaining to students with disabilities or other impairments. Part of the charge for the task force is to research and analyze relevant literature and benchmark comparable institutions around these issues. Another charge of the task force is to develop a transparent and coherent guide for addressing student behavior issues through conflict resolution strategies.

Questions

1. How should Jeremy's status with Student Disability Services play a role in the student conduct case? What privacy concerns would need to be addressed regarding this in the hearing process?
2. If Jeremy is found responsible for rules violations, what sanctions would be appropriate, educational, and restorative? Are there other administrative actions that could be considered instead of student conduct, and if so, why, what, and how?
3. How might Student Affairs staff assist the WGC move forward with the existing fracture caused by this incident?
4. Should accommodations of any sort be provided for students with disabilities such as Jeremy's in relation to their co-curricular involvements and experience?

Chapter 15

Keep Them on Campus

The Unintended Consequence
of a Residence Hall Policy

Lenee McCandless and Melissa A. Rychener

In the following case, a new residence hall employee tries to balance the needs of a student with the policies of his employer. As you are reading, think about how university policy affects students' lives. Also, consider the procedural challenges "helicopter parents" create.

"And that's a wrap!" says David Saunders, Assistant Area Coordinator at Southwestern State University, smiling to himself because he has always wanted to say that! He is helping a group of Latino students in his residence hall area who are preparing for a dance performance during Latin American Heritage Month. The performance is coming together well, and he's learning a lot. The choreographer is a student and a dance major, and David, a freshly minted Student Affairs M.A., is stepping in tonight because the choreographer is sick. Although David's role in the group is usually more related to the technical aspects such as setting up the stage and the music, tonight he is a more visible presence—and he's having fun with it. During a typical week, he goes back to his office to get work done during the practice, but he often finds himself watching at least part of the rehearsal. Growing up white in a small city in Indiana, he doesn't have much experience with Latin American culture, and he is curious and interested to learn more.

He notices one of the students, Gabriela, lingering after practice. He approaches her, and she says, "Que onda David?" He responds, "Nada mucho," and his pronunciation makes her laugh. "Et tu?" he says to her, and Gabriela makes a face and says she doesn't speak French. "Oops! My bad. I thought I was answering in Spanish! Well, what's going on? You aren't your usual energetic self."

Gabriela: I'm just tired. It's hard to sleep in the Smith Hall study lounge.

David: Yes, I would think so, though when I was a student, I was usually trying not to sleep while studying.

Gabriela: No, I'm not trying to sleep when I study. It's just that sometimes I can't sleep in my room, and I have to sleep somewhere.

David: Okay. But I don't get it. Why can't you sleep in your room?

Gabriela: My roommate sometimes has friends over. When I go back to my room after studying, sometimes I find someone sleeping in my bed. I feel bad to wake them up, so I go to the study lounge, but it isn't very comfortable.

David: I can imagine. . . . How long has this been going on?

Gabriela: Well, it started the first week of classes. Jessica, that's my roommate, she always has friends in our room, so I started studying in the library. When I came back from the library at night, her friends would be sleeping in my bed, and I wouldn't know what to do. I would just go sleep on the couch in the lounge.

David: Aargh, Gabriela! Why didn't you tell me sooner? This has been going on since the first week of school?

Gabriela: Well after a week of this, I talked to Jessica. She told me, "I'm sorry. My friends live off campus and get tired, and we all fall asleep eventually. You are usually out so late I don't know if you are coming back to the room." I told her that I just study late and that I want to stay in our room, and she told me that she would, "definitely make sure no one falls asleep in your bed again." It was a really quick conversation, but I felt like she listened.

David: I'm glad that you talked to Jessica and that she seemed receptive. Good for you. However, I am assuming this was not the end of the story since it sounds like the same thing happened last night?

Gabriela: For a while things were better, but starting this weekend, people started sleeping in my bed again. It also smells like they were smoking in the room. I hate the smell of smoke. I had a test today, and I was so tired because I slept in the lounge. I know I have to talk with Jessica again tonight . . .

David: Yes, Gabriela, please talk with her—about the after-hours guests and about smoking. If these are off-campus guests, they are not allowed to be in the residence halls after midnight, and smoking isn't allowed on campus. If you need help, reach out to your RA—or come see me again tomorrow.

Gabriela goes back to her residence hall, and David returns to his office to finish up for the night.

The next morning, he is back at work, when his boss, Anita Davis, the Area Coordinator, calls him into her office.

Anita: I just received a phone call from the mother of one of our residents. She is calling to complain about her daughter's roommate situation. Her daughter's name is Jessica Esposito, and she lives in Smith Hall. Do you know her?

David: I don't know her, but I may have heard something about her. . . . Has Jessica talked to her roommate or contacted her RA about the problem?

Anita: No, Mrs. Esposito is reaching out to me about a sensitive topic. She says that Jessica's roommate studies until late and keeps her up until all hours. This weekend, when the mom was visiting, she was sure that she smelled marijuana smoke in the room. She asked Jessica about this, and Jessica said it belonged to her roommate. Mrs. Esposito is calling because she doesn't want her daughter to get in trouble.

David: Actually, Jessica's roommate talked to me last night. She told me that she has been sleeping in the Smith Hall study lounge because her roommate has been having friends sleep in her bed. She also said that there was smoking taking place in the room, but she said she doesn't smoke. She didn't say anything about marijuana smoke.

Anita: David, I'd like you to ask Jessica's roommate about this . . .

David: Sure. I guess I can talk to Gabriela tonight after practice, and then I'll follow up with her hall director.

An hour before practice, Gabriela pokes her head into David's office.

David: Oh, hi Gabriela! You are here early. You look upset! Come in and have a seat. Can I get you something? What happened?

Gabriela: When I tried to talk to Jessica last night, like I said I would, she and her friend were in the room smoking marijuana! I didn't know what to do. I asked, "What are you doing," and she laughed and said, "Smoking, want some?" I told her no and said, "But you can't do that in here." She just kind of brushed it off and said, "It's okay. I know the RA. She doesn't care what we do. You should really smoke with us. This weed probably came from Mexico too." At this point I just got really upset and left and stayed in the room of my friend from the dance group. I don't want to go back there.

David:	I can understand why you are upset, and I am glad you left. Now it's important that I write up an incident report . . .
Gabriela:	No! I don't want to make a big deal about this. I just want to move.
David:	I can understand, but we need to follow the Residence Life guidelines for documentation. This will help speed up the process of a room change request.
Gabriela:	What if she says that I am lying? I don't have any proof! She's friends with the RA! And the marijuana is in my room! Even though I never even touched it, she already made it sound like it must be mine—since I am Mexican.
David:	But, it's not true, right? Her accusation is based on a stereotype, not you. You told me you don't smoke. Look, there's a whole process . . .
Gabriela:	Don't you understand? I can't get in trouble with the law! Even though I never had marijuana, what if something is found in the room and Jessica says it's not hers? What if she says it's mine?
David:	If you tell the truth, it will all work out!
Gabriela:	[scoffing] You actually believe that? Maybe in your world, but not in mine. David, I'm a "dreamer."
David:	What? A "dreamer"? Do you mean—
Gabriela:	Yes, I'm undocumented. I could get deported to a country I don't even know. You can't tell anyone.

David is reeling and not sure what to do. His cell phone buzzes, and he answers. It's Anita.

Anita:	Hi David. Good news. The room is clean.
David:	Oh, okay. What room? What happened?
Anita:	Well, it turns out that Jessica's mother called the RA when she didn't get what she wanted from our conversation. The RA talked to her hall director. Based on the mother's complaint and another resident's report of smelling smoke, campus police were called. When they too detected the smell of marijuana, they entered the room. They didn't find anything. Sounds like a situation we need to keep our eyes on.
David:	Yes, I definitely think we need to stay on top of this. It is good news that the room is clean. Thank you for letting me know.

David gets off the phone and turns to Gabriela.

David:	Nothing to worry about.
Gabriela:	What do you mean?

David: That was my boss, Anita. Your room was searched by campus police this afternoon, but nothing was found.

Gabriela: [looking pale] Okay. That was too close though. I still don't want to stay in my room.

David: [gets her a drink of water] Listen, I don't really know what your life is like. But I know that you were really scared. I can't make it right, but I can try to help you work on resolving your housing situation.

Gabriela: I won't go back to that room. Maybe I just don't belong in college at all.

David: Let's concentrate on figuring out how to proceed. Conflicts like these come up all the time, and students change rooms all the time. There's no need to question whether you should be at college. You are a good student, you study hard, and you have important academic goals.

Gabriela: Well, I'm not sure, but I guess I'll give it a try.

David: Well that's a start anyway. Speaking of getting a start, I better get the stage set up for rehearsal.

The next morning, David approaches Anita about Gabriela's dilemma. He explains that she is not comfortable in the room

David: Anita, I want to follow up on the situation with the roommates that came up yesterday. Jessica's roommate, Gabriela, is staying in a friend's room because of the problems that she is experiencing in her room. I think we need to fast-track a room change.

Anita: [sighing] Yeah, we can add her request to the pile on my desk [gestures to a stack of room change request forms]. This seems to be the case lately, students wanting to change rooms.

David: In this case, I don't think we should wait. The problems between Jessica and Gabriela are serious. Jessica is a junior and Gabriela is a freshman. There is suspected drug use. A parent is involved . . . I think it would be best to move one of the students to another room.

Anita: Don't get me started on Jessica's mother. She has been hovering over her daughter since she arrived on campus three years ago. Finally, this year Jessica has the residence hall her mother has always wanted her to have. And as you know, it is university policy that upperclassmen have first choice of rooms. Jessica chose this specific residence hall, and there are no other openings in Smith. If we do anything, we would have to move Gabriela.

David: That policy doesn't make much sense to me. Can't we make an exception?

Anita: The university really wants more upperclassmen to live on campus with the new suites because we lose revenue when they move off campus. However, we can make exceptions in the case of an incident report.

David: Isn't there an incident report from when the campus police checked the room? I understand that room requests are backed up at the moment. However, I'd really like to advocate for this situation being given priority. Since Gabriela will have to move, when will she be reassigned?

Anita: Gabriela will have to be added to the list. I would say a week hopefully, maybe a little longer.

David: A week or more? Even with the situation? Gabriela is concerned about the legal implications of her roommate smoking marijuana, and she isn't able to sleep in her room half of the time. I really don't want to send her back there for another few nights.

Anita: I'm sorry David; there's nothing I can do. Gabriela doesn't seem to be in any danger; she's just in an unfortunate situation. We're just too backed up, and I am trying my best. I suggest that you talk to the hall director about the marijuana situation, and I'll keep you posted on the room assignment.

When the conversation ends, David is in disbelief. So he just has to send Gabriela back to her room? That just doesn't seem right. He didn't want to do or say anything that would jeopardize Gabriela's safety, so he didn't discuss her status with his boss. However, David is feeling extremely disappointed with the outcome of the conversation. It seems that the pressure to fill the new halls has created unanticipated problems and a backup of room change requests. And to add another layer of complexity to an already difficult situation is Gabriela's undocumented status. He thinks to himself, "If someone had asked me a week ago about my opinions about 'dreamers', I might have been sympathetic to their plight, but it wouldn't have occurred to me that I could actually know someone who has to live with the fear of being deported. I wouldn't have considered how a system that I generally view as responsive and fair could be experienced as the opposite, especially by such a thoughtful, hard-working student."

He carefully composes an email to her, explaining the good news, that she will probably be permitted to move from her room, as well as the bad news, that it might take a couple of weeks. He asks her to stop by his office so that they can think about short-term options.

Later that afternoon, David is setting up for the Latin American dance rehearsal when someone taps him on the shoulder. A student he recognizes from the group hands him an envelope. "Gabriela wanted me to give this to you," she says. He thanks her, finishes setting up the sound system, and returns to his office to read the note, aware that Gabriela is not at rehearsal.

Dear David,

Thank you for everything you have tried to do for me. You are a really great advisor and the only person who works here that I could trust. I don't want you to be angry or to feel bad, but I decided to withdraw from my classes and go back home. I am too scared to stay on campus. I will enroll in the community college and live at home. My dreams are still alive, but I just can't stay on campus anymore. I hope you understand.

Sincerely,

Gabriela

Once again, David feels off balance. How could this be? A wonderful student is gone and her roommate, a student who breaks policies and has a helicopter parent, is here to stay. He feels like he failed Gabriela. Should he have told Anita that Gabriela is undocumented so that she would have better understood the urgency of the roommate problem? Gabriela asked him not to tell anyone, and he felt that he should honor her request. The outcome that Anita was trying to guard against—a student moving off campus—came to pass. Except that the student was Gabriela, a freshman student who could have lived on campus another three years. There must be a better way to manage residence hall roommate crises.

Questions

1. What are some of the residence hall policy issues that contributed to this situation?
2. How could David have handled this situation better? What could Anita have done differently?
3. What options do universities have in working with parents who advocate for their adult children? How does Jessica's mom's involvement affect the case?
4. Discuss the importance of and limits of confidentiality. What were David's ethical obligations in this case?

Chapter 16

Social Media Scandal

Felicia P. McKinney, Emma K. Coomes, and Stacy A. Jacob

In this case, a social media scandal creates a university-wide crisis. As you read the case, think about all the offices that are affected. Also, think about how a campus with a strong social media culture could utilize that culture to address the issues in the case.

Lexington University (LU) is a midsize institution. In comparison to its competitors, LU has a strong presence on social media platforms. There is a focus on high-quality content designed to showcase the current student experience to prospective students. LU is made up of 6,000 traditional-aged undergraduate students and less than 1,000 graduate students. It is a social media heavy campus where students, faculty, staff, clubs, organizations, and academic departments have Twitter, Instagram, and Facebook accounts. Campus-wide social media contests and classroom discussions via Twitter chats are commonplace at LU. Students are known to write their Twitter and Snapchat handles on their whiteboards in the residence halls, and Resident Assistants often create Twitter accounts for their floor (@MapleHallFloor2 for example) to help their residents connect with one another. The university has an official presence on Facebook, Twitter, Instagram, Snapchat, and YouTube—all managed by Social Media and Digital Communications Coordinator, Madison Clay.

While Madison does not have a formal background in marketing/communications, she received both her bachelor's in Psychology and her master's in Student Affairs from LU. Her knowledge of the university and her professional connections across campus are highly valuable in her work. She views the success of LU social media as a collaborative effort, believing that her job is to promote the excellent work that others do. Though she is a young professional, she has gained support from colleagues for the good work she does; however, she constantly has to prove the value of her work to upper-level administrators, who either do not see the value of social media, or have concerns about its uncontrollable nature.

In a meeting regarding the university's website redesign, Madison lobbied to put social media icons linked to LU's accounts on the homepage and Bob Terry, Director of Alumni Relations, commented, "Why would we direct people away from our website?" In addition, Mary Smith, Director of Public Affairs at LU, is particularly uncooperative because she thinks all social media platforms should be managed under her supervision. One of Mary's staff members manages the official Facebook page for LU, which is not done well. Typically, the account manager binge-posts on Fridays, and the posts are known for being long, and unappealing to LU's constituents. Mary is known for her top-down, highly bureaucratic structure in the Public Affairs Department, and rules with an iron fist.

When Madison presented updates on how she is using social media for recruitment at a quarterly Director's meeting, the Vice President of Student Affairs, Dave Wallace commented, "You're telling me anyone can say anything at any time, there's nothing we can do about it? If we're using these avenues for recruitment, we need to control what people see. This is a firestorm waiting to happen." While Dave is technically correct, the nature of social media does allow anyone who engages on those platforms to say anything at any time, Madison has not experienced any major incidents on LU social media platforms up to this point. She monitors LU's social media conversations, and unofficial twitter accounts like @luturnup that promote parties, but she knows that she cannot control the content that is posted. From her perspective, conversations about LU are happening on social media whether or not there is an official university presence. It's better to be monitoring and contributing to the conversation than to be left in the dark about what students are saying.

A major aspect of Madison's work involves personally interacting with individual prospective students on social media. Madison promotes popular recruitment hashtags that developed organically from the students for each incoming class—#lu18, #lu19, as well as #lubound. She is constantly working to explore how new social media platforms can be used to reach prospective students. Last year, Lexington recruited its finest first-year class in history. Madison and her supervisor Olivia Robinson, Director of Admissions, attribute some of this success to social media recruitment, as Madison has documented over 600 individual interactions with prospective students online.

While Madison is on the forefront of this area with few best practices to work from, she has developed a process for analyzing her work. She carefully documents every interaction with prospective students online, and works with Admissions to code each student in LU's student information management system. The results of her work have indicated that students who have been offered admission and interacted with LU on social media are significantly more likely to enroll. Madison also keeps up with national research on social media use to help her make data-driven decisions. She has found that while college websites are the best place for prospective students to find information such as admissions deadlines, tuition, and majors, social media is the best place to learn about student life. As indicated by research, Madison is sure that a well-managed social media presence and intentional interactions with prospective students give LU a competitive edge over other institutions that have not yet adopted the practice.

LU has no formal social media policy, community guidelines, directory, or crisis communication plan—all of which are important, large-scale projects that would require cross-campus collaboration from LU's senior administration, legal team, and, unfortunately, Mary. As someone on the forefront of a new and exciting area in higher education, Madison is always imagining the possibilities of expanding her work if she had support staff and additional resources. On top of a number of other marketing, video production, and website responsibilities, Madison is the sole manager of social media at LU, and has no staff to spread out her workload.

Alexis Jones is a first-year student at LU. She was excited to find out that she was accepted to LU, tweeting a picture of her acceptance letter as soon as she opened it in the mail. Upon arriving on campus, Alexis was surprised at how different college is from high school. For one, she feels like she "became" pretty—guys flirt with her and a football player even asked for her number. She's slowly getting used to this new kind of attention, and she and her roommate Sara spend a lot of time talking about cute guys. Alexis and Sara met on Twitter during a university-sponsored #lu19 Twitter chat. Both girls were relieved to have clicked with one another during the chat, and solidified their connection in person at orientation.

Over the last few weekends, Alexis and Sara have been going out to parties and enjoying the social aspect of college life. They don't know too many people on campus yet, but find out about parties from postings on Snapchat and the Twitter account @luturnup. Alexis is gaining a ton of new followers on Twitter, Instagram, and Snapchat, many of them are guys that she meets at parties. She's been featured on @lucrushes, a Twitter account where LU students submit their crushes for an anonymous account manager to post. Alexis quickly discovered that being "LU crushed" is a big deal on campus. When someone submitted a crush about her, four people took a screenshot and sent it to her within five minutes of it being posted.

Late Sunday morning, Alexis opens her eyes and barely makes it into the bathroom before throwing up.

Alexis: [groaning] I'm never drinking again. What happened last night? Do you remember how we got home?

Sara: [rolling over in bed] I think we left with Chris.
            Chris lives a few doors down from the girls, and has been sort-of-talking-to-but-not-officially-dating Sara.

Alexis: [looking at her phone] Well, thank god for Snapchat, let's find out what happened last night—OMG, how did this happen? It's all over Twitter!

Sara: [sitting up] What?

Alexis: [panicking she shows her phone to Sara] What I am I going to do?

At about the same time, Madison sits down at her desk with a warm cup of coffee. Planning to use this time to get ahead on the week, she opens her email and begins responding to a few coworkers. As she prepares to schedule Twitter content for the week, she begins scrolling through the @lu timeline. She stops on a photo with a caption that reads "#ALEXIngton's finest. so glad I chose this school." She clicks on the photo, originally posted from @lucrushes, and cringes to find that it has been retweeted 257 times in one hour.

A picture of Alexis is on Twitter flashing her breasts with all kinds of nasty comments. Alexis continues to read the comments about her from people in the LU community. She wonders if these are from people she knows, or people she's never met, and which is worse. She's embarrassed, angry, hurt, and upset all at once. Consumed by her iPhone, she barely notices Chris at the door before he says, "Morning ladies. I don't know about you, but last night hit me hard. Gould Hall pancakes are calling my name."

Alexis: My life is over and according to Twitter, you're the reason why!

Chris: Excuse me? What are you talking about drama queen?

Alexis: Oh, I don't know. Maybe the photo of me flashing my boobs that's all over the Internet. The photo that you took!

Chris: Listen, you may or not remember, but you handed me your phone to take a picture of you and Sara. It's not *my* fault you decided to flash your boobs on your own Snapchat before Sara got in the picture. It's not that big of a deal anyway. Just delete it.

Alexis: Not that big of a deal? This picture is all over Twitter. Someone put it on @LUcrushes and it's up to 281 retweets and 522 likes. Obviously, I just deleted it. Not like it's going to do any good! How could you post that? I was drunk! That's basically taking advantage of me.

Chris: Don't make it sound like I raped you, Alexis. All I did was take a photo that you asked me to.

Alexis: [crying] What am I going to do? I can't go to class and face people tomorrow. I just can't. I never want to leave my room again.

On Monday morning Alexis gets an email from Matthew Roberts the Graduate Resident Director in her hall that says, "Alexis, I'd like to meet with you this week. Please contact me within three days to set up a day and time. My office hours are posted on my door, 103 Lucot Hall."

"Ugh," Alexis groans as she reads her email. The last thing she feels like doing is talking to anyone, let alone the guy who is always preaching the importance of keeping your door open and "building community." Alexis thinks to herself, "Maybe people shouldn't always have their doors open. Maybe people want some freaking privacy and would be better off if they didn't try to make friends."

Sara goes off to her First-Year Experience class where everyone has clearly been talking about Alexis. One of Sara's classmates points her to the class's Twitter account@fye13.

@mandylu: @fye13 Is this Alexis girl your roommate @Sarasmiles?

Reply: @lucutiemax She is actually hot.

Reply: @froshpete Shoutout to @chrismason for showing us the goods and taking the pic seen round the world.

Reply: @shanesworld I can't stand desperate freshmen who think showing their tits will get them attention! What a whore!

Reply: @robrob When my brother tells me he should have went to LU bc of #ALEXIngton

Reply: @froshpete Half the football team was in the background. What do #ALEXIngton and a bus have in common? Everyone gets a ride.

Reply: @shanesworld Sluts will be sluts. Can we all move on now?

Sara's gasps, and her instructor asks her what's wrong. She stands up and yells, "You guys are such jerks!" and runs out of class. The professor, Dr. Hannah Jenkins, asks everyone to hang on a minute and goes out after Sara.

Hannah: Sara, what is wrong?

Sara: Those guys in class are such assholes. Did you see what they wrote about my roommate on Twitter to @fye13?

Hannah: No, honestly I have been busy all weekend and haven't checked. Sara shows Hannah the tweets.

Hannah: I can see why you are upset. Why don't you go back to your room and I will talk with everyone.

Hannah is a new professor and unsure about how to handle the situation, so she goes back to class and tells the students that she thinks there has been enough excitement for the day and they will talk about everything next Wednesday. She then says that she thinks everyone should think about the situation and how they presented themselves. After dismissing the class, she goes to talk to the Director of the FYE program.

Madison is aware of @LUcrushes and other anonymous accounts like it on campus, but knows there isn't much she can do other than monitor its activity. While she knows the image of topless girls drinking at parties is horrible for the institution, Madison can't help but sympathize with Alexis when thinking about her own not-so-smart choices in college. She takes a moment to be thankful that social media wasn't around to capture every move she made. On Tuesday, Madison sits in her office thinking, "How am I going to handle this? Maybe it will blow over before anyone higher up gets wind." She hears her iPhone Twitter notification sound three times in a row, and swipes right to view the @lu notifications. A tweet that she scheduled last week with the link to LU's first-year student application had been quote tweeted nine times, and @lu had been mentioned four times since the tweet went out five minutes ago. Current students were responding to the scheduled tweet with the infamous photo of Alexis, and comments like:

@jasondefrancis:	Real reasons to come to LU: the beer is cheap and the girls are cheaper #lu20 #ALEXIngton
@ninadancer35	I'm embarrassed to be at a university that cares more about recruiting new students than helping current ones. Apply somewhere else, #LU20.
@chrisdrinksallday:	Ladies: photo required with your admission application. See below for preferred body type. #lubound
Reply:	@ashleymarie: OMG that's not funny that girl lives in my building and I heard she was raped.
Reply:	@chrisdrinksallday: Wow that's fucked up, shouldn't be out showing it all off I guess.
Reply:	@ashleymarie: You're an asshole.

Dave Wallace's phone starts ringing. In the last hour and a half, he has fielded calls from the Director of Residence Life; the Director of the FYE program; a new professor; the Director of Student Conduct; Mary Smith, the Director of Public Affairs; Bob Terry, the Director of Alumni Relations; Olivia Robinson, the Director of Admissions; and Alexis Jones's mother. The one person he has not heard from is Madison Clay. Dave picks up the phone and calls her, letting Madison know that there will be an emergency meeting in one hour in his conference room and she should be prepared to speak.

An hour later, Madison grips her notepad as she walks into the conference room. After everyone is settled, Dave says, "I would like Madison to brief you all on the situation." "Thank you all for taking the time to meet today," Madison takes a deep breath and says, "As you all know, a topless photo of Alexis Jones has exploded all over the internet. She's a first-year chemical engineering student living in Lucot Hall. She has quickly developed a reputation on campus, and this is known primarily from social media posts by LU students. These posts also suggest that Alexis may have been assaulted. In addition to the picture, students have taken to social media to engage around this matter and have begun to use our recruitment hashtags to influence prospective students. There isn't much I or anyone can do to filter what students are saying on social media. What we need—"

Before she can finish her thought, Mary Smith interrupts by saying, "See what happens when you put a girl with no communication expertise in charge of such things."

Dave then says, "Mary, I think that was a little harsh. Instead of pointing fingers we all need to figure out how we are going to fix this mess."

Questions

1. What responsibility does a college or university have to the developmental needs of students as they experiment with social media?
2. With the advent of social media, universities are often caught between formal and informal communication. How should they ideally balance the formal and informal?
3. How can universities began to tackle large-scale issues that touch several offices? Develop an action plan that reflects collaboration across the offices represented in this case.
4. How can Madison use her skills and knowledge to help the situation?

Chapter 17

Roommates From Different Worlds

Ryan Morgado and Stacy A. Jacob

In the following case, symbolic objects start conversations between two roommates who are from different backgrounds. As you read the case, think about how the various staff members in the case compound the problem. Can Karla and Sissy be helped or was the situation doomed from the beginning?

Anna, like many eldest sisters in the South, goes by the nickname Sissy. Sissy is an academically talented, 18-year-old, white female from a small, rural town in Alabama. She lives with her stay-at-home mom, stepfather, and two younger stepsisters. Sissy's family, like most of the families that live in her town, have been there for generations and do not travel often. Sissy has never been more than two hours away from her hometown.

Sissy's mother left Alabama after high school to go out West and live for two years in Denver, Colorado, where she met Sissy's biological father. The relationship between Sissy's mother and biological father dissipated when Sissy's mother found out she was pregnant. She moved back home to Alabama, and quickly married her high-school sweetheart, Bob. Although Sissy's biological father has always supported her, she has only met him twice when he was in Alabama for business. She speaks to him on the phone a few times a year. He is nice; but her biological father and her mother seem to be of two different worlds—he is a wealthy, well-traveled, and liberal entrepreneur and Sissy's mother is a pastor's wife in a small town with conservative values. Pastor Bob is kind and loving father and Sissy has always considered him to be her "daddy."

Sissy earned a few small scholarships for college, has a college savings account, and as the daughter of a pastor, she knows that several religious colleges of her denomination would offer her discounted tuition. She feels lucky that she will be able to go to a private, Christian college for the price of a state school. At the beginning of her senior year, Sissy's biological father offered to cover all of her college costs on the condition that she attend his alma mater, California University (CU), because he believes that CU is the root of his success in the world.

It is a generous offer, but scary for Sissy as she had always pictured herself at a small, Christian college in the South. She wants to study early childhood education and hopes she will meet a nice man like her daddy. Sissy and her parents talk a lot about the decision. All of them are worried about her going to CU, but they know that a free education (at a school that has a well-known early childhood education program) would allow her to keep her savings for a down payment on a house, or maybe even more school someday. Sissy ultimately decides to attend CU. Her parents remind her that she was raised right and will be fine anywhere she goes to school.

CU is a large, public, comprehensive school in an urban environment in Northern California. CU has a diverse student population with 32% Asian American, 27% Caucasian, 23% Hispanic, 10% African American, 2% Native American, and 6% other. The mission statement specifically states that diversity and inclusion are a main focus of the university. CU echoes this commitment with social justice figures such as Eleanor Roosevelt and Rosa Parks represented as statues and monuments on the campus. It also has several buildings named after them.

There are over 200 clubs and organizations on campus and many of those clubs represent various minority student populations in sexual identity, gender, race, ethnicity, culture, and religion. Faculty and staff diversity on campus closely resembles the student population with 24% Asian American, 20% Caucasian, 25% Hispanic, 23% African American, 5% Native American, and 3% other. CU's various departments host programs and events centered around educating their students on social justice and immersion—giving students an opportunity to expose themselves to many facets of identity and the concepts of power and privilege. Students seem to be open and willing to explore areas of identity that may not be familiar to them.

Sissy's parents and her biological father all help her move into her room in a traditional residence hall named Davion Hall. She gets to move in a full day before many of the students because she lives over 300 miles from campus. When her family leaves, Sissy quietly goes about decorating her room—being careful to keep everything on one side. As the eldest of three sisters, she knows better than to cross over into another girl's space! She makes her bed with the new pink sheets and fluffy comforter her mom helped her pick out, puts out pictures of her friends and family, and hangs up a poster her best friend gave her that says, "Alabama girls: Love like crazy. Use our manners. Say grace. Sweeten our tea. Listen to mamma and daddy. Count our blessings. Match our pearls to our monograms." Then, she pulls out the wrapped-up present her parents gave her as they left. It is a brand-new, leather-bound family Bible. She opens it up, and inside her mom has calligraphed her family tree on the special pages in the front. She hugs it, cries a little, and places it on the bookshelves above her bed alongside Emily Post, Flannery O'Connor, Eudora Welty, and Harper Lee. She calls her parents, and thanks them for the beautiful gift. They reassure her that she will be fine, and she goes to bed.

The next day Sissy makes her bed, gets dressed, and goes exploring on campus. College is so different; she has never seen so many different people and the food in the cafeteria is so exotic—she tries Indian food for the first time, decides it is delicious, and walks back to her room. When she gets there, she sees that her roommate has moved in. The other side of the room contains pictures of a biracial family, a black mother and a white father, and what appear to be two older brothers. Her roommate has hung a poster that says, "In this house we believe: Black lives matter. Women's rights are human rights. No person is illegal. Love is love. Kindness is everything." There are also lots of books about being a feminist. Sissy is a little worried as she is pretty sure she has never known a feminist. "Well," she thinks, "at least I know we agree on kindness." At that moment the door opens and in walks a girl.

Karla: Oh hey, I'm Karla.
Sissy: Hi Karla, I'm Sissy. It's nice to meet you.
Karla: Soooooo—I guess we are roommates?
Sissy: I guess so.
Karla: It looks like you are from Alabama [Karla points at Sissy's poster]. Sounds like it too, from your accent.
Sissy: Umm yeah, where are you from?
Karla: About 30 minutes from here.
Sissy: Whew, I am pretty nervous; we seem to be different people, [Sissy points back at Karla's poster] but, we agree on the kindness thing!

Karla laughs, and they begin getting to know each other. Sissy finds out that Karla's two older brothers graduated from CU and advised her that the success of your first year depends heavily on your relationship with your roommate. Karla finds out that Sissy has two younger sisters. They laugh about being the oldest and the youngest of their siblings. They have fun, but they each acknowledge that they want to get along and are worried about their difference. They decide to take it slow, be kind (like Karla's poster says), and try to become good friends on the advice of Karla's brother.

At first, everything is great and Karla and Sissy have nightly roommate chats. Karla realizes, from listening to Sissy's stories, what a different world CU must be for her and enjoys that Sissy feels comfortable asking her all sorts of questions as she learns about the world. It's always something different from day to day. Like, "Guess what Karla, I stopped and read a plaque on the statue by the art building. Have you ever heard of Cesar Chavez? Whoa, his life has got me thinking." Sissy also seems to make friends easily and every time Karla comes home there is a different person that Sissy is having a deep and earnest conversation with. The person leaves and Sissy says something like, "Wow I never met a Filipino person before." After a while, however, Karla feels like she never has any alone time and sometimes, even though Sissy is kind and polite, Sissy asks offensive questions without realizing it.

Karla is tired of always helping Sissy, sometimes uncomfortable, but she really wants to make the relationship work. Not knowing how to handle the situation, Karla decides to go to her Resident Advisor (RA), Lucy.

Karla: Hey Lucy, you said to come to you whenever we have problems, right?

Lucy: Of course Karla, what's going on?

Karla: Well, there is something going on between Sissy and me, nothing that big of a deal, but sometimes I'm uncomfortable being in our room.

Lucy: What's going on?

Karla: It's just that we are really different. She come from this really small world and kind of doesn't know anything, so she is always asking me questions. Like, "why is it not okay to refer to herself as a girl?" "What does it mean to take back the word 'bitch'?" "What is social justice?" She is always polite about it and thanks me for helping her but I am just tired of all the questions. Oh and every time I come home there is always some person in our room. I feel like I never get to be alone.

Lucy: Well, did you say anything to her?

Karla: No, I don't want to create any problems in our room, you know? How can I tell her how I'm feeling without hurting her feelings?

Lucy can tell by the look on Karla's face that she wants her to talk to Sissy.

Lucy: Well, how about I talk to her for you? I can try to help before you talk to her directly.

Karla: That sounds great Lucy! Thanks so much for your help. Let me know what happens after you talk to Sissy.

Karla leaves the conversation relieved, she doesn't have to confront Sissy and Lucy is going to help. However, Lucy is now anxious and stressed that she promised something she doesn't feel ready to take on. She is nervous as a first-year RA and wants to do a good job and become friends with her residents. Because Lucy's supervisor, Ricky, wants the RAs to be more autonomous and independent, she doesn't approach him for help.

Two weeks go by and Karla notices that Lucy seems to be avoiding her. She runs into Lucy in the elevator and asks her about the conversation Lucy said she would have with Sissy. Lucy says she just has not had the time to do it between her RA job and classes. Karla's not really sure how to move forward with the situation, but that night Sissy and Karla are in their room together and begin to have a conversation.

Sissy:	What was it like growing up out here?
Karla:	Well, most of my family is out here, I love the city, and the people out here are much nicer than I've experienced in other places.
Sissy:	Yeah, I've noticed that too, everyone is so polite. Can I ask you a question?
Karla:	Okay.
Sissy:	Well, it's just that I love kids so much. I mean I like some of the feminist things you tell me about, but I don't think I can be one because I don't believe in abortion and I like boys.
Karla:	What do you mean you like boys?
Sissy:	Well, you are a feminist right, doesn't that also mean you are a lesbian?
Karla:	[visibly frustrated now] What? Feminism doesn't make me a lesbian or pro-choice, it just means I think men and women should be treated equally.
Sissy:	Well I am not so sure about "equal." I mean I want a boyfriend who is a gentleman and opens doors and pays for dates.
Karla:	I'm sorry, I just can't do this right now. I can't educate you about everything!

Karla storms out and leaves the room upset. She doesn't understand how Sissy could say anything like that. Sissy is puzzled by Karla's reaction; she thought they were friends and Karla has always been so helpful. She figures that Karla will calm down and realize that she wasn't trying to be offensive.

Since Lucy was of no help, Karla decides it's time to go higher up the ranks and contacts the RD of her building, Ricky. Ricky promptly sets up a time for them to meet the next day.

Ricky:	Hi Karla, what can I do for you today?
Karla:	Well, I'm having some roommate issues and I'm not sure what to do at this point.

Ricky: Well, talk to me about what's going on.

Karla: My roommate Sissy is from a really small town in Alabama and is a fish out of water here. She is always asking me questions, and I try to be helpful, but today she told me she thought I was a lesbian because I am a feminist. I went to my RA to figure out how to handle the situation and she said she was going to talk to Sissy, but it's been two weeks and Lucy hasn't done anything.

Ricky: Uh-huh. Go on.

Karla: I care about Sissy and she is a nice girl, but it's not my job to educate her. I feel like a battery, and she is draining me.

Ricky: So it sounds like you feel as if Sissy needs to go figure out some things for herself.

Karla: Yeah. She just doesn't seem to realize that she hurts me sometimes, even though she is nice about it.

Ricky: First off, did you try saying anything to Sissy yet?

Karla: No, I'm worried about making her upset.

Ricky: Well, I apologize that Lucy hasn't been more responsive. She should take more care in following up with her promises. What we can do from here is plan to facilitate a roommate mediation meeting between you and Sissy to see if you can come to any common understanding about the situation.

Karla: I would like that; I feel like having an outsider there would help.

Ricky: Of course. Until we can get it set up, can I suggest finding a student organization for you to go to for some support and guidance—the Feminist Majority Foundation?

Ricky is disappointed to hear how Lucy handled the situation. Part of him fears that Lucy felt uncomfortable because she is a new RA. He knows that Lucy is responsible for her own actions, but he can't shake the feeling that there is more he could have done to prepare RAs for complex diversity issues. At the beginning of last spring semester, Ricky and some of the other RDs pleaded with the previous Director of Residence Life to add more diversity and social justice training components to RA training. Unfortunately, the transition to the new Director of Residence Life, Ruben Ortega, didn't allow time for new opportunities such as RA training about diversity and social justice. Ricky was excited that one of Ruben's goals was to work with a multicultural student body and felt like they could make some headway bringing a more robust diversity and social justice training for the RAs.

Ruben seemed receptive of the concepts that Ricky brought to him but didn't seem to care about them in the same way that Ricky did. Ruben also stated a hesitance to implement a change like this since he hasn't been here a full year.

Ruben: I understand your concern, but I'm under the impression that the campus climate for diversity is pretty good.

Ricky: True, but we should think about how training like this can help prepare our RAs to handle the complexity of these issues.

Ruben: I understand, Ricky, but I was not hired to place my time and energy into matters like this. I was hired to oversee the administrative end of our department. Take it up with your assistant director. If she brings it to my attention, we'll see where we can place it on the list of things to do.

Ricky felt defeated and wasn't sure what to do next. The assistant director he reports to tends to be more concerned about numbers and administration, like Ruben. Ricky knows that this situation might have turned out differently if they had a stronger diversity and social justice training for their RAs. He only hopes that Ruben and the rest of the Department of Residence Life will take the social justice component more seriously after this. And now he has to think about how to help Lucy gain confidence in addressing the conflict between Karla and Sissy. How can they help Sissy find answers to her questions without burdening Karla? How can they support Karla in establishing boundaries that help her to feel comfortable in her room?

Karla decides to check in on the organization on campus called the Feminist Majority Foundation that was suggested by Ricky. She sets up a meeting with the Feminist Majority Foundation president, Amy.

Karla: My roommate is extremely ignorant and I don't know what to say to her anymore. I tried talking with my RA, but she didn't help when I came to her for the first issue.

Amy: What all happened with you and your roommate?

Karla explains the situation to Amy who suggests setting up a meeting with the rest of the Feminist Majority Foundation group saying, "The more people we have, the better the ideas could be."

Karla is unsure about the whole idea of making a huge statement about the situation, but she is relieved she found someone who understands where she is coming from and wants to help her. Amy feels this issue cannot be left unaddressed by her group. She plans on talking with Residence Life to see how Karla's situation is being addressed and how they are currently training their RAs on feminist issues. Amy wants to ensure that the students, faculty, and staff of CU realize how serious these issues are. She tells Karla, "We will help you." But she is not sure how and thinks to herself, "I get why Karla is upset, even though her roommate is nice, it is not Karla's job to educate this woman. She must be exhausted." Amy realizes Karla is looking for someone to relate to and that can help her through this stressful situation.

There needs to be training and dialogue happening here and she doesn't know what to do. She thinks that maybe their faculty advisor can help pull in the support they need from the faculty and staff on campus. She wants to bring situations like Karla's to light so everyone can learn.

Ricky comes into work the next morning to find an email from Amy. He is concerned now that the student body is getting involved. Ricky hopes this incident will be enough to convince Ruben to start implementing more social justice trainings for RAs and can be used as material to educate students and student leaders, like Lucy.

Questions

1. In this case, Lucy is ill equipped to work with Karla and Sissy, but she feels uncomfortable saying so. Pretend you are Ricky and come up with a list of expectations for your RAs that would both illustrate how they must be independent and able to ask for help when they need it.
2. What actions could Ricky take to help Karla and Sissy get to know one another given what you know about diversity? Given what you know about student development theory?
3. How could Ricky create support for diversity training for his RAs? What might that training look like?
4. What would you do to help Karla? How would you support Sissy?

Chapter 18

Disability Service Animals
and Emotional Support Pets

Janine N. Muri and Michael G. Ignelzi

When emergent changes and situations run ahead of existing law and/or university policies and processes, how can an institution best respond in the interests of students? What should guide decisions by campus professionals when guidance is ambiguous or nonexistent?

SETTING

Singer University is a small, private university with roughly 3,500 students. The campus is located in a small metropolitan area in the Midwest. The campus is a predominantly white institution (PWI) but has been slowly increasing its ethnic student diversity due to recruitment and support initiatives targeting underrepresented populations. A somewhat neglected population, however, has been students with disabilities even though enrollment numbers in this group have also been increasing.

The Office for Students with Disabilities (OSD) at SU serves 9% of the student population. Most of the students served have documented learning disabilities, but there is a small population of students with physical disabilities and a growing group of students with mental health and/or emotional issues. Resources in the office are limited. There is only one full-time staff member (the director), a part-time administrative assistant, and a handful of student workers. The office is located in an older building on the outskirts of campus, which makes it inconvenient for access, particularly for students with mobility issues.

The Disabilities Office tries to accommodate each of its students, to the best of its ability, within the context of the law. Students seeking accommodations must set up an appointment with the director, at which time the director allocates accommodations depending on the student's documented disability and needs.

CHARACTERS

Jake: Visually impaired student. He is not completely blind and is able to see shapes and shadows. Jake is a 22-year-old senior student.

Loki: Service dog. Loki is a six-year-old, 75-pound German shepherd. Loki had previously completed a yearlong service dog training program specific to serving a visually impaired handler. Loki has been with Jake since he completed the program five years ago. Loki also goes through short refresher courses every two years.

Meg: 19-year-old sophomore student, who was recently diagnosed with anxiety.

Ruby: Emotional support pet. Ruby is a two-year-old, five-pound Pomeranian. She was a high school graduation gift to Meg. Ruby has never had any formal training.

Nicole: Director of the Office for Students with Disabilities. Nicole has been in this position for three years, since graduating with a master's degree in Student Affairs in Higher Education.

Ellen: Director of Residence Life. Ellen has been at SU for the past five years. She previously worked as a Resident Director at another institution after completing her M.A. program in Student Affairs.

Jody: Nurse.

Lilith, Jo, and Cassie: Meg's friends.

CASE

Jake, a visually impaired student, has been attending SU for the past five years. He is a senior and will be graduating in the spring. Jake's guide dog, Loki, is a 75-pound German shepherd that has been with Jake since he began college. Jake needs Loki to navigate successfully around campus and around town. Like many service dogs, Loki knows that when his harness is on it is time for work. Many people on campus know Jake and Loki; Loki is always happy to see and interact with his human friends when he is "off duty".

Meg is currently in her second year at SU. This fall she has a new companion, Ruby. Ruby is a two-year-old Pomeranian that Meg received as a high school graduation gift. Meg struggled academically during her freshman year. Toward the end of the spring semester, she started to experience some generalized anxiety. Over summer break, she explained to her parents that her classes were difficult and the professors were giving her too much work. She told her parents how she was feeling anxious. Concerned for their daughter's well-being, her parents had her see the family doctor. The doctor diagnosed her with anxiety and prescribed a low-dose anxiety medication. Still worried about their daughter, Meg's parents did some research on ways to help with anxiety. During their research, they came across information on animals being used for emotional support. They made a comment about this to Meg, which prompted her to do her own research on emotional support animals. On the Service Dog Central webpage, Meg found the following:

> An Emotional Support Animal [ESA] is a dog or other common domestic animal that provides therapeutic support to a disabled or elderly owner through companionship, non-judgmental positive regard, affection, and a focus in life. If a doctor determines that a patient with a disabling mental illness would benefit from the companionship of an emotional support animal, the doctor can write letters supporting a request by the patient to keep the ESA in "no pets" housing or to travel with the ESA in the cabin of an aircraft.
>
> ESAs are not task trained like service dogs are. In fact little training at all is required so long as the animal is reasonably well behaved by pet standards. This means the animal is fully toilet trained and has no bad habits that would disturb neighbors such as frequent or lengthy episodes of barking. The animal should not pose a danger to other tenants or to workmen. But there is no requirement for fancy heeling or mitigating tasks since emotional support animals are not generally taken anywhere pets would not ordinarily go without permission (the exception being to fly in the cabin of an aircraft, even if the airline does not ordinarily accept pets).
>
> [http://servicedogcentral.org/content/node/256]

After doing her research, Meg concluded that Ruby could be registered as an emotional support dog. She and her mom went back to her doctor and asked him to write a letter saying an emotional support animal was in her best interest. Since the doctor did not see the harm in it, he wrote the letter. Meg then registered Ruby online as an emotional support dog in order to have Ruby at school with her. The process was inexpensive and simple, and all she needed was the letter from the doctor. Once Ruby was registered, Meg contacted SU to inform them that she would be bringing Ruby with her in the fall. She was told that she would have to contact Nicole, the Director of the Disabilities Office, to discuss this situation.

All students requesting accommodations through the Disabilities Office must make an appointment with the Director. Nicole goes over the student's disability and discusses the accommodations that are available. Meg scheduled her appointment the week before residence hall move-in day.

Nicole: Thanks for coming in today, Meg. Before we get started, do you have documentation from your doctor?

Meg: Yep. [As she pulls out the paperwork from her purse, out pops a small fluffy dog.]

Nicole: Oh, who do we have here? [slightly confused at the sight of the small dog]

Meg: This is Ruby. She is my emotional support dog.

Nicole: Emotional support? [She flips through the paperwork Meg has given her. A letter from Meg's doctor explained she was diagnosed with anxiety over the summer and he suggested the use of an emotional support animal.]

Meg: Yes. I was diagnosed with anxiety. I have a hard time being away from home and focusing on my schoolwork. My parents suggested, and my doctor agreed, that I should get an emotional support dog. Well, I already had Ruby so we got her registered.

Nicole has heard a lot about emotional support pets in the past couple of years, but this was the first request for accommodation her office had received. She knew the law, as reflected in the Americans with Disabilities Act (ADA), defined and approved the use of service animals, but the regulations regarding therapy and emotional support animals were somewhat unclear.

Nicole: Okay, so tell me about Ruby and what she does for you?

Meg: She helps me cope with being away from home. Sometimes I just need to hold her to settle me down.

Nicole: [nods in understanding] All right. You said you had her registered, what is she registered for? And does she have documentation?

Meg: She is registered as an emotional support pet. And yes I do have documentation for her. It's in the paperwork I just gave you.

Nicole: So I assume she will be living with you in the residence hall?

Meg: Yes.

Nicole: Okay [making a mental note to call Residence Life and give them a heads-up about the dog]. So let's discuss your other accommodations . . .

Before Meg leaves, Nicole has her sign a release form saying that she is allowed to discuss her accommodations with other offices on campus as needed. This form allows Nicole to discuss the emotional support dog with Residence Life and SU's legal counsel.

Nicole's first call is to SU's legal counsel. She needs their opinion on what the current law is regarding emotional support animals. They explain to her that under federal law the residence halls fall under the Fair Housing Act (FHA) that was implemented by the Department of Housing and Urban Development (HUD). According to the FHA, anyone with animals used to assist people with disabilities cannot be discriminated against. And since there has not been a distinction made among service animals, therapy animals, and emotional support animals, for now they are all in the same category. The only time an animal can be excluded from resident areas is if the animal poses a threat to the health and safety of others. The counsel's advice is to allow Meg to bring Ruby with her. The reasoning is that it is easier and cheaper to accommodate this than it would be if Meg and her family complain or file suit for discrimination. Nicole's next call was to Ellen, the Director of Residence Life.

Nicole: Hey Ellen, I just wanted to let you know that we have a returning student this year that will be accompanied by an emotional support dog. It's just a little dog; hopefully, it won't cause too much of a problem.

Ellen: All right, I will make a note to keep an eye out for a small dog. [jokingly] You know pretty soon every student is going to be showing up with their family pets. Seriously though, I do have concerns about having untrained animals in the residence halls, not to mention the problems animals can create for some residents that have allergies or animal phobias.

Nicole: I'm sorry Ellen, I am sure it is difficult to have to worry about animals in the residence halls. The concept of emotional support animals is relatively new, and the laws and regulations are not very clear. I have been advised by SU legal counsel to accommodate this request.

By coincidence, Meg and Jake were assigned to the same residence hall that fall. They live on different floors, but have access to the same common areas. When Jake and Loki are not on their residence hall floor, Loki is on his leash. The same cannot be said for Ruby. Since she is so tiny and fits in Meg's purse, she is usually not on a leash and when in the residence hall Meg lets her wander.

Loki and Ruby have met a few times. While Loki is an extremely friendly dog, he has been trained to ignore dogs while on duty. Ruby has not had any formal training and has not been socialized much with other dogs. Being true to her Pomeranian characteristics, she does not see herself as a small dog. Her personality and demeanor are loud and bossy. This mixture along with being ignored by Loki has led Ruby to be aggressive when she sees Loki. As soon as Loki comes into the room, Ruby is in his face yipping.

Most of the time Loki ignores her, as he is trained to do. On occasion, he has given her a low grumble to get her to back off.

At the beginning of each school year, Nicole, the Director of the Disabilities Office, tries to meet with all of the students to make sure that they are ready for the new academic year. As usual, Nicole looks forward to Jake and Loki's appointment. Jake never has any complaints and if he has a problem, he is not demanding in its resolution. In their meeting, Jake brings up the new dog on campus.

Jake: I'm sure you already know, but there is a new dog on campus. She is small and yippy.

Nicole: [chuckles] Ruby, yes she is quite the character.

Jake: She lives in my building. I know it is just the beginning of the year and everyone is trying to figure things out, but she is always running around the residence hall. I tried to tell the RA and she said she would talk to her owner, but nothing ever came of that. I don't want to cause a problem . . .

Nicole: Jake, you are not causing a problem. I will call over to Residence Life and see what is going on.

Jake: I am just afraid of Loki being around her. I can feel him tense up when she is around.

Nicole: Are you worried that he is going to hurt her?

Jake: No, I don't think so. I mean he has never showed aggression toward another dog before. But he is so much bigger than Ruby. Maybe he senses me getting tense because I am afraid of what could happen, and that causes him to tense up.

Nicole: That is a possibility. You two have a close relationship and it is his job to be aware of how you are feeling. But I am sure that Loki would never purposely hurt her or anyone for that matter; he is such a well-trained service animal.

Jake: I suppose you are right.

Nicole: I do appreciate you telling me this, though. [She makes note of the conversation and Jake's concern over Loki and Ruby in his file.]

Nicole intended to share with Ellen in Residence Life what Jake had told her, but she was so busy with other student appointments and accommodation requests, that her follow-up with Ellen was delayed.

It was a couple of weeks into the fall semester. Meg and her friends were in the common area of the residence hall. As usual, Ruby was running around while Meg was preoccupied with her friends and not paying attention to her. As Jake and Loki walked into the common area, Ruby rushed Loki and jumped straight into his face. Ruby continued her yipping and Jake tried to get her away from Ruby since Meg did not interrupt her conversation to help. As Ruby continued to jump and yip, she accidently nipped Jake. In the commotion of a yipping dog, high stress levels, and now a hurt Jake, Loki jumped into action. Loki grabbed Ruby with his mouth, and ended up seriously hurting Ruby. Once Meg heard the cries of her dog, she and her friends hurried over to see what had happened. Loki quickly realized his mistake and dropped Ruby. Jake was able to get Loki away from the situation and yelled for help. One of Meg's friends, Cassie, immediately called campus security. After yelling a few choice words at Jake and Loki, Meg left with Ruby to take her to a vet.

By the time Ellen and campus security got there, Meg and Ruby were gone. But Meg's friends stayed behind to tell their stories. They had been in the room when the incident happened and wanted their stories on record, even though they really did not see what happened. Jake and Loki were also still present. Jake knew he had to talk to Ellen and most likely campus security, since Loki was involved. However, Ellen sent Jake to the health center to have the dog bite looked at and cleaned.

At the health center, Nurse Jody cleaned up the dog bite and filed her report. Since Ruby is so small, the bite was fairly insignificant and did not require stitches. After a quick clean of the wound, a Band-Aid was applied, and Jake was sent back to his residence hall.

Back at the residence hall, Ellen listened to the stories of Meg's friends along with minute-to-minute updates from Meg on Ruby's condition via texts to Lilith, one of Meg's friends. All of Meg's friends were placing the blame on Loki. They reported to Ellen that everything was fine until Loki entered the room and then he just snapped and attacked Ruby.

Cassie: We were over there talking. And then all of the sudden we heard Ruby crying. It was the worst sound I have ever heard in my life!

Jo: Yeah, we were just minding our own business.

Ellen: So, did any of you see what actually happened? [The girls look at each other, but stay quiet.]

Lilith: Meg just texted me; they just got to the emergency vet office. Oh, I can't believe this!

Ellen: Thank you for the update, Lilith. Is there anything you can tell me about what happened?

Lilith: What else do you need to know? Loki attacked poor Ruby! She is so sweet. [Looking down to her phone] Meg says Ruby just went into surgery.

Jo: Oh poor Ruby! I can't even imagine what Meg is going through. Oh God, what if that dog had attacked one of us?

Ellen: Let's not think about that [trying to defuse the situation]. Look, maybe you girls should head back to your rooms. We can talk again tomorrow once things have settled down.

When Jake and Loki arrived back at the residence hall, Ellen asked him to return to his room and wait for her there. By the time Ellen got to Jake, she had received news that Ruby should make a full recovery. However, because of the amount of blood lost, Ruby would have to stay at the vet for a few days.

Ellen: Hey Jake. Are you and Loki okay?

Jake: Yes ma'am. We're fine. Have you heard how Ruby is?

Ellen: She just got out of surgery; she should be okay. Jake, can you tell me what happened? I have known Loki for at least four years now and this seems extremely out of character for him.

Jake: I don't know what happened. I knew that there was tension between the two dogs but I never thought that he would ever hurt her. Everything happened so fast. We walked into the common area and Ruby came running over, like she normally does. She jumps and nips at Loki's face, I know he doesn't like it so I always try to keep our distance. But today I couldn't get Ruby to settle, and she nipped my hand. Not hard or intentional or anything. But I think that is what set Loki off because that is when he grabbed her. Oh, I just don't know what I will do if something happens to Ruby.

Ellen: Ruby should be fine. How is Loki?

Jake: He's okay. I think he knows he did something he wasn't supposed to do. I'm not going to lose Loki because of this, am I?

Ellen: Please don't worry about that, Jake. I know how important Loki is to you, and I'm also not convinced he did anything wrong. [As Ellen left she made sure to acknowledge Loki. She put her hand down signaling for him to come over. He did but slowly and with his head and tail down; he gave her hand a small lick and laid down.]

As a temporary measure, Ellen decides to move Jake and Loki to a different residence hall to minimize further contact with Meg and Ruby. Ellen heard from Meg's friends that Meg was still shaken by the attack on Ruby. Apparently, at her parent's direction, she and Ruby returned home while Ruby was recovering. Ellen had reached out to Meg, but Meg was not responding.

Ellen was consulting with Nicole, as well as others on campus, regarding how to address and move forward from this unfortunate, novel situation. About a week after the incident, Meg and her parents file a lawsuit against Jake and Singer University. The suit alleges that a vicious dog was wrongly permitted on campus. Damages are being sought for Ruby's veterinary bills and emotional trauma caused to Meg because of the attack on her dog.

Questions

1. Once university legal counsel advised Nicole to allow Meg to bring her emotional support dog to campus, what actions could she and others have taken to better manage the situation?
2. How should Singer University respond to the lawsuit and adjust its policies/practices moving forward?
3. How can institutions and their Student Affairs professionals balance the competing needs and/or interests of students in situations such as this?

REFERENCE

Service Dog Central. (n.d.). *Emotional Support Animals.* Retrieved from http://servicedogcentral.org/content/node/256

Chapter 19

Swept Away by an International Student Crisis

Lauren Perri and Melissa A. Rychener

Consider how the university in this case could have been better prepared to respond to a crisis of this nature. Also, consider the role that professional organizations can play in helping institutions, particularly smaller institutions, set policy and craft institutional responses.

Salow University is a small, private university in the Southeastern United States with a student population of just over 3,000. Seventeen international students from 10 different countries are currently enrolled as degree-seeking undergraduates. Although international student numbers are few, their financial contribution is significant because they typically pay full tuition. Salow's president, William Roth, is aware of this lucrative revenue stream and has increased international recruitment. He is in frequent contact with the international office and keeps close tabs on international student numbers.

Beatriz Gomes, who originally came to the United States as an international student from Brazil, is the international student advisor and the admissions representative in the small Office of International Education. She and the director of the office, Adam Grice, are under increased scrutiny as President Roth seeks to expand international recruitment efforts and retain current international students.

The increased pressure on the Office of International Education has made Beatriz's already-full plate seem almost unmanageable. Beatriz juggles international admissions, orientation, immigration recordkeeping, and advising international students about cultural adjustment and immigration rules. She tries to be an advocate for international students, but she sometimes feels unsupported in this task. Adam is often abroad, recruiting students and negotiating international agreements, and when he is on campus, he is often in meetings with the executive team or writing revenue projections. The communication within the office is almost nonexistent, though Adam has communicated to Beatriz that he expects her to take on more travel for international recruitment in the next year. Beatriz quietly wonders who will support the students when she is traveling.

This semester, there are six new full-time, degree-seeking international students at Salow, and three of these students are from Japan. Having Japanese students at Salow is the direct result of recruitment trips that Adam made to Japan last year. Ten years ago, Salow had 20 Japanese students, but that number had dwindled to none in the past few years due to the lack of institutional support for maintaining alliances with international institutions. Now that the current administration sees the benefit in investing in international relationships, Salow again has a presence at recruitment fairs in Japan and other countries. Although President Roth sees this as a "good start," he expects international student numbers to continue to increase.

After welcoming the new international students, Beatriz's first task is to register them for classes. She has found that this isn't always easy. Because international students arrive on campus after most U.S. students have already registered, many classes are filled. She then has to work with academic advisors, most of whom are also faculty, to ask them to lift enrollment caps. Some faculty are resistant to having international students in their courses, claiming it is difficult to work through the language and cultural barriers; and others simply resist allowing international students into closed classes because they see it as unfair to other students who were unable to register for a full course. In contrast, one of the faculty members in the English Department, Dr. Cindy Solman, is always happy to have international students in her classes and is willing to lift the enrollment cap. Dr. Solman seems to embrace her informal role as the go-to faculty member for the international office.

Yumi Watanabe, one of the new Japanese students, is having some difficulty adjusting to life in the United States. She is determined academically and has not missed any class sessions. However, during her weekly international student advising meetings with Beatriz, Yumi has reported that she is having trouble making friends aside from the two other Japanese students—Haru and Suka. Although Yumi's challenges in navigating friendships with U.S. students is not uncommon for new international students, it has been Beatriz's experience that international students have a better experience at Salow and are more likely to persist to degree completion if they find some way to connect to their U.S. peers.

Yumi is in Dr. Solman's 9:00 a.m. writing class every Wednesday and Friday. Dr. Solman told Beatriz that Yumi is a good student, but she hasn't yet adjusted to the U.S. classroom. Yumi follows directions exactly, but to a fault. She has a hard time with creative writing assignments and making decisions on her own; she always wants Dr. Solman's opinion. As an academic advisor, Dr. Solman has not had much contact with Yumi other than their initial meeting to get to know one another and confirm her fall class schedule. Unfortunately for Yumi, she did not have much time to adjust before tragedy struck and disrupted her entire life.

The day, Saturday, September 23, begins like any other day. However, by 4:00 pm, everything changes. Beatriz receives a text that reads, "Breaking News: A massive earthquake and tsunami in Japan. Thousands are feared dead." Immediately, Beatriz's thoughts go to the Japanese students. She remembers that Yumi is from the area affected by the earthquake. Leaving her weekend plans aside, Beatriz drives to campus, calling Yumi on her way. Yumi doesn't answer. Beatriz calls the other two students to make sure their families are safe—thankfully, they are. When she arrives on campus, Beatriz finds Yumi with an RA, and Martha O'Connor, Director of Residence Life.

Yumi is staring into the distance when Beatriz approaches her. As Beatriz sits down next to her, Yumi turns to her and says, "I can't find my family. My father . . . my mother . . . my sister. What do I do? What do I do?" Beatriz reassures Yumi that she will do all that she can to help her to contact her family and provide her support. Beatriz sits with Yumi, and after a couple of hours, Yumi seems calmer. However, Beatriz doesn't quite know what to do to help Yumi to locate her family; she's never experienced something like this before. Beatriz stays with Yumi for the rest of the day, and when she leaves to go back home, she knows that Martha and the rest of the residence hall staff will be there for her.

SUNDAY, SEPTEMBER 24

Early on Sunday, Beatriz returns to Salow. She needs to get herself organized and think through the next steps for Yumi. On the way, she buys things for breakfast, takes them to her office, and immediately calls Martha O'Connor in Residence Life to check on how things went with Yumi the night before. Yumi's RA stayed up with her until Yumi finally fell asleep around 5:00 a.m. Beatriz asks if Martha could have one of the RAs walk Yumi over to her office when she wakes up.

At 10:15 am, Yumi appears at Beatriz's office. She looks exhausted, understandably. Beatriz offers her breakfast, hoping the food will distract her, if only momentarily. Yumi refuses the food and simply stares blankly at the wall behind Beatriz. She seems to be in a daze. Yumi flatly explains that she still has not heard anything from her family and the news reports have estimated the number of dead at over 10,000. She expresses that she fears the worst has happened. Beatriz spends a few hours with Yumi, continually encouraging her not to lose hope, to think positively, and to keep busy. Yumi seems lost though. She asks Beatriz what she is supposed to do now. Her friends, the two other Japanese students, Haru and Suka, come by the office to pick her up for the afternoon.

MONDAY, SEPTEMBER 25

On Monday morning, Beatriz and Adam hold an emergency meeting with Residence Life staff, the counselor from the Counseling Center, and the Health Center staff to make them aware of what is going on. Martha expresses her concern that Yumi hasn't eaten since the disaster, according to Yumi's roommate. As of right now, Yumi is still in limbo—she doesn't know the whereabouts or status of her family, having heard nothing for the past two days. Beatriz's colleague from the Counseling Center suggested that they encourage Yumi to make small decisions each day, to empower her to have autonomy, and to be positive with Yumi. When everything else is out of control, a student needs some bit of control or power. Beatriz also seeks out the two other Japanese students, as they seem to be Yumi's only friends on campus. Beatriz speaks with them privately and asks them to continue to be a source of support for Yumi and to encourage her to think positively.

THE SUBSEQUENT DAYS

Over the next couple of days, Beatriz checks in with Yumi frequently, but there is little news coming out of the region where Yumi's family lives. Yumi doesn't look good. As the days go by, she is becoming more and more dazed and sleep-deprived. When Beatriz asks about whether she's been sleeping, Yumi says she has homework and studying to do. Beatriz gently suggests she see the counselor, but Yumi refuses, saying she doesn't want to talk about it, and Beatriz doesn't push her. On Thursday, Yumi comes to the International Education Office. Beatriz can sense upon seeing Yumi that something has changed.

Yumi: I'm going home to look for my family. They need me. I must help my country too.

Beatriz: You want to go home to look for your family and help the rescue efforts?

Yumi: Yes. Dr. Solman and my classmates will help me. They will get money for me. And Suka and Haru say they will come too to help me.

Beatriz: So you reached out to your classmates so that they know what you are going through? I'm so glad you did that. It was very generous of them to offer to help pay for your ticket, but we need to talk about that . . .

Yumi: Yes, I want to go home, but I don't want my classmates to know about my family's situation. I don't want to talk about it.

Beatriz: I understand that you're feeling helpless and worried, and I can understand your wish to keep your worries to yourself. However, I think it might help to reach out to others.

Also, I think we should discuss your wish to go back to Japan and find your family. Even though the main airports have reopened, train travel to your city may not be available. Also, people are being told to stay away due to radiation. I worry that it is not safe for you, Yumi.

Yumi: Yes, but my family needs me now.

Beatriz is unsure of how these plans have come about, but clearly others are involved beyond what she was aware of. Beatriz doesn't want to cast aside Yumi's plan, as she knows how important it is for a student in crisis to feel they have some control, but she is genuinely worried for Yumi's safety if she goes back to Japan. She doubts that Haru and Suka's families would want them to abandon their academic plans and return with their classmate to a country in chaos. She also is concerned that Dr. Solman has made promises to Yumi without consulting Beatriz and her colleagues about the institutional response. Has Dr. Solman shared Yumi's story with her classmates without her knowledge and consent? After Yumi leaves Beatriz's office, Beatriz calls Dr. Solman.

Beatriz: Hi Cindy, this is Beatriz Gomes. I'm calling to follow up on a conversation that I just had with Yumi Watanabe.

Dr. Solman: Oh yes! Poor Yumi! Her classmates are so glad to help support her to get home to her family. Families need to stick together at times like these! Yumi looks so sad! If it were my daughter, I'd want her back with me as soon as possible!

Beatriz: Thank you for being so kind to Yumi. I know that you are always there for international students. In this case, however, I think we need to be cautious about how to proceed. We don't know whether Yumi would be able to get to her community at all, and we don't even know if her family survived.

Dr. Solman: Well, surely they survived! I really hadn't thought about the traveling logistics . . .

Beatriz: Have you talked with Yumi's classmates about her situation?

Dr. Solman: Of course. I told them all about it. I'm meeting with some students tomorrow to start planning the fundraiser.

Beatriz: Yumi has expressed her desire to keep her situation confidential. Perhaps you should wait to meet with the students until we have more information . . .

Dr. Solman: I was only thinking of Yumi! I feel like you are saying that I've mishandled things!

Beatriz: Dr. Solman, I am trying to manage a situation that feels like it's spinning out of control. Maybe it's better that Yumi's classmates know. She certainly could use the support . . . however, I think we need to respect her wishes . . .

Dr. Solman: Yes, I see.

After getting off the phone with Cindy Solman, Beatriz goes to Adam's office to tell him what has transpired. She explains that Dr. Solman has offered to hold a fundraiser to help buy a plane ticket for Yumi and that Suka and Haru, the other Japanese students, have offered to go with Yumi back to Japan. Adam's strong reaction surprises Beatriz. Beatriz assumed Adam would be upset at Dr. Solman's rash, perhaps uninformed offer, but Adam is adamant.

Adam: There is absolutely no reason that they should be leaving Salow . . . we can't afford to lose three students right now. It isn't Dr. Solman's place to advise these students.

Beatriz: [finally reaching her limit] Although I, too, have strong concerns about Yumi's plans to return home, and I question Dr. Solman's judgment here, I do not question her intention. Dr. Solman is trying to help Yumi, which is more than I can say about you. Putting profit over students' welfare at a time like this! We need to work together for Yumi's well-being, and I need your help to figure out how to do that.

Adam appears shocked that Beatriz has spoken to him so directly. Beatriz is actually surprised at herself. She looks down.

Adam: [talking more softly now] I hear what you are saying, Beatriz. I know you have been working hard to respond to a very difficult situation. I'm sorry I haven't been more involved.

Beatriz: It's okay, Adam. But what should we do? I'd like to think about this together.

Adam: Let me clear my schedule for this afternoon. Maybe we can reach out to our contacts in Japan . . .

Beatriz: You know, I was thinking that maybe we could connect with universities in our region with a larger Japanese student population to see what they are doing.

Adam: I'd like you to get back in touch with Dr. Solman tell her that we appreciate her proactive approach to supporting international students. Ask her to come to a meeting tomorrow morning with the new International Student Task Force. I'm going to contact President Roth.

On the way back to her office to call Cindy Solman, Beatriz thinks about the turn of events and the creation of an International Student Task Force. Although the enormity of the crisis remains, Beatriz feels strangely hopeful that Yumi—and she—have more support than they realized.

Questions

1. How did Dr. Solman's "good intentions" get in the way? Do you think she should be included on an International Student Task Force? Why or why not?

2. Read back through the case and make a list of what we know about Yumi's personality, her culture, and her adjustment to Salow. Based on this analysis, what do you think Yumi's three greatest needs are? What resources could help you gain a better understanding of Yumi's situation and her options?

3. Why is Beatriz so isolated in her response to this crisis? How did she broaden her base of support? What could she have done proactively in her role prior to the crisis unfolding?

4. Going forward, how can the university be more proactive in responding to international student crises? How can the university leverage its relationships with other institutions and professional organizations in crisis preparation and response?

Chapter 20

Orientation Leaders and Staff Diversity

Emily Price and Stacy A. Jacob

The following case is a first-person narrative in which a new student affairs professional is asked to add a staff member to their team without considering a previous competitive hiring process. As you read the case, think about how you would react to such a request. Was the request unethical or is there a higher purpose that is more important? Is it more important to help the university achieve their stated goals or to develop a student team?

Less than a year ago, I accepted a position as the Director of Orientation at Reeds University (RU), a midsize public institution founded in the early 1900s. After working at an idyllic, small liberal arts institution, I was attracted to Reeds and its traditional feel. I was ecstatic when I was offered a directorship and couldn't wait to begin working at RU.

The students, faculty, and staff at RU are predominantly white; however, RU has been working on creating a more diverse student population through admissions efforts and the demographics have begun to change. Recently, the institution has also focused on diversity awareness and education—forming several committees and task forces. The result of these efforts is a new mission statement and strategic goals that emphasize diversity. As a new hire in a position that is highly visible, I was asked lots of questions about diversity, and it was made clear to me that my position was to support the new mission and vision of the university. I felt well prepared for this interview and to serve in a position that was publically supportive of initiatives around diversity—I had graduated from a student affairs program three years before that was well known for specializing in diversity and social justice. Whenever I attend national conferences, it is clear to me that my master's program was on the cutting edge of these initiatives.

My new supervisor, Robin, is the Dean of Enrollment Management. She has been at the institution for about 20 years, working her way up to this position. She and I have begun to develop our working relationship; however, I am still uncomfortable showing disinterest in her initiatives or telling her when I disagree with her. Lots of people call her a micromanager; I just think she has high expectations. Robin always seems calm and in control; and frankly, next to her, I feel like a bit of a crumpled mess. She seems to value the ideas and visions of everyone in the office, and is knowledgeable about the Reeds campus culture, but sometimes I think she is not always up on the latest issues and trends in the field of student affairs.

I supervise one Orientation Coordinator, Pete. I was lucky to be able to hire him a month after I became the director. He is a first-year graduate student in a counseling program on campus.

Our first-year orientation program has three spring Saturday programs and four two-day June programs. The June programs include an optional overnight experience followed by the one-day program. The majority of the Orientation Leader (OL) training occurs over a four-day period in June, but there are two OL training sessions in March before the spring programs take place.

We began advertising the OL positions at the beginning of the spring semester. We worked hard to advertise the positions and provide applications in prime locations on campus. We also did an email blast and provided the application online. After talking with Robin, I learned that there has not been much diversity in the OL staff. Pete and I worked hard to meet with the directors of the identity centers across campus, to get out the word about the OL position—asking each center to send us candidates for the OL positions. In these meetings, Pete and I quickly learned that students in campus leadership positions are not representative of the diversity present on campus. However, there is often pressure from the administration to include a diverse group of students in leadership positions, whether the application pool is diverse or not. As we began advertising the OL positions, Robin reiterated that I should have diversity in the OL staff.

Of the 35 students that applied for the 15 positions, 10 were students of color, LGBT students, nontraditional age, or first-generation college students. Pete and I were pretty excited that our visits to the identity centers seemed to be working! Only 26 of the 35 students were eligible for an interview based on the application criteria (cumulative GPA, campus involvement, and credible references). Pete and I had two weeks of interviews with those eligible candidates. After all of the interviews were finished, we met to discuss all of the candidates to determine the OL staff. In choosing a staff, we discussed the candidates' perceived personalities, academic majors, strengths, and weaknesses. We took extra care to really think about diversity. Overall, we tried to balance a number of things and come up with a staff that was both a great representation of our student body and a staff that we felt would work well with us and with each other. Pete and I chose a team that included six students who represented various types of diversity—two African American students, one Asian student, two first-generation college students, and one self-identified gay male student. We also achieved an even balance of men to women. The following day, I called all of the team members to offer them the position. They were all excited to be selected. Since I was new to the campus and my position, I was both excited and anxious about managing my first OL staff.

We began staff training in early March, a few weeks before the first Orientation program. Pete and I spent the majority of the training time discussing the responsibilities and expectations of the OLs. I was anxious about the team creating a bond. In our last training session before our first Orientation, we reviewed everything that was about to happen, so there was little time for socialization among the team members. I observed them interacting with one another, and I was uncertain if they had established a team bond. I was hopeful that it would eventually happen.

The first three Orientation programs were successful with no major issues. The teams bonded well. In fact, they seemed closer than any other group I have worked with in the past. I think a lot of the bonding happened after the first orientation session. Late that evening, we were cleaning up, and one of the OLs, James, said, "I can't believe I am having so much fun and getting along so well with all of you. As a black man, this is the first time I have felt comfortable on this campus."

Everyone stopped, and just sort of sat down, and started sharing. We talked for about three hours and it was amazing to see students really open up and share their thoughts and feelings. After that night, we ended each of the next two orientation sessions with a rap session on the students' request. I was happy that I not only had a great team that was bonding, but also that we were discussing real issues. I was also thankful for my social justice training in graduate school. I think it helped me facilitate some really meaningful rap sessions.

Robin seemed to be pleased with the progression of the team and their efforts, but she continued to express concern about the diversity of the team. I explained our recruitment and decision-making processes but when I look back on the conversation, I realize that Robin and I have different ideas about diversity. Our conversation went something like this:

Robin: I'm worried; we still need more students of color on the OL staff. With all of the campus emphasis on diversity, we need to find more of these students to participate in these leadership positions.

Me: I agree, but I can only work with the students who completed the application process. Aside from the application criteria, I want to make sure that we have a solid, effective OL staff. We advertised in all of the prime locations on campus, there are applications available online, and Pete and I personally visited with all the directors of the identity centers. I want to make sure to hire students who can commit to all of the programs and training sessions or who seem to be a good fit. I think the process we designed helps ensure we get the best people.

Robin: I can see what you're saying; however, the administration wants to have more diversity in our student leadership. Remember, OLs need to visually represent our diversity to the public. We will revisit this at some point to talk about ways to work on changing the situation. I know that the OL staff is more diverse than ever, but we need to do better.

I was uneasy after this conversation. I understand that we are working toward a more inclusive campus, but as I had tried explaining, I believed that I did everything I could to advertise the Orientation Leader positions to the entire campus. I believe Robin understood what I was saying, but had a sneaking suspicion that Pete's and my definition of diversity was different from Robin's. I was pretty certain that her definition only included students of color, while Pete and I considered GLBT status and gender as aspects of diversity that are important to represent in a diverse team. I took a few minutes to recoup, decided that I could not change the way things were currently, and began preparing for our June training and programs.

Waiting until June to conduct the four-day training and host four two-day Orientation programs created a lot of emotions for me. I was excited to begin this next phase of Orientation, especially with the OLs that represented the university so well and worked so hard in March. I was also a little anxious again because the team had not been together during this time period, and I hoped the bond was still there.

A week before the OLs came back to campus, Robin shared with me that she had a student in mind to add to the team. Her name was Angela, and she was an African American who had an extensive list of campus involvement. She did not apply for the OL position because she had conflicts last spring. Based on Robin's description of Angela, it sounded as if we would have interviewed Angela during the hiring process. As Robin was talking, it became clear to me that she was not suggesting I think about hiring Angela, she was giving me a subtle directive to hire Angela for the summer.

I was not uncomfortable disagreeing with Robin and I realized at that moment that hiring more students of color was a major issue to her and she was determined to address it. I agreed to include Angela on the team.

When the team came back to campus, I was aware that the OLs noticed Angela, but they were also focused on moving in to their residence hall rooms. We held a meeting that night, and I introduced Angela to the team—explaining that she would be an additional team member. The OLs expressed excitement, but I sensed tension and confusion about why an additional person was brought onto the team. I didn't feel that it was necessary to explain and Angela was not aware of why she was asked to be part of the team; Robin had simply told Angela that she would make a great OL and then said she would talk to me about creating an opportunity for her. As we got ready for the summer Orientation sessions, it seemed as if the OLs were including Angela.

Our first session went smoothly. Angela caught on quickly and seemed to be settling in fine. Everyone seemed to be getting along and working together well. The afternoon before our second session, Angela approached me; visibly upset, she pulled me aside in the lobby of the residence hall as our guests were checking in for their stay, and asked if we could talk. She and I walked into an office down the hall, and I shut the door so we could speak privately.

Angela:	I don't know if I can be on the team anymore. I don't think any of the leaders like me.
Me:	Tell me what's going on. What happened?
Angela:	I was trying to get the bags ready for tomorrow and Madison was packing them in the box for tomorrow. I was talking to Brad and I didn't realize that I was forgetting the book they get for fall. There were like eight bags I didn't do right. Madison realized that the bags were missing something and said, "Angela, your bags aren't finished." So, I went over to check them and realized what was missing. So I said, "Oh, I'm sorry, let me put the books in really quick." Then, Madison said, "How about you stop talking and focus on the bags like you're supposed to?" I was caught off guard by that because it wasn't like I was forgetting the books on purpose. So, I said, "I'm sorry. I'm fixing them right now." Then she said, "Well, if you had been here from the beginning, you would've known that you're supposed to focus on your job, not chitchat with people and get distracted from your responsibility." Then, she just left the room.
Me:	Of course you didn't mean to, I don't doubt that. But I also understand Madison is concerned because we only have limited time to get everything ready for the program the next day. I'm thinking that she might have been worried about that.
Angela:	I totally understand that, but I feel like she overreacted. I think it's because I wasn't hired from the beginning.

Me: So you feel that Madison reacted like that because you weren't part of the staff in the spring?

Angela: Yeah. I was really excited when Robin started talking with me about becoming an OL. I wanted to be part of the team, and I looked forward to making friends. But, as training went on, I felt like I was on the outside and nobody wanted me in. Then, well, um, this.

Me: I'm sorry. I don't think that Madison was intentionally making you feel unwelcome. Do you want me to talk to her about this? What do you think the best approach would be?

Angela: Yeah, I would like you to talk to her. I don't think she will listen to anything I have to say, but since you are in charge, she'll listen to you.

Me: All right, well I will discuss this with her once I find her and try to understand where she is coming from. If you want, you can take a short break in your room.

Angela: Okay, thanks.

A few minutes passed before I found Madison and I asked her to come talk with me.

Me: I just spoke with Angela about earlier when you two were preparing the giveaway bags. I want to talk with you about that.

Madison: Well, first off, I want to say I'm sorry, I think I overreacted.

Me: Well, from what I understand, you got upset that she was forgetting the book when she was stuffing the bags. Correct?

Madison: Yes. It seemed like she wasn't paying attention because she was talking to Brad. And I knew we had to get the bags done, so I just kept getting more aggravated.

Me: So, you were angry that she was talking and not paying full attention to her responsibility.

Madison: Yes.

Me: Is that why you ended up yelling at her?

Madison: Yes—well, no, not the only reason. I'm upset that she was just brought onto the team out of nowhere. I mean, I don't think she wasn't just picked out of a hat; she's learned stuff really quick. But I worked really hard to be hired as an OL, and then all of a sudden, there's someone new, out of nowhere. Especially because it wasn't like someone else left and they had to be replaced.

Me: You're right; Angela was hired on to the team after the original hiring. But, she's been very involved on campus and will certainly contribute to the team and the programs in a significant way. And we can be even more effective as a team of 16 than 15, right?

Madison: I know—I feel bad. But, some of us were upset because, like I said, it seemed out of the blue. After we all worked so hard in the spring and really started becoming friends. Here comes someone new that we don't know and after all our rap sessions; how can she just fit in?

Me: So, you all have talked about Angela?

Madison: Yes. We weren't freaking out about it; I think we just all felt a little confused. Well, maybe some of us were a *little* angry and upset because we all worked really hard to be an OL. I can't help being a little mad about it.

After this conversation, I began formulating ways to create a discussion with the OLs about this issue. As I was preparing for a discussion, I also began thinking about what could be done in the future to essentially prevent this from happening. How could I attempt to diffuse the situation and work to create a cohesive team for the remainder of Orientation? In the long term, what changes can I make to my recruitment strategies so that this situation can be avoided in the future? How can I talk with Robin and explore this issue of diversity with her?

Questions

1. The young professional in the story is struggling because she and her supervisor view diversity in different ways. Which professional's actions do you agree with? Explain. Discuss why each person's viewpoint might be important.
2. If you were asked to do something by a supervisor that might upset your student staff, how would you justify your actions to the staff? In this case, being forthright could harm several students in the case. How would you work with those students if you were transparent about the situation?
3. The young professional in this case at times seems to question herself. If you were her supervisor, how might you help the young professional grow and learn?
4. If you were in a work situation where you felt that you need to challenge authority, what strategies would you use or plans would you make to do so?

Chapter 21

The College Admissions Process
Search and Satisfaction

Denise N. Sanata and Molly A. Mistretta

This case explores two different perspectives. The first is that of a first-generation college student as she makes her college selection and transitions to life at college. The other perspective is that of a young professional in retention services who struggles in her attempt to help students transition to life in college. How can colleges and universities better meet the needs of students like Julie?

INTRODUCTION: JULIE'S ADMISSION PROCESS

Applewood is a small town with a population of around 2,000 people, two hours north of the nearest major metropolitan area. Applewood High School draws students from the town and the surrounding rural area, graduating about 100 students per year. Julie Scott, who spent her entire life in Applewood, loves her small hometown experience. Her father, Tim, is the town supervisor, overseeing Applewood's public works, including town streets and utilities. Her mother, Sue, is a secretary at the town's elementary school. Although neither attended college, they are able to provide Julie with a comfortable middle-class upbringing.

Although Julie knows almost everyone in town, she is not an outgoing person. She has a couple close friends and only participates in a few extra-curricular activities. Her best friend is Taylor Thomas—a neighbor since elementary school.

Julie received mostly Cs and Bs in high school, but she never struggled with her coursework. She feels that she is ready to attend college upon graduation, and trusts that she will succeed if she sets her mind to it. Julie is actively involved in the school newspaper and is on the yearbook committee. She finds the work fun and interesting. She is not certain of what she would like to study in college, but thinks that she might enjoy something related to writing or communications.

At home, Julie has the support of her parents. Julie is the older of two children, and this will be the first experience Tim and Sue have with the college application process. Even though they lack knowledge about the process, Tim and Sue are both supportive when it comes to Julie's intention to go to college. Julie knows that her parents love and support her, but she also knows that they do not know the first thing about college, let alone choosing the right one, so she will need to take the lead in the college application process.

MONROE UNIVERSITY: OVERVIEW

Monroe University (MU) is a large, urban research institution with approximately 18,000 undergraduate students. The university is spread throughout a large and thriving downtown area. There are two big hospital complexes, as well as many restaurants, apartment buildings, and retail stores scattered among Monroe University facilities. Thus, the campus has a busy, city-like feel.

Monroe University's new president, Dr. Caldwell, hopes to encourage more of a collaborative approach among staff, faculty, and administrators at MU. One of his main goals upon starting work at Monroe University is to increase enrollment and retention numbers, both of which have been decreasing in recent years. Enrollment numbers are still better than other public institutions in the area, but retention numbers are at an all-time low.

Monroe currently offers open enrollment for in-state students—meaning there is no minimum test score, grade point average (GPA), or certain class rank required to be admitted to the university. Because of these criteria (or lack of), faculty and administrators believe that many of the students who are admitted to the university are not academically ready for college.

JULIE'S COLLEGE APPLICATION PROCESS

Julie, like most incoming freshman, is unaware of any of the enrollment or retention issues at MU. As she continues her college search, Julie realizes that application deadlines are fast approaching, and she decides that she should start to get serious about applying to colleges. So far, she has done all of her research on potential colleges by browsing the Internet in her spare time—finding this tactic to be the easiest, most convenient way of finding information about colleges. Julie browsed the websites of several different colleges in her area, but none have interested her as much as Monroe University.

Julie began seriously considering Monroe University after discussing it with Taylor; the two of them have talked about rooming together. Julie decides to take a closer look at Monroe's website to find more details on the university. As she browses through the Campus Life section, she is excited to find that there are brand-new residence halls on campus in which she could potentially get her own bedroom and bathroom. She loves that the students and professors on the web pages look so happy and inviting. While searching for majors, she is excited to learn that the Communication Department has brand-new facilities for students.

In the Admissions section of Monroe's website, Julie discovers an option to take a virtual tour of the university. Here, she can see practically every section of the campus and follow links to pictures and videos of each campus building, as well as descriptions of the departments and activities within them. As she browses, Julie becomes progressively more excited and interested in becoming a student at MU. After taking the tour, Julie finds a link to Monroe's Facebook page. She browses through the page and finds that there are thousands of "likes" for Monroe University. There are many students commenting on the activities they are involved in at MU, and eagerly talking about upcoming programs and events. The Monroe University Office of Student Activities staff posted information about opportunities to connect with others on campus through student programming. Julie sees that Monroe has its own Twitter account, which is also linked with Instagram. Julie loves the convenience of finding everything that she needs to know about MU online, and she sees no real need to take an in-person tour of the university when she can do it in the comfort of her own home.

Julie decides to apply for admission and reveals her decision to her parents. They are excited to hear that she has made her decision and is taking the initiative to apply on her own. They support Julie in applying to Monroe, and tell her that they think she'll do great there. Julie goes back to school the next day and tells Taylor about her search and application to Monroe.

Julie: I applied to Monroe last night! Their dorms look awesome! You have to check them out. And it was so easy—everything was online, I didn't even have to make a phone call or schedule a visit. I'm starting to get so excited!

Taylor: Me too! I'm going on a visit with my parents next Saturday. I told them I definitely want to go there, but they're making me go on a tour first. I'm so excited you're going too! We should totally look into rooming together.

Julie: I know! The new residence halls look awesome. And we can get our own rooms and bathroom so we wouldn't get sick of each other!

Julie and Taylor continue to keep each other updated on their application and admission status. After anxiously waiting for her acceptance letter, Julie is finally offered admission at Monroe University. She and Taylor plan to room together in one of the brand-new residence halls where they will each have their own bedroom and bathroom and share a common living room and kitchen area.

After accepting admission to Monroe, Julie is invited to join a Facebook group for incoming MU freshman. The group has over 2,000 members, and Julie feels slightly overwhelmed. She wonders, *how can so many people be in this group?* Julie is excited and anxious about attending college and has mixed feelings about what to expect. Julie hopes that college will be different from high school and that she will meet new friends with whom she has things in common. She imagines that everyone else at Monroe will be looking to make friends too.

JULIE'S EXPERIENCE AT MONROE

The first few weeks living on campus are mediocre for Julie. She adjusts to living with Taylor in their new residence hall, but struggles to make many friends outside of the few acquaintances she passes daily in her building. Since Julie and Taylor have their own bedroom and bathroom, as do all of the other girls on their floor, there is not as much interaction in her residence hall as she had expected. Julie feels especially shy and timid throughout the first couple of weeks. She had envisioned her freshman peers being much more inviting and eager to get to know her.

One thing Julie overlooked about Monroe was the size of the place; she did not realize just how many students would be walking around campus. She feels like everyone already has friends and no one wants to get to know her. She is not sure if she is the only one, but she feels lonely and isolated. Julie misses the comfort of her own home and her family. She is not enjoying herself most of the time at Monroe. Julie tries talking to Taylor about her situation, but Taylor seems more occupied with other things and isn't much help. Taylor seems annoyed with Julie and says, "Maybe you should get out and go do something, Julie. I'm thinking about joining a sorority. You need to get out there and find something to do on your own, too." Julie feels like Taylor is always too busy for her. She is always hanging out with other girls on the floor who also plan to rush sororities. Julie is uncomfortable with the amount of drinking they do and is not interested in hanging around them as much as Taylor is.

After six full weeks of being at Monroe, Julie finds little to no change in her happiness at the university. She has not made any new friends, and spends most of her time catching up on readings to better understand the material. She has always received passing grades in high school without putting forth much effort, but college is different. Julie spends most classes frantically writing notes during her professors' confusing lectures. Professors are never clear about what information will be on exams, and they are always asking the students for their opinions instead of telling them what they should learn. Her professors intimidate her because none try to get to know her, or any of the other students, on a personal level. On average, there are between 1 and 200 students in each of Julie's introductory courses. In her high school classes, Julie had never experienced a class size larger than 20 students. She has heard of "feeling like a number" and now she knows what it means. She starts falling further and further behind academically as the semester progresses.

Julie truly believes that the main reason for her loneliness is that she just doesn't fit in at Monroe. There are too many students on campus to get to know anyone, and everyone is so busy. Also, Julie feels uneasy about how different the students at Monroe are. She thought she was totally open and willing to meet people who are different from her; but now that she is completely immersed in a diverse student body, she struggles to make friends with those she has little in common with. She does not know how to begin talking to them, and she worries that she would offend others from different cultures than hers. In her hometown almost all of people around her were the same as her: white, middle-class, and Christian, which is definitely not the case at Monroe.

Julie is enrolled in a mandatory first-year seminar class, and they often have guest speakers from different areas of the university and community talk with them about common issues for new students. This was the seventh week of classes, and Julie is dissatisfied with her decision to attend Monroe University. As she enters her seminar class, Julie's professor explains that they would have a staff member from the Office of Retention Services presenting to them. Julie has never heard of this office before, and she becomes interested after hearing a little bit about what the guest speaker does.

OLIVIA BARNES, RETENTION STAFF MEMBER

Olivia has worked in the Office of Retention Services (ORS) for two years with three other full-time staff members. The ORS is overwhelmed with a heavy caseload of students needing services, along with the responsibility of implementing the newly acquired retention software, and coordinating programming and outreach.

In an effort to recruit more students in a variety of ways, the Admissions Office has created several social media accounts including a university Facebook page and an Admissions Facebook page, a Monroe Twitter account, and a #monroe Instagram hashtag for students to post pictures of themselves and friends on campus. Olivia was recruited by the Admissions Office to assist with the development of these accounts because of her youth and experience with technology. She considers herself technology-savvy and believes that she can bring a more innovative perspective to the Admissions Office's online accounts.

Near the beginning of her presentation to Julie's first seminar class, Olivia states, "We are here to help you. We know that the transition from high school to college can be a tough one, and we really want you to be happy here. Monroe is a great place to be, and we want to ensure that our students succeed." As she listened to the speaker, Julie becomes more and more interested. There is something about Olivia that seems genuine. She thinks that Olivia can make things better so that she would actually start enjoying her time in college. After Olivia finished with her presentation, Julie decides to approach her and see if she could learn more about what the office does, and possibly schedule an appointment to speak with someone.

Julie: Hi, I'm Julie. I'm kind of interested in learning more about what your office does. I'm not sure if I'm doing something wrong, but I'm not enjoying myself all that much here. I thought maybe there was something you could do to help.

Olivia: We see many students, especially first-years, who are experiencing a tough time at Monroe. Don't get down on yourself! I'd be happy to set up a meeting with you if that would help.

Julie: That'd be great. Thanks so much!

Olivia is extremely busy. Her calendar is filled each day with student meetings, staff/department meetings, and presentations. Olivia is overwhelmed with balancing the work of her own office plus helping out with Admissions' social media accounts. She barely has time to meet with students face-to-face. Olivia does not want to let anyone down, and she accepts her heavy workload and level of responsibility without question.

OLIVIA'S MEETING WITH JULIE

On the day that Julie comes to the Office of Retention Services, Olivia's mind is focused on several different tasks, which has been common during the past couple of weeks. Julie waits in the lobby area for fifteen minutes before Olivia comes to greet her. She has been working on updating multiple websites and got stuck in a meeting with her colleagues.

Olivia: Hi, Julie! I'm so sorry about the wait. Things are so crazy around here! Come on in. So tell me a little bit about how you found yourself at Monroe in the first place?

Julie: Well, I actually had a friend in high school who wanted to come here, and we room together now—which is a whole different story. Anyway, I was interested partly because she was, and I decided to do some research on Monroe. I looked everything up online. I took an online tour, looked up majors, housing, all of it online. The decision seemed so easy back then! Now, it's just so different than it seemed when I applied. I'm just not happy.

Olivia: I see. Why do you think you are feeling unhappy?

Julie: Well, I guess I knew this place was big, but I honestly had no idea how big. It's so different from my little town back home. I kind of just feel like I don't matter here. None of my professors pay attention to me, and my classes are so hard! Classes are nothing like they were in high school. I seriously spend all of my time in my room catching up on homework, and it never seems like I get enough done. Most of the stuff we talk about in class is way over my head, and most of my professors talk so fast I can barely keep up.

As Julie explains her unhappiness to Olivia, she notices that Olivia's computer and phone seems to be making a dinging sound every couple of minutes, which is distracting.

Olivia: [Trying to turn off the sounds from her computer and phone as she responds] You know Julie, I'm really sorry to hear this, but a lot of students experience these struggles in college. It sounds like this environment is a lot different from what you're used to back home. Can you tell me more about that?

Julie: I thought I would like the change of going to a big school and meeting a lot of new people. But I just don't feel like I fit in. I miss being close to my family. I miss only having to go down the street to go to the store. Here I have to walk like a half hour to get anywhere! I just feel like this place isn't right for me at all.

Olivia: I see what you're saying. Have you tried getting involved on campus? I can show you some online resources for getting involved. This really helps students in your situation. I would highly suggest it.

Julie: I know, and I've heard that before. I don't know if that will help. When it comes down to it, I just really want to leave. I don't know if it is worth me coming back next semester.

Olivia: Julie, I know things seem extremely challenging right now, but I encourage you to try using some of the resources offered to you before you give up. We have a tutoring center here that can help you if you are struggling with your classes, and I would strongly suggest you get involved with at least one organization on campus. Why don't you try to do these things and we can plan to meet again in another couple of weeks?

Julie agrees, but leaves the office feeling disappointed. Talking with Olivia didn't help her feel much better. She feels like Olivia was rushing her out of her office. This made Julie feel even more convinced that no one at Monroe had time for her or wanted to get to know her. She thought to herself, "Olivia didn't even do anything for me, she just told me to 'get involved.' I'm tired of people telling me to do that." After talking with Olivia, Julie feels even more like just a number at this huge, overwhelming place, and she leaves with a sense of hopelessness.

Olivia finishes the meeting feeling overwhelmed. She goes throughout her day getting as many of her tasks done as she can, and leaves work mentally and physically exhausted. As she reflects on her day during her commute home, Olivia feels uneasy about her meeting with Julie. She realizes that she probably did not devote the time that she should have to Julie. Julie's story is one of many that she hears all too often.

Questions

1. How does Julie's background, and her college choice process, contribute to her problems at Monroe? Evaluate how these processes led to Julie's current issues.

2. Do you agree with the advice Olivia gave Julie regarding the struggles she was experiencing at Monroe? What other avenues of support might Julie benefit from? What would you have said if you were Olivia?

3. How might organizational and environmental factors at Monroe contribute to the retention issues at the institution? Assess and create a list of the issues.

4. What are the benefits and drawbacks of social media use in enrolling and retaining students? Generate a pros and cons list.

Chapter 22

Identity Expression
Safer to Wait Until After Graduation?
Meridia D. Sanders and Melissa A. Rychener

As you read the following case, consider the advisor's competing alliances: to her university, her department, her student. What role do external constituents such as internship supervisors play in advocating for or challenging the actions of a university?

Basra Khalid and Brooke Campbell are back on campus at Carolina State University (CSU) for summer semester, each taking two classes in Athletic Training, the major they plan to declare. Basra is retaking one course for a better grade, and a second so that she can have a lighter spring semester. Brooke needs these credits because she studied abroad during the spring semester. They have been roommates in an off-campus apartment for a year, and they will live together this summer and during their junior year.

Brooke, a white upper-class North Carolina native, has a long family history in the medical field. Her father, Nigel Campbell, is well known in the athletic training field for his work with professional athletes. He spends several weeks each summer volunteering with Doctors Without Borders, a French medical relief program. Inspired by her dad's travel and service, Brooke spent her spring semester in Quito, Ecuador learning Spanish and exploring this culturally diverse country.

Basra, a Somali-American student whose family came to the United States as refugees when she was four years old, grew up in St. Paul, Minnesota. Basra has found needed comradery within the African American Student Association (AASA). Although she didn't always consider herself

"African American," connecting instead to the Somali community and her Muslim faith, she has found the AASA community to be her home away from home. She now proudly identifies herself as African American. She has also enjoyed her friendship with her roommate, Brooke.

Brooke and Basra met during their second semester of freshman year, while studying for a human anatomy class. The two discovered they were in the same major and had similar aspirations about their work in athletic training. Studying together and enjoying each other's company cemented their relationship and led them to become roommates.

In her Muslim family, Basra grew up wearing the hijab. Upon leaving for college, her family gave her the choice of whether to continue wearing it, and she decided not to. Throughout her childhood, she was constantly teased about her religious practice and clothing. Her decision not to wear the hijab was liberating for her; she finally felt that she could blend with the crowd. Her family accepted her decision and hoped that she would continue with her other religious practices. Her mother told her privately that she supported Basra's decision and hoped that it would keep her safer. She was concerned that Basra would face discrimination if she could be easily identified as Muslim.

During the spring semester of her sophomore year, Basra completed a sociology course that emphasized self-reflection and identity. After the semester, she went home to Minnesota where she celebrated Ramadan with her family. Due to her sociology course, and her experience with her Somali community in June, Basra made the personal decision to begin wearing the hijab again. She saw this as her responsibility to reclaim her Muslim identity through religious practice and dress. Basra wrote in her last course reflection paper:

> I used to think that not wearing the hijab was freedom because I fit in with everyone else. Although I was no longer teased, stared at, or considered an outsider, I realized that I was losing an important part of myself. In this class we discussed societal expectations. I wanted to feel accepted in society, but the loss of my Muslim identity is too high of a price to pay.

SUMMER SEMESTER—AT THE APARTMENT

When Basra and Brooke met in their apartment for the first time after Brooke's semester abroad and Basra's visit home, Brooke immediately noticed the difference in her friend's appearance. The opportunity for a conversation presented itself later that evening when Brooke came into the living room where Basra was writing in her journal.

Brooke: What are you doing?
Basra: Journaling.

Brooke: Class hasn't started and you already want to write?

Basra: [laughing] Well I guess so, but I journal a lot now. I took a sociology class this spring, and we had to do it as a requirement of the class. I enjoyed it so I still do.

Brooke: Well that's cool. Hey, can I ask you a question?

Basra: Yeah, sure. What's up?

Brooke: I noticed you're wearing that head scarf . . .

Basra: Hijab

Brooke: Yeah, sorry, of course. Hijab.

Basra: What about it?

Brooke: [feeling nervous] I don't know. I guess . . . well, why are you wearing it?

Basra: Because it's part of my culture; part of my faith.

Brooke: I mean I knew you were Muslim, but I just thought you were different from them.

Basra: [Becoming frustrated] What do you mean by *them*? What are you saying Brooke?

Brooke: [stumbling through her words] I am not trying to offend you or be insensitive. After studying abroad, I am more curious about the differences I notice, and I notice that you look different, and I want to understand why. I have never talked to someone who has worn a hijab before. I mean, I thought you didn't have to wear any of that stuff because I have never seen you wear it.

Basra: Listen. I realize that it looks weird to you, but this is really important to me. I did a lot of thinking while I was at home . . .

Brooke: About?

Basra: Well, it's my choice to wear the hijab. This is a part of my culture. The hijab represents modesty and me respecting myself and my faith. This is my decision and no one forced me to wear it, and no one will force me not to wear it. Although not all Muslim women wear the hijab, it is part of who I am as a Muslim woman. We are halfway through college and most of my friends have no idea about my beliefs. I don't feel that I need to hide in silence. . . . You know?

Brooke: Wow. I understand, I mean it is kind of cool. Can anybody wear one?

Basra: [laughs] If they want to, they can. Who is going to stop them?

Basra was encouraged by how well her first conversation about the hijab went. Brooke was excited to have learned something new about her roommate, and proud of herself for having the courage to ask about something that she didn't understand.

ADVISING CENTER—FRIDAY, JUNE 28

Academic Advisor Angela Singleton has been at CSU for almost 10 years as the primary advisor for students interested in health disciplines. Angela is passionate about student success and is known for going the extra mile for her students. As the only African American advisor in Health Sciences, she plays an official and unofficial role as an advocate for students of color. She also serves as the secretary for the President's Commission for Diversity and Inclusion.

Angela and the other advisors are under pressure to increase the number of advisees that they see each day. The new interim supervisor, Darwin, is a newly minted Ph.D. who appears eager to demonstrate that he runs a tight ship. Angela thinks that this pressure to get advisees in and out is affecting the quality of her advising sessions. It is hard to build a relationship of trust with students in such a short time.

FIRST DAY OF CLASS—MONDAY, JULY 1

"Introductory seminar" was one of the final courses athletic training students had to take prior to declaring the major. This seminar is taught by Dr. Ray Ford, a white male and a tenured full professor, who serves as the Athletic Training Program Coordinator. He has been at CSU for over 18 years, is one of the leading researchers in the field, and is a notoriously demanding professor. Dr. Ford stresses to his students the importance of professionalism and representing the department well, and he focused on this in his opening remarks on the first day of introductory seminar.

Dr. Ford: Here in the Athletic Training Department, we take great pride in being the best, and that will not change! In this course you will do a field observation, and I will ensure that you are ready to formally declare your athletic training major. I expect everyone to be in class every day on time and ready. I expect you all to be professionally dressed at all times in your program T-shirt and shorts. No hats, no hoodies, sunglasses, and so on. You all should know by now, but I want to reiterate that you represent this program and people are watching you at all times.

Basra stayed after class the first day due to her concerns about the expressed required dress for fieldwork. Dr. Ford did not recognize her, even though he previously had her in class.

Basra: Dr. Ford, do you have a minute?
Dr. Ford: Yeah, let's make it fast. What's your name again?

Basra:	My name is Basra. I took Intro to Body Mechanics with you last fall.
Dr. Ford:	Oh, okay, yeah I remember you. I didn't recognize you with that thing covering your head. Why are you wearing it anyway?
Basra:	It's a hijab. It's part of my cultural and religious beliefs, and that is what I wanted to talk to you about [Dr. Ford nods]. Because of my religious beliefs, I am unable to wear shorts anymore. Will that be okay? And I was also wondering if there was a long sleeve polo or T-shirt option for the senior Athletic Training shirts?
Dr. Ford:	As long as you dress professionally and in line with the department expectations, I do not care what you wear. You have to talk to the Athletic Training Club about shirts and things of that nature. Is there anything else Basra because I have to get to a meeting.
Basra:	[fearful to ask about her hijab] No, that's all.
Dr. Ford:	Okay [walks away to his office].

SPRING SENIOR ENROLLMENT DAY—AUGUST 12

The summer term was a good one for both Basra and Brooke. Basra did her field observation at Brooke's father's sports injury practice and was able to make subtle changes to the uniform to accommodate her religious beliefs. In addition to wearing her hijab, she substituted long pants for shorts and wore a long-sleeved shirt under her T-shirt. Nobody raised concerns about these changes, and she felt really good. Brooke was able to spend a day observing the trainers for the CSU football team's summer training camp. They both ended up with a 3.2 in their major classes, just above the GPA required for students wishing to declare an athletic training major. Upon completion of their course, both women needed to register for fall classes.

When registration opened, Basra logged on to the student portal, but for some reason the system sent her an error message that said, "restricted, department permission required." Basra assumed it was just a system glitch and decided to go to the advising center to see Ms. Singleton.

Angela:	Hi Basra, what can I help you with?
Basra:	Well, last night I tried to register for my approved course schedule, and I kept getting an error message.
Angela:	Well that's odd. I wonder why it would not let you on. I will take a look. [Looks at computer screen] It looks like the department forgot to remove the permission hold for you. I will call Dr. Ford

and see what's going on [calls office number and leaves a voice-mail for Dr. Ford]. Basra, hopefully Dr. Ford will call me back sometime today. If you see Dr. Ford before then, mention it to him and see what he says.

Basra: Okay I will. Thank you. Ms. Singleton, can I ask you something [Basra says hesitantly]?

Angela: Of course you can.

Basra: Do you think wearing my hijab is unprofessional?

Angela: No, that is part of your culture and your beliefs. Who or what makes you think it is unprofessional?

Basra: Oh no . . . no one, I was just wondering.

Angela: Basra, if someone or something is bothering you, you can tell me.

Angela's boss, Darwin, knocks at the door and lets Angela know her next appointment is waiting.

Angela: Thank you Darwin, I will be out as soon as I am finished here.

Darwin: Okay, I will let the student know you will just be another minute.

Angela hates when Darwin pops in like to remind her to finish up quickly. She is afraid that his interruption may have derailed the discussion with Basra, since she appears to be packing up her things.

Basra: Well thank you, Ms. Singleton, and please let me know when you hear back from Dr. Ford [as she packs up her things].

Angela: Basra, are you sure everything is okay?

Basra: Absolutely. I will stop by Dr. Ford's office sometime tomorrow and see what's going on, if I do not hear back from you. See you later! [Walks out the door.]

Angela did not feel comfortable with the way that the conversation ended. She wanted to know what was behind Basra's question about whether her hijab was unprofessional. Angela made a note to check in with Basra later to revisit the topic.

ADVISING CENTER—AUGUST 15

Angela had sent an email to Basra, instructing her to go meet with Ray Ford, because she still had not heard from him. Angela was bothered by Ray's lack of response, so she decided to go talk to Darwin and see if he knew anything, "since he tries to keep his nose in everyone's business any-way", she thought to herself. Darwin called Ray to see what was going on, and Ray answered the phone on the first ring. Although Angela was frustrated that Ray answered the phone immediately when Darwin called (but did not return her call or email), she was hopeful that Basra's registration problem would be solved. Shortly after hanging up, Darwin told Angela that Basra was not permitted to enroll because she had not been accepted as an athletic training major. Ray said that Basra should have received an email from him requesting that she schedule a meeting. Angela thanked Darwin and went back to her office:

Angela: [thinking to herself] Basra did not say anything about changing her major when we spoke last. I wonder if she got Ray's email? Why did he not call me back? How unprofessional! Basra will be a junior, she has the required GPA, and from what I have observed she has done everything she is supposed to in that program. Something just does not seem right about this. I need to check in with Basra.

VISIT TO DR. FORD—AUGUST 14 (GOING BACK ONE DAY)

Basra decided to follow Angela's suggestion and stop by Dr. Ford's office during his office hours.

Dr. Ford: Basra, come in. I was just emailing you to request a meeting.
Basra: Okay, a meeting with me . . . about what?
Dr. Ford: Well, come in, have a seat. [Basra does as instructed.] We just finished up our student program review. Based on your observed academic performance and professionalism, we, the Athletic Training Department, have decided not to admit you into the program.
Basra: [shocked and confused] But, what is this based on? How did— why am I just now being told?
Dr. Ford: In our last review, several faculty members brought up concerns about your academic performance and demonstrated professionalism in their course [Basra listens on in shock]. Showing up late to class and underperforming on exams will not be acceptable.
Basra: [in tears] I'm confused. This does not make sense! No one ever told me I was doing anything wrong. I was late to a few classes here and there, but I was never on academic probation. I made the required grade point average and have taken all required classes. I did all of my homework and assignments, and I was always in class. What exactly did I do wrong?

Dr. Ford: Basra, I just explained what was wrong. Based on the student review process, the faculty have determined that you are unfit for the professional nature of the program and the field. Please schedule an appointment with the advising center to review other major options.

Basra: This program is the whole reason I came to CSU. What am I supposed to do?

Basra leaves the office in a state of shock.

BACK AT THE APARTMENT—AUGUST 16

Brooke walks in looking for Basra because they were supposed to meet for lunch to celebrate successfully completing their courses. She finds Basra in her room journaling.

Basra: [writing in journal] How did this happen? What did I do? I mean I know I had to retake a course, but I had the GPA! This can't be my fault. I know Dr. Ford is a professional, and he has been doing this for years. If he says that I am not fit for this field, then I guess I am not fit for this field. What am I going to tell my parents? What am I going to do now?

Brooke knocks on the door.

Basra: I don't really want to talk right now.

Brooke: What's going on? You missed our lunch today, and my dad told me that you aren't going to be an athletic training major. Is that true? What happened? Tell me.

Basra: [crying] I went to see Dr. Ford because I had a hold on my account and couldn't register for classes. He said the faculty has determined that I am unfit for the professional nature of the program and the field.

Brooke: What! Why, how?

Basra: He said several faculty members brought up concerns about my academic performance and demonstrated professionalism in their courses—whatever that means.

Brooke: Oh my gosh. I am so sorry. I have never gotten a letter from the department besides my acceptance letter. There has to be something you can do. I am going to call my dad and see if he can help with anything.

| Basra: | Don't bother. Dr. Ford is the program coordinator, if he is telling me this, then there is nothing I can do. |

Basra's phone rings and it is Ms. Singleton.

Basra:	Hi, Ms. Singleton.
Angela:	Hello Basra. What happened when you met with Dr. Ford?
Basra:	He basically told me I was kicked out of the program because the faculty determined that I am unfit for the professional nature of the program and the field.
Angela:	WHAT? What rationale did he give? What was the reasoning?
Basra:	Some faculty thought I was unable to demonstrate knowledge of the coursework and that I was not a good fit for the program. I don't even understand what's going on. I need to figure out a new major because I obviously cannot finish this one.
Angela:	He said what? Basra, I am so sorry this happened to you. I will find out more because this is just not right. Please come by my office tomorrow.

Angela hangs up and thinks about what Basra just told her. She thinks about the last conversation she had with Basra and her question about whether the hijab is professional. She calls Dr. Ford and leaves another voicemail for him to call back about an urgent matter. Darwin walks by and Angela calls him in. She explains what happened with Basra. Angela explains that she thinks there is no legitimate reason for Basra's denial to the program and that this is actually an act of discrimination. Darwin tells her, "Calm down and don't make such strong allegations." He also assures her that he will check into the matter. Angela, unsatisfied with Darwin's response, returns to her office and emails the chair of the President's Commission for Diversity and Inclusion with the subject, "Discrimination in an Academic Department."

BACK AT THE APARTMENT—LATER ON AUGUST 15

Brooke just hung up with her dad, who had talked with Dr. Ford. Dr. Ford told him that Basra was not accepted into the program because "she was unprofessional and unfit for the field; she didn't represent the program well and dressed unprofessionally." He did not mention anything about the coursework. Dr. Campbell, Brooke's dad, thought that Basra was extremely professional when she did her observation at his workplace. He found Dr. Ford's decision to be out of place and had requested a meeting with the Dean. Brooke told Basra what she found out. Basra said to Brooke, "My mom was right, I should have waited to wear my hijab."

Questions

1. Why were Angela Singleton and Brooke's dad so concerned when Pat Ford said that Basra was not admitted because she was "unprofessional" or "not a good fit"? What did they think Dr. Ford was really saying?
2. Was it reasonable for Angela to act on her assumptions about Dr. Ford's actions? What does Angela risk by questioning the ethics of a powerful faculty member? Does her ethical responsibility to defend a student's rights justify this risk? Under what circumstances would you risk your job or your career to advocate for a student or for a cause you believe in?
3. Why do you think that Angela Singleton was considered an "unofficial" advisor by students of color?
4. What are some possible downsides of increasing efficiency and advisor load in terms of advising quality?

Chapter 23

A Young Black Woman's Experience in a Historically White Sorority

Lesli Somerset and Molly A. Mistretta

A student of color struggles to navigate social experiences on a predominantly white campus. As she experiences micro-aggressions on campus, she turns to her sorority sisters for understanding and support. Why doesn't she find the support she expected?

How can institutions promote cross-cultural understanding without relying on students of color to educate their peers? Think about the various perspectives characters view the problems in this case and how it influences their responses.

ON CAMPUS

It was a beautiful fall day on the campus of Ellington University, and Aaliyah was enjoying the short walk along the edge of the quad as she headed toward her late afternoon class. It had been a good start to the school year, and with three weeks of the semester under her belt, she was glad that things were settling into a normal routine. The beginning of the school year had been rather hectic. She arrived before classes started due to her role as a mentor for the ADVANCE Program. The ADVANCE Program, sponsored by the Multicultural Office at Ellington, serves as a transition program assisting new students of color with their adjustment to life on campus, both academically and socially. Aaliyah enjoyed helping the new students and was kept pretty busy with meetings and social activities through the first day of classes.

The first week of classes also kicked off the beginning of sorority recruitment. Aaliyah is a member of Delta Nu, a National Panhellenic (NPC), majority white sorority at Ellington. As the chair of her sorority's membership recruitment committee, Aaliyah had many late nights planning and hosting Delta Nu recruitment events. Recalling her own experiences as a new student exploring Greek Life on campus the previous year, Aaliyah knew the sorority recruitment process can be overwhelming for new students. She wanted potential members to see the aspects of the sorority that had appealed to her: the close-knit community of sisters, a sisterhood that represented a wide variety of interests and abilities, and a supportive environment in which to navigate the challenges of college life. Aaliyah was glad they had met quota on Bid Day, which meant her role was over for the year. Now her time was largely her own.

While many of her fellow black students thought her choice to join a predominantly white sorority was odd, Aaliyah was comfortable with it. Growing up, Aaliyah lived in a white majority neighborhood and attended a racially diverse high school. She also grew up in a racially diverse family; the idea of race was never something she gave much thought. She was black, but she had biracial cousins, white aunts and uncles, and strong friendships with both the white and black students in high school.

Looking across the lawn, she saw Laila, one of her fellow ADVANCE mentors. Aaliyah waved. She was looking forward to reconnecting with the friends she had made through the programs offered by the Multicultural Office. Laila waved back at her.

Laila:	Hey stranger! I haven't seen you since the Multicultural Office's ice cream social last week! What's going on?
Aaliyah:	I'm good. The past few weeks I've been crazy busy with sorority recruitment. This year they've really buckled down on us showing up to everything, but luckily things are starting to slow down.
Laila:	Oh yeah. I forgot they use you as their poster child.
Aaliyah:	Poster child? What's that supposed to mean?
Laila:	You know that they use you and that other light-skinned girl as the face of diversity in the sorority you're a part of. I don't even know why. It's not like they're bringing in any more of us.
Aaliyah:	Can you believe at the Activities Fair last week, the college president asked our chapter president if Delta Nu was diverse. Her answer was, "Yes, we have two black girls in our sorority now and Aaliyah is even on our E-Board". Ashanti and I both cringed but still kept our "face" on. We have a potential new member, so the college president will now be able to say we have *three* black girls in our sorority.

Aaliyah was used to having these conversations. Although it did not feel good to admit, there were times when she agreed with Laila's comments.

Laila: Why am I not surprised? They've got you all asking, "How high?" when they say jump. With your matching sparkly shirts you all wear in the pictures I see on your Instagram, are you even a real black girl anymore?

Aaliyah: [Jokingly] What does my skin look like?

Comments like this really got to Aaliyah, but she didn't want to make a big deal so she usually just laughed them off. However, the more times she had to hear her friends question her blackness, the more she started to question it herself.

Aaliyah: Anyway, my schedule will be pretty open in the next few weeks. We should definitely get together. What are your plans for this weekend?

Laila: I'm planning on going to the Theta's Pajama Jam this weekend! You should come! I hear everyone will be going. It's going to be Friday at ten.

Another ADVANCE mentor approaches the two women talking, overhears their conversation, and jumps right in. Chris is a brother of Theta Nu Theta, a historically black fraternity.

Chris: Yeah, it's going to be great! A bunch of our brothers are coming up for it. Everyone who's anyone will be there.

Aaliyah: That sounds fun! My sorority is mixing with Sigma Alpha Chi [a predominantly white fraternity] that night. They're our homecoming partners, so I'll probably have to show up a little later than ten. Can I text you when I'm on my way to meet up?

Chris: Why don't you just invite your sisters to come? All are welcome. It's $3 before midnight and $5 after that.

Aliyah had found herself in this conversation a lot of times over the past year. She had tried to get her sorority sisters to come to events hosted by the National Pan-Hellenic Council (NPHC), a council of historically black Greek letter organizations, more times than she could remember, but never had anyone take her up on the invitations.

Aaliyah: Chris you know how that goes. I don't even know why you asked.

Chris: Yeah, you're right. You need to get out of that and come back to our side. I heard that Kappa Alpha Kappa is having formal recruitment this year, you could join them!

Aaliyah: And on that note I'm out. I'll just continue to live my double life for now. But I will text you guys about the Pajama Jam. And P.S., I am on both sides.

THE MIXER

Later at the mixer, Aaliyah, her sorority sister Elle, who is her "Big", and a fellow sorority member, Brooke, are walking to their mixer with Sigma Alpha Chi, an Interfraternity Council (IFC) majority white fraternity.

Elle: Little! Are you coming with us to Anna's party after the mixer?

Aaliyah: I don't think so, Big. I was planning on only staying at Sigma Alpha for a little while tonight so I could head to another event happening on campus.

Brooke: Where are you going?

Aaliyah: Theta Nu Theta's Pajama Jam . . . but I promise I'll at least stay at the Sigma Alpha mixer for an hour.

Elle: It's okay, Little. I think it's cool that you're friends with them.

Aaliyah knew by "them" that her sorority big sister meant the black fraternity brothers.

The three girls join the majority of their sisters at the Sigma Alpha Chi house. About an hour passes. Aaliyah goes outside to let Elle and Brooke know that she is planning on catching a ride that will take her to the Pajama Jam. Elle and Brooke are outside talking with someone she assumed to be a new pledge for Sigma Alpha.

Aaliyah: Hey Big! You guys good? I just called for a ride to come pick me up to take me to the Pajama Jam. It should be here in five to ten minutes.

Elle: Little! You have to meet Teddy! This is one of Sigma Alpha's new members. He just started pledging. [Elle leaned in to whisper in Aaliyah's ear.] OMG, OMG! Isn't he cute? He was asking about you! You should go for him!

Although it was pretty evident that Teddy had been drinking, Aaliyah plays along and introduces herself.

Aaliyah: Hey Teddy, my name is Aaliyah, I'm Elle's Little. Where are you from?

Teddy: Hi, Aaliyah. I'm from Tyndall, so not too far.

Aaliyah: No way! I'm from North Robinson! We played you all in football all the time! Small world!

Teddy: [turns to Elle and Brooke] I like this sorority sister of yours! Where have you been hiding her? [He laughs and throws his arm around Aaliyah.] Get it? How could they hide *you*?

Aaliyah rolls her eyes at this. Reminding herself that Teddy is drunk and she would need to make allowances for his behavior, Aaliyah decides to be nice and get herself out of there as fast as she could.

Aaliyah: Well, maybe I'll catch you around, Teddy.

Aaliyah begins to slide away from the group, but Teddy tightens up his hold on her.

Teddy: Let's hang out more. I like you. You're not like the other black girls I knew back home. You are not, like, *black*-black. You hang out with blacks *and* whites, which I think is pretty cool.

Aaliyah looks over at her friends for help out of this situation, but Elle and Brooke giggle.

Brooke: That is what makes Aaliyah such a great sister. She is friends with everyone on campus. Everyone loves her.

Elle: We're going to check out the drink situation around here. We'll be back. Aaliyah, want anything? Teddy, you be good to my Little.

Elle winks suggestively at Aaliyah as she leaves. "Great, now I'm stuck with Teddy", Aaliyah thinks. Aaliyah watches them walk away, wondering why her sisters think that she'd be interested in Teddy. Cute does not make up for his racist remarks. Aaliyah suddenly feels Teddy playing with her hair.

Teddy: These dreads look cool on you. Is this your real hair?

Aaliyah: [tries stepping away] Actually, they are braids.

Moving back in toward Aaliyah, and still playing with her hair, Teddy leans down and whispers in her ear.

Teddy: Don't go to your other party. We can get out of here and go back to my apartment. I want to hang out with you more. I've never been with a black girl before. I bet we can have a lot of fun together.

Angry, Aaliyah turns and walks away. As she does, she meets Elle and Brooke who are bringing back drinks.

Aaliyah: I'm out of here. That guy is disgusting.

She tells her sorority sisters what Teddy said to her.

Elle: What are you talking about? He thinks you're cool! He's hot and it looks like he is into you! Don't leave now. Are you crazy?

Frustrated, Aaliyah tries to explain her perspective.

Aaliyah: Look, I'm not interested in being something he can check off of some sexual wish list. Black girl . . . *Check!* It's insulting.
Brooke: I'm sure he doesn't mean it in a bad way. It's not a big deal. Give him another chance! I can tell he really likes you.
Aaliyah: No, I don't think he's kidding, and I'm really not interested.

Aaliyah was getting angry as she realized her friends really didn't understand why this was upsetting for her.

Elle: [wanting to diffuse the situation] Okay, there's no need to get all mad about this, Little. He's been drinking. You can't take anything he says too seriously. Give him another chance when he's sober. It looks like your ride is here. Are you about ready to go?
Aaliyah: Yes, I couldn't be more ready! Are you guys going to leave too?
Elle: I think Brooke and I are going to hang around a little longer, but please text me when you get to your destination safe?

Aaliyah walked to the car barely holding the tears back. She looked out the car window to see Brooke and Elle still laughing and talking to Teddy. She realized that she was much more upset about her friends than she was about what Teddy said. She did not understand how her friends—her sorority sisters—could let a random guy disrespect her without defending her and show such a lack of support for her afterward. Did they care about her feelings? Couldn't they see how upset she was? Aaliyah could not decide if her sisters just didn't know or didn't care about what happened, but either way she knew it would be a while before she got over it.

THETA NU THETA PAJAMA JAM

Aaliyah decided she wouldn't let the incident ruin her night and proceeded to the Pajama Jam. When she arrived she started to search for Laila.

Laila: Aaliyah! I'm so glad that you made it! You came just in time! Chris and . . . Aaliyah! Have you been crying? What happened?

Aaliyah and Laila duck outside where it is quiet. Aaliyah filled Laila in on the night's happenings.

Laila: Oh my God, girl. If this does not tell you why you need to be done with them, I do not know what will! You'll never fit in, and you know this will keep happening. I just got one word for you. QUIT! Go straight to Maya Peterson to discuss this. You know she handles all of the black issues in the Greek community, and she will understand why you are quitting.

Aaliyah had never considered disaffiliation from her sorority, but after listening to Laila, maybe it was something to think about. What Laila was saying did make a lot of sense. Maybe leaving Delta Nu was in her best interest. She never imagined that joining a predominantly white sorority would be so problematic. Maybe she should go to the Office of Greek Affairs just to explore what it would mean to disaffiliate. Aaliyah decided to stop in the office first thing Monday morning.

OFFICE FOR GREEK AFFAIRS

Charlotte Preston is the Director of the Office for Student Leadership and Greek Affairs. Charlotte has been at Ellington for a little over a year and has a great deal of experience in working with majority white fraternities and sororities through her positions at two other small colleges. However, Ellington is the first institution that Charlotte has worked at that also has historically black NPHC organizations. With no experience in working with NPHC groups, Charlotte relies heavily on Maya Peterson, who serves as an admissions counselor at Ellington. Maya is African American and an alumna of Ellington who was heavily involved with her NPHC sorority as a student. Over the last five years, Maya has served as a volunteer advisor for the NPHC groups, and is glad that Charlotte has asked her to continue in this role.

Charlotte: Good morning, Aaliyah. What can I help you with this morning?
Aaliyah: Hi Charlotte. Is Maya in? I need to talk to her. I think I want to disaffiliate from my sorority. Things there have just been

causing me additional stress lately, and I am not sure I can do it anymore.

Charlotte: Oh no, you're always wearing your letters so proudly around this office! Maya is not here, but will be stopping by later. However, I would be the one for you to talk to anyway. Disaffiliation is a really big step. I wouldn't want you to make a bad decision if we can avoid it. Why don't you tell me a little more about why you think you should quit?

Aaliyah goes into detail and describes what happened over the weekend at Sigma Alpha Chi's mixer. She finishes by saying,

Aaliyah: And I do love my sisters. My Big has been such a support system for me since I came here, and I love being a part of something bigger than myself, but being a minority student in an all-white Greek organization is hard. I feel like none of my sisters recognize how hard it is for me at times, especially because I want to stay connected to the black side of campus. I always have to justify why I am in a white sorority to my black friends, and there's no one to vent to because I can't tell my white sisters that it irritates the hell out of me when I get looks for sitting with them in the dining hall when everyone else who looks like me is at a separate group of tables.

For any other organization like the Biology Club or the Programming Board, there is only one of each so no one judges you for joining or scrutinizes you because you don't have to choose between the black biology club and the white biology club. I just don't feel my white sisters get what it is like to be black on this campus. I don't want to have to be hesitant in sharing my sorority successes with my black friends and act like it doesn't bother me when my white friends say things that I find ignorant or insensitive. I can't continue to live this double life.

Charlotte: Wow! It sounds like you are overwhelmed. From being in a sorority in my younger years, I can understand why you might feel agitated right now. The girl drama that happens when you are around a group of women all the time can be a lot and can cause us to make impulsive decisions.

Aaliyah: I'm not agitated, and it's not drama. I am just confused and tired.

Charlotte: Whatever the case may be, I'd rather you take some time and make the right decision, than make the wrong one impulsively. While it might be a struggle today, think about how much your sisters are learning from you! Like you said, they have no idea what it is like to be black. They don't understand how it feels to be a minority in a mostly white group or how some of the things they or others say might be hurtful to you. You are in a position to educate them on that and change their entire perspective. Because you have embraced a variety of campus experiences yourself, you are helping to integrate the campus and are a role model for other minority students. I'll put you on my calendar for next Friday at two. We can talk further about this.

Realizing that this wasn't the way she hoped this conversation would go, Aaliyah managed to keep her tears back until she got out of the Office for Greek Affairs. As she leaves, she passes Maya Peterson in the hallway of the campus center.

Maya: Aaliyah, are you okay? Talk to me. What's going on? You seem really upset.

Aaliyah stopped and filled Maya in on her meeting with Charlotte and the weekend's events.

Aaliyah: And now I just feel really unheard and feel even more stressed out knowing that I am considered a role model by the university, and I am expected to make my sorority more educated and diverse.
Maya: Aaliyah, I am so sorry for how you are feeling and what you have been going through. I'd like to help you figure things out.

Questions

1. What are some steps that Maya could take in working with Aaliyah? What are some limits to Maya's ability to assist Aaliyah in this situation?
2. How effective was Charlotte's response to Aaliyah's concerns? Why is it problematic for her to expect Aaliyah to educate her sorority sisters about her experiences as a black woman?
3. What are examples of micro aggressions/implicit biases in this case? How did these micro aggressions contribute to Aaliyah's decision to disaffiliate from her sorority?

Chapter 24

Helping Students, Setting Professional Boundaries in an Unsupportive Environment

Morgan E. Weber and Michael G. Ignelzi

As you read this case, think about the balance between helping a troubled student and setting appropriate professional boundaries. Also, reflect on what forms developmental support should entail for students, and the effects overburdened campus resources can have on providing such support. Additionally, consider person-environment fit issues between a new professional and their workplace.

I, Elizabeth Andrews, am a Residence Life Coordinator at Newton State University. Newton is a large, public institution that enrolls approximately 18,000 students. About 7,000 undergraduates live in the residence halls on campus. I oversee a residence hall of 600 students. Most of Newtown's undergraduate students are from in state. The majority of my resident students' family homes are within a two-hour radius of the institution.

I started working at Newton in Residence Life this fall, after completing my graduate program in student affairs at Centre State University. My assigned building is on North campus, which consists of a collection of five large residence halls housing approximately 3,000 students. I report to the Area Coordinator for North campus, Ryan Amos.

My residence hall director and supervisor during my time as a graduate assistant at Centre State University encouraged me to be intentional in my interactions with students. He challenged me to do my best work, not just the minimum to get by. He had a clear developmental philosophy and approach, and always seemed to put the interests of students first. My professional orientation, based on my coursework and supervision, came to mirror his commitment to student development and support of students as the primary goal of our work in student affairs.

After working a couple of months in my job at Newton, it seems to me that the Residence Life operation, or at least the Residence Life office leadership, does not have a strong developmental orientation. I would characterize the department culture as policy/rule oriented, expedient, and conflict avoidant. From what I have heard and seen, Patricia Jones, the Director of Residence Life, above all, wants student issues resolved quickly and neatly. Ryan, my direct supervisor, seems more committed to developmentally supporting students, but is highly concerned about handling situations in ways that his superiors, mainly Patricia, will approve. While I feel somewhat disheartened by this situation, I am trying to stay focused on working with my residents and RAs in a manner consistent with my understanding of what would best help and support them.

Two months into the fall semester, on a Sunday afternoon, I return to the residence hall and am stopped by a Student Desk Worker (SDW) who alerts me that a resident is in the hallway crying. The SDW informs me that the University Police have just spoken with the distraught student, but left the residence hall to address an issue elsewhere. While I am speaking with the SDW, the front desk telephone rings. After hanging up the phone, the SDW tells me that the upset student has called the police and requested that the officer return to the residence hall. The officer told the SDW that he would not be able to return to the building for a while. I leave in search of the student.

I find the resident, Kasey Stodden, crying in the hallway being consoled by her friend, Melissa Downy. I ask Kasey why she is upset. Kasey replies, "My boyfriend just broke up with me." I ask Kasey and Melissa to come to my office where we can speak more privately. I prompt Kasey for more information on the situation:

Elizabeth:	So you're upset because your boyfriend broke up with you?
Kasey:	Well—he wasn't really my boyfriend. I met this guy, Landon, online, through a chat site in June. We talked a lot and he's come to visit me since I've been here at Newton. But my parents have been really upset about the situation because of his age—I told them about a month ago that I haven't been talking to him anymore, but we've still been in contact. My parents don't know that he's visited me here.

Elizabeth: Okay, so you've been talking to a guy that you met
                    online, but your parents aren't aware that you're still
                    talking to him. You said they disapproved of him
                    because of his age, how old is he?

Kasey: He's 32. I tried to keep the fact that I was talking to
                    him a secret from my parents, but he got mad at me
                    one day and called my house. He told my mom that
                    we had been talking and my parents flipped out on me.
                    They were so mad at me for talking to him, so I told
                    them that I would stop. I kept talking to him though
                    and now [Kasey begins to cry again and reaches for a
                    tissue] I'm afraid he's going to call my house because
                    he's pissed with me right now. I'm going to get in even
                    more trouble with my parents if he calls them. They're
                    going to kill me if they find out.

Elizabeth: You said Landon was upset with you. Why do you
                    think that?

Kasey: Well, he came to visit me this weekend. After he was
                    here for a while, I realized I didn't want to be around
                    him anymore. I asked him to leave, but he didn't.
                    That's when I texted Melissa and asked her for help.
                    She told me that I should tell him I was going to call
                    the police if he didn't leave. I was starting to get scared
                    about what might happen—he still wouldn't leave, so
                    I called the police. Landon left before the officer got
                    here. I told Officer Coatsworth my situation, and that
                    I didn't want Landon to come around anymore. The
                    officer left to see if Landon was still on campus and
                    said he would tell Landon that he was not to contact
                    me anymore.

Melissa [to Kasey]: I just hate seeing him upset you like this Kasey. Enough
                    is enough!

Kasey calms down and is no longer crying. I talk with Kasey about how
the issue will be handled. I inform Kasey that the police will make sure that
Landon knows that he is not to contact her anymore. I also try to calm
Kasey's fears about Landon returning to the building reminding Kasey that
the SDWs carefully monitor who enters the building and know to call the
police if Landon tries to enter. I begin to tell Kasey that she may want to
consider making an appointment at the Counseling Center to discuss her
situation and related anxiety. I don't share with Kasey that it seems to
me she is displaying intense feelings and contradictory behaviors that are
concerning. Kasey's cell phone begins to ring. Once Kasey realizes that the

call is from a blocked phone number, she begins to cry again. Barely able to catch her breath, Kasey communicates that she believes Landon is trying to contact her. Panicked, Kasey says she believes Landon will now call her parents.

As Melissa and I work to calm Kasey, Officer Coatsworth knocks on my office door. He tells Kasey that he tried to call her cell phone, but she had not answered. Kasey is relieved that it was Officer Coatsworth who had called her, and not Landon. Officer Coatsworth explains that Landon left his jacket in Kasey's room and requested that Kasey retrieve the jacket, so the officer could return it to Landon. Kasey leaves with Officer Coatsworth, while Melissa and I wait for the two to return to my office. Melissa takes this opportunity to express to me that Kasey has been having ongoing problems with Landon. Melissa tells me that she believes Kasey is downplaying the situation and a number of residents on Kasey's floor are worried about Kasey's relationship with Landon.

Officer Coatsworth returns to my office with Kasey and Landon's jacket. Before the officer leaves, I privately ask for some clarification about the directives that have been given to Landon. The officer explains that Landon was told to have no communication with Kasey. I ask if Landon has been issued a "No Contact" order. Officer Coatsworth curtly replies that such orders can only be issued through the Office of Judicial Conduct and that the director, Lindsay Deighan, will work with Kasey to issue the order. I ask if the officer told Landon that he is not to return to the residence hall. Officer Coatsworth, clearly annoyed by my questions, says, "Yeah he knows not to return. Any other questions or can I leave now? I have more important things to deal with than this girl and her dramatic breakup. Tell her to call us if he contacts her again, okay?" I am somewhat shocked by the officer's bluntness and seeming lack of concern. Residence Life and the University Police work together on a regular basis, but apparently the offices do not communicate well with one another. I understand from my Resident Director colleagues that officers frequently take their frustrations out with the Residence Life building staff.

After the officer leaves, I tell Kasey that I will check in with her and express that if she needs anything for the rest of the day, the RA on duty will be able to reach me. I ask if Kasey is feeling better and if she feels comfortable returning to her room. Kasey says that she is "feeling a lot better" and is going to take a nap and work on her homework.

Half an hour later, as I am typing an incident report about Kasey's situation to send to my supervisor, an RA contacts me asking me to come to her room. I arrive to find Kasey crying so hard she is barely intelligible. I ask what is wrong to which Kasey replies, "He contacted me on a chat site and said, 'I love you.' He's going to call my house now, I just know it." I tell Kasey that she needs to call the police and update Officer Coatsworth. Kasey calls

Officer Coatsworth and explains what happened. Kasey then reports, "Officer Coatsworth said Landon is getting arrested. I didn't want to get him in trouble. I just wanted him to leave me alone. I don't want him to go to jail." I remind Kasey that Landon brought this on himself; it was his choice to contact Kasey despite Officer Coatsworth's warning. Kasey eventually calms down. I tell her that she should block Landon on Facebook, Twitter, and any other chat sites, so that he cannot contact her. Kasey says she will do so as soon as she gets back to her room. Kasey thanks me for listening and leaves.

On Monday morning, Kasey stops by my office. Kasey explains that the night before had been awful, as Landon had called her house to apologize to her parents. "My parents were so upset. I contacted Officer Coatsworth to call them to explain what the police were doing to address this. That calmed them down a little," Kasey comments. Realizing the amount of stress that Kasey is experiencing, I again remind Kasey of the Student Counseling Center. I know that the Student Counseling Center will provide Kasey with extra support as she deals with her breakup, but I worry that Kasey will not be able to get a prompt appointment. The Student Counseling Center is understaffed and overbooked. Students often wait weeks before being able to get an appointment with a counselor. "You can call right now and schedule an appointment; if you'd like, you can use my office phone," I urge. Kasey calls and secures the first available appointment, which is three weeks away. Kasey leaves for class.

A few days later, I meet with Kasey to check in with her. I prompt her for details about how she is doing.

Elizabeth: I just wanted to check in and see how you're doing? I know it's probably been a difficult week for you.

Kasey: I'm okay. Things are better with Landon. He sent me a bag of candy and a new keychain, but he's been indirectly tweeting about me—since he can't mention me directly without getting in trouble. I feel bad, I didn't mean to get him in so much trouble, I just wanted him to leave me alone because I was afraid my parents would find out we were still talking. They found out anyway, so it really doesn't matter.

Elizabeth: So, he's contacted you again? You told me you'd blocked him on Twitter.

Kasey: I did, but I unblocked him since things were going well. He's not contacting me directly, so it's okay.

Elizabeth: You should block him again. I don't want him to be tempted to contact you. It's better that way. Have you met with Lindsay Deighan from Judicial Conduct to file a formal "No Contact" order?

Kasey: Yeah—I will. It's not a big deal.
Elizabeth: Okay Kasey, make sure you block him on Twitter and Facebook and all the other chat sites.

As Kasey leaves for class, I once again, express that if Kasey needs anything I am available. I know that since Kasey's appointment at the Student Counseling Center is still almost two weeks away, I am Kasey's primary support person for now. Later that night, I am in my residence hall apartment relaxing when I decide to check my email. I receive the following message from Kasey sent just minutes prior:

> Officer Coatsworth told my parents there was a hearing and he didn't tell me anything. I don't see why they need to know; it's not their business. I just got screamed at and now I feel worse. I just want this to be over. I was told there wouldn't be court??? I don't want court. I just want him to go away and my parents to stay out of it. Please help me.

I am beginning to feel that Kasey is relying on me too much; and I'm also frustrated that Kasey seems to be complicating the situation. After all, Kasey had unblocked Landon on Twitter and accepted gifts from him. I decide that I will wait until later that night to respond to the email knowing that Kasey knows to contact an RA who could then call the Resident Director on duty, if she needs to talk to someone immediately.

Twenty minutes later, my phone rings and the RA on duty asks me if I could come to my office to speak with Kasey, as she specifically asked for me. Slightly frustrated, I meet Kasey in my office.

Elizabeth: Kasey, what's going on?
Kasey: I sent you an email like twenty minutes ago—I'm going to have to go to court because of everything with Landon. My parents just called me furious because apparently Office Coatsworth called them to say that I have to go to a preliminary hearing. I don't want to go to court! I never wanted Landon to be arrested; I just wanted him to leave me alone. And I don't understand why my parents found out about this before I did. Officer Coatsworth never told me that I'd have to go to court. I don't want to see Landon in court. What's going to happen in court?
Elizabeth: I understand that this has been a really difficult week for you. I can see why you'd be apprehensive about going to court, but I'm not sure what is going to take place in court. I don't feel comfortable speculating on what will happen. You need to talk to Officer Coatsworth; he may be able to answer your questions about the legal process.

Kasey: I'm just so mad at him. My parents are on my case again since they spoke with him. Why would he tell them I'd have to go to court before he told me? I just wanted Officer Coatsworth to tell my parents that Landon had been told not to contact me again.

Elizabeth: I'm not sure why Officer Coatsworth spoke with your parents before he talked with you. You'll really need to speak with him about this. I'd suggest you call him now, but I don't believe he works the night shift, so I'd suggest you email him tonight and he'll get back to you tomorrow.

Kasey: Do I have to go to court though? I don't want to do that.

Elizabeth: Kasey, I know you really need answers, but I can't answer questions about the legal process because I'm not familiar enough with it.

Kasey: Can I call another police officer to talk with me?

Because Kasey is so upset, I reluctantly decide to contact the dispatcher myself. I explain that a student has some follow-up questions about a situation that transpired over the weekend and ask that an officer be sent to the building when it is convenient.

A few minutes later, Officer Kelly reports to my office. Kasey asks Officer Kelly about the court process and he stresses that it will be quick. She will just have to give a brief statement and she will not have to see Landon. Kasey seems more at ease after hearing this and asks the officer why Officer Coatsworth involved her parents. Officer Kelly says he does not feel comfortable answering that question, and that Kasey should speak with Officer Coatsworth directly. Kasey replies, "I just don't understand why he even needed to talk to my parents." Officer Kelly gets aggravated with Kasey responding, "He involved your parents because you asked him too—didn't you? You told him to call your parents and tell them that you'd told Landon not to contact you anymore, right? Can't you see you're a major part of the problem here? Stop pointing fingers." Kasey begins to cry and sensing that this is only making the problem worse, I thank Officer Kelly for coming to speak with Kasey and walk him out of the building. Out of earshot from Kasey, Officer Kelly comments, "She's nuts. Coatsworth called her parents because she told him to. Silly girl just needs to constantly be the center of attention. I mean seriously, how pathetic do you have to be to go on to some sketchy website to meet men. She has *major* issues. You should drag her to the Counseling Center right now."

I return to speak with Kasey and Kasey's RA. Kasey has calmed down again and said that she would call Officer Coatsworth in the morning, if she does not receive a response to her email. The RA comments that she is about to go hang out with some other residents on the floor and Kasey is welcome to join her. Kasey tells her RA that she would prefer to just go back to her room and be alone. I tell Kasey that she can schedule a meeting if she wants to talk more.

The next afternoon, I am working on some paperwork in my office. Kasey stops by my office, again unannounced.

Elizabeth: Hey Kasey, how are you doing today?

Kasey: I'm okay. I talked with Officer Coatsworth, he didn't tell my parents as much as I thought he did. They exaggerated—I didn't go to my classes this morning though. I just couldn't get out of bed. I can't stop thinking about everything with Landon and my parents. I threw up this morning because I was so stressed out. He's still subtweeting about me—he keeps complaining on Twitter about being arrested. I feel bad; he really didn't need to be arrested. I still don't want to go to court.

Elizabeth: So you haven't blocked him on Twitter? Kasey, we had this discussion, you need to block him. Every time you get on Twitter you're reminded of the situation. You need to block him and keep him blocked.

Kasey: Yeah. I know.

Elizabeth: You said you didn't go to your classes this morning. Are those the first classes you've missed?

Kasey: I was too tired to go. I've missed three classes—well three of each class. I just can't focus in class. My classes are a lot harder than high school, and I can't stop thinking about Landon and everything in class. It doesn't even make sense for me to go to class if I can't pay attention and learn.

Elizabeth: I know you're drained and exhausted from everything, but you really need to go to class. You're only going to get behind and then have to work really hard to catch up. Take some time this weekend to catch up on your schoolwork, then you won't be so overwhelmed. Do you have any plans for the weekend? I know there are some cool events going on on-campus; it might be fun to go to one as a break from studying.

Kasey: I'm going to my 3:00 p.m. class, don't worry. I'm going to just hang out in my room this weekend. A lot of people on my floor are going to this big off-campus party, but I'm not into that. I went to one of those weekend events a couple weekends ago. It was sooo lame!

Elizabeth: Well, you have class in twenty minutes; I don't want to keep you. Your RA has some things planned for the floor this weekend; you should try to go if you can. The events are different every weekend, and you might have fun this time.

Kasey: Okay, I'm sure I'll see you this weekend.

Elizabeth: I have a lot going on this weekend, if I don't see you I'll check in with you on Monday.

Kasey leaves for class, and I am perplexed. Kasey's situation seems to be getting more complicated each day. Kasey's appointment at the Student Counseling Center is still over two weeks away. Kasey continues to allow Landon to have access on Twitter and Facebook, which I just cannot understand. I am glad to help Kasey, but feel that I need to begin to set some boundaries with her. I am responsible for another 599 residents and need to be available to them as well. I am left wondering how I can assist Kasey while also setting limits.

I am looking forward to talking the situation over with Ryan on Monday. He has been out of the office at a conference all week and I have not been able to consult with him. I considered speaking with Patricia about the situation, but chose not too because I am concerned that the advice or, more likely, directive she would give would not be helpful, and that she would be upset with my handling of the situation.

As I am preparing to leave for the weekend, I receive a phone call from Patricia.

Elizabeth: Hello, Patricia.

Patricia: What's the situation with Kasey Stodden? Is she yours?

Elizabeth: Yes, she's my resident. She just went through a complicated breakup. She has an appointment scheduled at the Counseling Center, but she can't get seen for another two weeks. I've been working with her a lot to help her cope.

Patricia: I just got a phone call from the Chief of Police. He said she's been a complete pain for his officers to deal with. I don't need the ongoing tension between the police and our office to be complicated by this drama. The Chief said he talked with Lindsay Deighan in Conduct. Why hasn't Kasey filed a formal "No Contact" order through the Conduct Office? You need to get her over there to do that. You need to fix this so the police get off my back.

After this exchange, I feel upset and angry. I think the police were disrespectful while handling Kasey's situation, and now they are the ones complaining? Furthermore, Patricia doesn't seem at all concerned about Kasey. I feel defeated. I know that I probably could have handled this situation more effectively, but I have been trying hard to assist and support Kasey. I feel alone in all of this.

Questions

1. What is your assessment of how Elizabeth attempted to support Kasey? What did she do that was developmentally sound and not developmentally sound?
2. Since Elizabeth's supervisor was unavailable, did she make the correct decision in not consulting Patricia? What other individuals and/or resources might she have utilized to support her?
3. What are the appropriate boundaries and limits for a student affairs professional in supporting a student with emotional and behavioral issues such as those displayed by Kasey?
4. What options moving forward are open to Elizabeth now that she fully realizes the poor person/environment fit she is experiencing, along with problematic resource support for her students and herself?

Chapter 25

Student or Athlete? An Advising Dilemma in the Basketball Program

Brandy A. Wilson and Michael G. Ignelzi

In reading this case, think about how you might handle a situation where the unwritten policies or actions in your office conflicted with the stated mission/goals. As a new professional, how would you balance your professional responsibilities with the associated risks of taking needed action?

SETTING

Green University is a midsize public institution of around 9,000 students. Athletic events bring unity and a sense of pride to the entire campus. Even though most intercollegiate athletic teams at Green are Division II level, intercollegiate competition is highly valued at Green by students, faculty, and staff. The teams and games bring the campus community together, but a particular team, the men's basketball team, has also brought valued recognition and revenue to the institution because of their winning record and postseason success over the past several years.

CHARACTERS

> **Sheila Conrad:** Academic advisor who also works with transition services/programs for underrepresented students. This is her first professional job after receiving an M. A. in Student Affairs.

Lisa Westry: Academic advisor who also manages the tutoring center.

James Williams: Director of the Academic Services Department. He has been working at the institution for over 15 years and has been in his current position for five.

Lamar Moore: First-year, African American student on men's basketball team.

Anthony Pierce: Second-year, African American student on men's basketball team.

Coach Hardy: Men's head basketball coach.

CASE

The Academic Services Department attempts to support the academic success of students. This department is where tutoring services, academic skills workshops, first-year transition courses, and a number of other services are housed. Also, the department oversees the exploratory/undecided program, which is for students who have not yet declared a major or have recently switched from a major to undeclared. All first-year students start out in the exploratory/undecided program because they are unable to officially declare a major until they complete two semesters of undergraduate work. However, students are permitted to take courses within their intended major department.

Academic advisors work closely with students to help them fulfill liberal studies requirements and choose a major based on their interests, goals, and abilities. Advisors meet with students to discuss their degree audits and the liberal studies guide, their academic progress, selection of courses for the following semester, and areas of academic interests. All of this is discussed prior to giving students a registration pin number that will allow them to register for courses. It is important that students understand the registration process, requirements, policies, and procedures before registering.

In the advisement center, there are five advisors and a director. Each advisor advises anywhere from 200–220 students in addition to having a particular area of additional responsibility. Sheila Conrad's additional focus area is underrepresented students (e.g., students of color, low SES students) and their successful transition to academic life at the university. All of the advisors report to James Williams, the Director of Academic Services. James is well liked and respected on campus. He is an active intercollegiate athletic booster and is particularly passionate about Green College basketball.

When Sheila was hired as an advisor to work with transition services/ programs for underrepresented students, she was ecstatic. In the first staff meeting (a week before classes started), Sheila was welcomed to the department by the other staff members. James led the meeting, covering things to expect during the upcoming semester. James also encouraged the advisors to continue to develop their own individual styles of advising, and gave them the freedom to be creative in that process. At the same time, he cautioned the advisors to ensure their approach to working with students aligned with the mission/goals of the office and institution. The mission/goals and roles of this office are as follows:

> Academic Advising is an essential part of Green University's commitment to the process of educating students. Advisors help students to select proper courses, to choose appropriate majors based on their career interests, to understand university academic policies and procedures, and to cope with the transition to college. The foundation of the advising process is the relationship between the advisor and the student. The advisor should encourage the advisee to maintain regular contact with her/him in order to foster a strong and continued relationship, and to promote a more meaningful undergraduate experience. The advisor helps students to review, select, and reach their educational objectives in a professional, helpful, and mutually respectful atmosphere that allows students to: 1) Become well informed about policies and procedures, curricular options, and academic program requirements; 2) Clearly define their educational objectives; 3) Plan programs that incorporate their interests, abilities, and career goals; 4) Make full use of the facilities and resources available at Green University.

From this meeting, Sheila learned that James was not a micromanager; she really liked that fact because she valued her ability to work independently.

In the first couple of months, Sheila was happy with how things were going. She felt connected with her colleagues and was pleased with how well she was adjusting to her duties. Everything seemed to be going well until registration rolled around. For about three weeks straight in November, the advisors were meeting all day with students about scheduling. During the first week of registration, Sheila met with Lamar Moore, an African American student who played on the basketball team. It was his first year and he explained to Sheila that he had a strong interest in business. Sheila and Lamar talked about his particular business interests, what area of business he wanted to focus on, and how things were going this current semester. He needed a 3.0 to declare this major and, based on his current academic progress, Sheila was confident he would have no problem obtaining that QPA by the academic year's end.

Lamar was goal-oriented and seemed to have his academic and future plans mapped out. However, he was concerned that he would not get into the business major based on what he was told about the courses. Sheila told him that he could take a few of the required courses in the spring semester, but he said that was impossible. Sheila had a hard time understanding why it was impossible. Lamar was on the right track as far as credits; he was able to register early because of his athletic status, so classes would be open; and the courses were at levels that he would be permitted to take. Sheila asked Lamar why it was impossible to take any business courses.

Lamar: My coach won't let us take certain courses. He actually sent me here to get my registration pin number from you so that we could choose courses.

Sheila: Tell me a little bit more about him not letting you take certain courses. We will get to the pin number later.

Lamar: Coach has the courses we should take mapped out and he pretty much makes our schedules.

Sheila: Does he know that you are considering business?

Lamar: Yeah, he knows . . . when I received my original schedule this summer, I was enrolled in a business course based on my interest, but Coach had me change my schedule early this semester because he feels that many of the courses that the department requires will be too hard to manage, especially when the season really gets going.

Sheila: Okay, I see. How do you feel about your Coach changing your schedule? Are you okay with it?

Lamar: I mean, I know I want to go into business, but I want to play ball and remain eligible because that is what's paying my tuition. Coach says that as long as I graduate with something that will be better than a lot of people out there with no degree at all.

Sheila: Do you believe that you would be able to handle the workload? Or are your choices influenced by what you are hearing from others? Because based on our conversation, I think you are very driven and motivated and know what you want, but the courses conflicting with basketball is what is getting in the way.

Lamar: Honestly, I think I can handle it but Coach is not hearing any of it. Believe me, he is not that understanding. Plus, he has been working with players for a while now, so I'm sure he knows what he is talking about. He told me from the beginning that business is not the route to take.

Sheila: What are most of the other players' majors?

Lamar: General Studies.

Sheila: By choice?

Lamar: Some. I think that's the major coach wants me to choose, too, because he says that's the one that will allow me to be successful in school and on the team.

Sheila: Now, Lamar, I haven't been advising that long, but I can tell you with confidence that there are a number of students that have had successful athletic careers at college while graduating from programs that are a bit challenging, especially students with a strong work ethic and drive, such as yours.

Lamar: I guess I didn't think too much about that.

Sheila: Before you make a decision, I want you to do a little research. I'm sure you know of athletes that have attended different colleges. Look up the majors that those individuals achieved degrees in. It does not have to just be basketball, but check it out and tell me what you find.

Lamar: Okay. I will.

After talking a bit more with Lamar, she gave him his pin number and told him that ultimately the choice of courses and major that he chooses is up to him. This appointment made Sheila upset because she felt Lamar would likely excel in whatever he majored in. Sheila had a problem with the basketball coach telling Lamar, or any student, that certain majors were too difficult without even giving students an opportunity to take courses in the major. She hoped her interactions with Lamar might influence him to do what was best for him.

During the second week of registration, Sheila met with a student named Anthony Pierce, another African American student, who played for the basketball team. Anthony was a second-year undeclared major with a QPA of 2.2. Sheila figured that because he was a sophomore, he already understood the registration process and how things worked.

Sheila: Did you bring your degree audit with you?

Anthony: No, I don't know what that is. I just need my registration pin number.

Shelia: Well before I give you your pin, we need to go over your degree audit to see what liberal studies courses you still need to take. Considering that you will be a second semester sophomore, it is also time to start looking into a major.

Anthony: I don't need to do all of that. My coach will handle it for me.

Sheila: Well, let's just look over it so you can get an understanding for the direction you're headed in.

Anthony: Okay. Whatever.

Sheila: It looks like you are running out of classes to take within the liberal studies program. Have you started thinking about a major?

Anthony: No. My coach is going to put me in one so that I can still get out of here on time.

Sheila: Oh, okay [hesitantly]. Well, what are some of your interests?

Anthony: I really like my law and ethics class.

Sheila: How is that course going? What do you like about it?

Anthony: I'm not doing good in it; I'm failing right now, but I really like law.

Sheila: Well, have you talked to the professor about how to bring your grade up?

Anthony: I don't need to. My coach does that type of stuff [looks at his phone]. I really need my pin. I have practice in ten minutes.

Sheila wasn't certain what to do. She was uncomfortable giving him the pin under these conditions, but she thought perhaps this student was struggling (especially with his QPA being so low) or was high-risk for leaving, so the coach was really trying to assist. When she thought of Lamar, however, and how the coach was handling things for him even though he was driven and seemed to be on the right track, she decided not to give Anthony the pin number. She told him to schedule another meeting with her when he had more time so that they could discuss his goals, plans, and courses in more detail and then she would give him his registration pin. Anthony stormed out of the office without saying a word.

Sheila decided that she needed more information to give her better insight on what she had experienced with these two basketball players. She compiled major, retention, and graduation data for all players on the college basketball roster for the past five years. The data showed that the large majority of basketball players graduated within five years. All players that were enrolled longer than five years had either withdrawn, failed out, or simply did not complete their degree program. Furthermore, the players that did graduate, with only a couple of exceptions, were all graduating with degrees in General Studies. General Studies at Green was an interdisciplinary studies major with a wide offering of university courses that could be counted toward the degree. It was also routinely granted to students who were unsuccessful in completing the requirements of other majors, but had enough overall credits to graduate.

This information suggested to her that the coach had a clear pattern regarding what academic major he wanted his players in. General Studies had been the "go-to" major for the basketball team for at least the past five years, so the coach was likely familiar with particular courses (and professors) that made acquiring this degree relatively easy for his players. The data also indicated that the coach was fairly successful in graduating his athletes, if they graduated within four or five years (coincidentally, the length of their athletic eligibility), but wholly unsuccessful with those who took longer. Sheila wondered if Coach Hardy wasn't as supportive or engaged with his athletes once they were no longer eligible to play. These statistics troubled Sheila greatly, but she wanted to further test her assumptions.

Sheila decided to share her data with Lisa, one of her advising colleagues in the office. Lisa said she wasn't particularly surprised, as she had heard stories from basketball players in her advising work with them that was consistent with what Sheila had discovered. She also told Sheila that although some of the advisors see this as a problem, others do not, and no one was really interested in making waves about it.

Sheila: But, this is clearly a problem, Lisa. These students are being "told" what classes to take and what to major in by Coach Hardy, even if they express other interests or abilities. This isn't consistent with encouraging students to find a self-chosen, satisfying major/career direction or with our mission as academic advisors.

Lisa: I don't disagree with you, Sheila, but this is bigger than either of us. James knows what's going on. He and Coach Hardy are very tight, so Hardy keeps him posted. James thinks the coach is doing a fine job with these students. James is one of the biggest fans of the basketball program, and the college and community are also in love with this team. Everyone at the institution seems happy because we are graduating most of our African American basketball students and winning games. No one is choosing to look at this as closely as you have.

Sheila: So we are supposed to just give them the registration pins and then leave it alone?

Lisa: I'm afraid that is how it goes. Just let them have their pins.

While Sheila was contemplating what, if anything, she could do, she got a call from James demanding to meet with her right away. James told Sheila that he received a call from an angry Coach Hardy about the advising session that took place with Anthony. Coach Hardy was particularly angry that Anthony did not receive his registration pin number. Sheila tried to explain why she did not give Anthony the pin number, but James said that Coach Hardy manages his own players around registration. He apologized for not making Sheila aware of this process, and asked her to give the basketball players their pin numbers when they request them.

Sheila: But is Coach Hardy really handling it best for these students? They receive their pin numbers and are just sent away with no advising. It is left up to the coach to map out these students' college and, ultimately, future plans. Aren't you concerned that these students can't make important academic decisions for themselves? They don't even seem to know the academic policies and procedures here.

James: Look, Coach Hardy knows a lot about the academic programs here and how to advise his players. He has an impressive record of retaining and graduating his athletes, and at the same time, gets them to excel on the court. Just look at his winning record as basketball coach here.

Sheila: I met with a first-year basketball player recently who indicated a strong interest in a business major, but said the coach wouldn't allow him to take any business classes to explore that potential major. He said that Coach Hardy wanted to him to major in General Studies instead. It doesn't sound to me like he is listening to this student's interests or considering his academic potential.

James: Coach Hardy knows these students and their potential both on and off the court better than we do; he recruits them, spends significant time with them, and gets to know them intimately. He has to consider what is best for the student academically in relation to their performance on the team. Coach Hardy is largely judged on winning basketball games, which he has demonstrated he is quite good at. I know he cares about his players, and I think he does a great job of balancing concern for them and concern for the team.

Sheila: Based on what I've seen, I'm not so sure. You hired me to focus on the academic transition needs of underrepresented students, and I'm concerned these students are not being supported appropriately and in the ways we try to support other students.

James: [raising his voice] Look, Sheila, the coach called me and I told him I would handle this. Coach Hardy provides many of his players with an opportunity to receive a college education that they couldn't access or afford any other way. I suggest that you not stir things up about this. You recently arrived at Green, and you don't seem to understand the culture here. The success of the basketball program means a great deal to the campus community. You need to let this go, and do what I am asking regarding these students. I would like to see you succeed professionally here, but this is not the way to accomplish that.

Sheila: But . . .

James: Let's just pretend this never happened.

Sheila left this meeting upset and confused. She asked herself, "Is the entire institution aware of and okay with this practice?" She chose not to share with James what she had discovered about the history of academic choices and progress patterns of students on the basketball team. It was clear from their conversation that he wasn't open to her concerns, and she was afraid he would be quite angry that she had done this investigation. She thought back to the first staff meeting when they were told to advise students consistent with the goals/mission of the office. Those developmental learning goals were clearly not being followed in this instance. Sheila strongly felt she had a professional responsibility to address this situation, but she was realizing that doing so might jeopardize her relationship with her supervisor, and ultimately, her job. She also wasn't certain how she could further raise this issue in a way that could make a meaningful difference. She tried to let it go, but it continued to bother her.

Questions

1. Did Sheila make the right decision in not sharing her investigative findings with James Williams?
2. If Sheila decides to further pursue her concerns about Coach Hardy's advising of the students on the basketball team, what are her best options for an effective outcome?
3. If you were in Sheila's position, how would you decide whether to take the professional risk involved in pursuing this issue further?

Index for Case Chapters

The following case chapter index categorizes all of the cases in this book (Chapters 4–25) by functional area(s) focused on in the case, higher education institution type where the case occurs, student populations central to the case, salient issues contained in the case, and theoretical content areas relevant to analyzing the case.

The numbers noted after a particular index term/category refer to the chapter numbers of the cases connected to that index term/category. This index allows you to find cases, by chapter, which match your interests for a particular case among the aforementioned categories.

Author Biographies

Michael G. Ignelzi is Professor of Student Affairs in Higher Education in the Department of Counseling and Development at Slippery Rock University, where he has been a member of the faculty for the past 23 years. He previously worked as a student affairs practitioner (Resident Director, Director of Residence Life, Dean of Students). His research interests center on professional development and supervision of student affairs educators; application of developmental theory to teaching and learning; professional ethics; and moral reasoning and education. Michael earned a B.A. in Psychology from the University of California, Riverside, a M.A. in Student Personnel Work from The Ohio State University, and an Ed.D. in Human Development and Psychology from Harvard University.

Melissa A. Rychener, was a tenured Assistant Professor in the Student Affairs in Higher Education Master of Arts program at Slippery Rock University, and she is currently Coordinator of the Intercultural Preparation and Competency Curriculum at Duquesne University. Her research interests focus on how students become interculturally competent through cultural immersion experiences; she is also interested in career trajectory issues for women and people of color in higher education. Melissa began her student affairs career in residence life and spent more than a decade working in international education as a foreign student and study abroad advisor. Melissa graduated from Trinity University with a B.A. in English and minors in History and Women's Studies. She received an M.A. in Higher Education and Student Affairs and a Ph.D. in Higher Education from The Ohio State University.

Molly A. Mistretta is currently an Assistant Professor of Student Affairs in Higher Education/Clinical Mental Health Counseling in the Department of Counseling and Development at Slippery Rock University of Pennsylvania. Prior to that, she was a student affairs practitioner for 11 years, primarily in the areas of residence life, student leadership development, and student retention. Her primary research interests focus on college choice, compassion fatigue in the helping professions, and the use of effective pedagogical practices in graduate education. Molly earned a B.A. in Political Science from Westminster College (PA), an M.S. in Higher Education and Student Affairs from Indiana University, and a Ph.D. in Administrative and Policy Studies from the University of Pittsburgh.

Stacy A. Jacob is an Assistant Professor of Student Affairs in Higher Education and the Graduate Coordinator for the Department of Counseling and Development at Slippery Rock University of Pennsylvania. Her administrative career spanned several functional areas of higher education including admissions, residence life, Greek Life, and academic support. Her main research interests are the Scholarship of Teaching and Learning (SoTL) specifically in the field of higher education/student affairs, college choice, and the history of higher education. Stacy earned a B.A. in Communication Arts from Austin College, a M.A. in Educational Leadership from the University of New Orleans and a Ph.D. in Higher Education from Indiana University.

CO-AUTHOR BIOGRAPHIES

Jordan W. Brooks is currently the Assistant Director of Intercultural Affairs at Grinnell College.

Kerri Butler is currently a head women's soccer coach for Chattanooga Football Club Academy.

Anne C. Cassin is currently the Associate Director of New Student and Family Programs at Texas Woman's University.

Stefanie M. Centola is currently a Residence Director at Niagara University.

Emma K. Coomes is currently a Student Success Coach at Stevenson University.

Renee K. (Austin) Coyne is currently Assistant Director of Career Education and Development at Slippery Rock University.

Correy Dandoy is currently the Coordinator of Undergraduate Programs in the Department of Philosophy at Carnegie Mellon University.

Caitlin Barbour Ginter is currently the Assistant Director for External Marketing at The Key School.

Sara Gould is currently the Assistant Director for Career and Industry Engagement at the University of Florida.

Kristin M. Gregory is currently the Assistant Director of First Year and Transition Programs at Stetson University.

Deron T. Jackson is currently a Financial Service Representative for Fortis Lux Financial, a member of the Mass Mutual Financial Group. Previously, Deron served as the Assistant Coordinator for Leadership Development at the University of Pittsburgh.

Todd E. Kamenash is currently the Assistant Dean of Students and Director of Student Conduct at Kent State University.

Lenee McCandless is currently the Assistant Director of International Education at Allegheny College.

Felicia P. McKinney is currently the Social Media Manager at Point Park University.

Ryan Morgado is currently the Assistant Director of Student Activities at Rice University.

Janine N. Muri is a Commercial Property Manager at the Sampson Morris Group.

Lauren Perri is currently an Education Abroad Advisor for the Office of Global Education at Kent State University.

Emily Price is currently an Assistant Director of Transfer Admissions at Slippery Rock University.

Denise N. Sanata is currently an Academic Adviser and First-Year Experience Instructor for the College of Science at Coastal Carolina University.

Meridia D. Sanders is currently the Program Coordinator for the Office of First Year Experience at the University of Pittsburgh.

Lesli Somerset is currently the Coordinator of Career Development-Student Counseling, Outreach, and Resources at Chatham University.

Morgan E. Weber is currently the Disability Specialist at Ursuline College.

Kara Werkmeister is currently an Instructor and Residence Hall Director at Old Dominion University.

Brandy A. Wilson is currently Academic Advisor for the Information Systems Program at Carnegie Mellon University.

Index